JOHN VOLPE
The Life of an Immigrant's Son

JOHN VOLPE

The Life of an Immigrant's Son

by Kathleen Kilgore

A division of Yankee Publishing, Inc.
Dublin, New Hampshire 03444

Designed by Jill Shaffer

Yankee Publishing Incorporated
Dublin, New Hampshire 03444

First Edition
Copyright 1987 by Kathleen Kilgore Houton
An authorized biography

Library of Congress Catalogue Card Number: 86-51014

ISBN: 0-89909-121-0

Table of Contents

The dream of the return to Italy has rested largely on the love of family and home, and the new births, especially when the children have so far grown up as to recognize a tie of their own, create a home. Very rarely do these foreign-born children seek out Italian citizenship. And if, on the contrary, as happens abundantly in Argentina and the United States, the children become infused with the demonstrative patriotism of the new nation, then the parents too may come to regard Italy as a country without a morrow, and America as the country of strides and glamour. So at last, the bright colors of the dream may fade, and the dream itself be forgot.

— Robert Foerster
The Italian Immigration of Our Times, 1969

CHAPTER I

Birds of Passage

I N AUGUST 1905, the hilltop village of Pescosansonesco in the Abruzzi region of southern Italy baked white in the dusty heat, but the families of Benedetto and Volpe were not working in the tiny terraced plots of figs and grapes they had dug from the bare hillsides. The families stood solemnly in the close heat of the small church after the civil ceremony at the town hall, as the priest married Filomena Benedetto, age twenty-four, to Vito Volpe, age twenty-five.

There were no wedding photographs, but a portrait of the couple taken two years later shows a thick-bodied, muscular young man, awkward in a vested suit and high-buttoned collar, with his hands squarely on his knees, facing the camera like a challenge. He is quite dark, with a fashionably bushy black handlebar moustache and a mass of dark hair. Beside him sits a slim, fine-featured woman in an upswept hairdo, her glossy black hair topped with a straw hat like an upturned pie plate. She wears a dark, high-necked Victorian dress, and her first baby is wrapped in a tight white bundle on her knee, one tiny arm flung out as it tries to wriggle away.

Although the families were as poor as the other villagers, at her wedding ceremony Filomena Benedetto wore, not homemade clothes, but a seamstress's white wedding gown, having walked several miles down the mountainside to the village of Chieti for the fittings. Filomena wished

7

to make the wedding an important event, for it was more than the beginning of her new life and another generation of villagers. She and her future husband had already made the decision to leave Pescosansonesco and not return.

The voyage would be Filomena's first, but Vito was already a seasoned emigrant, an "American." He had made two decisions: to emigrate and then to settle permanently. The first decision was not difficult; in fact, it was almost a foregone conclusion. Vito Volpe had served his two years in the army, as an orderly. He had had two years of schooling (Filomena, like most southern Italian peasant girls, had none). He was strong, intelligent, ambitious, and in Pescosansonesco would be lucky to get a hundred days' work a year for the rest of his life as a farm laborer for the local landlord. And the way out of Pescosansonesco was already open and well-traveled.

The decision to make a permanent home in the United States was not typical for a young man of Vito's time. Most southern Italians fantasized a triumphal return to their villages, and a few really did come back to build "American" houses complete with plumbing and electricity. There were even a few retired Americans in Pescosansonesco. Vito cherished no such dreams. He was an adopted child, a rarity in a village where an extra mouth to feed was a heavy burden. Within the family, he had been treated as an equal with his brothers, but it was rumored in the village that his real father was the mayor of a neighboring town and his mother a servant. In a class-stratified society, he was neither peasant nor landlord. But in the United States, he and his sons could forge their own identity.

In 1888, the Italian legislature had passed a law permitting any Italian citizen to emigrate except young men who had not completed military service, but exceptions to the draft law were not hard to come by. There was no need for a passport, visa, or physical exam, or even money to pay passage. Under the padrone system, Italian agents for labor contractors in the United States advanced the emigrant the price of his one-way ticket from Naples to New York in exchange for enough work to repay the loan plus a high rate of interest. In 1885, the U.S. Congress, already aware of abuses, had excluded contract laborers from entering the country, but this law proved impossible to enforce, and the padrone system flourished until after World War I. Even the most naive contadino was drilled by the other men in his group on the steerage passage that the correct answer to the American examiner's question "Do you have a job waiting for you?" or "Is someone paying your passage?" was no.

Emigrants could avoid falling into the hands of the padrones by paying their own passage. But in 1904, a steerage ticket from Naples to New York cost from $27 to $39, or the value of about one hundred days' labor in southern Italy — the income a farm laborer might make in a year.[1] A fortunate few might be sent a ticket from a relative already established. This did not happen to Vito Volpe, for his only American relative was as poor as his family in Italy. There was work in the United States, but not wealth at first. Between 1900 and 1910, the average Italian-American family's income was about $600 a year, or less than half that of a native born family.[2] But the Italians still came.

There was both pull from abroad and push from at home. For the five million Italians who emigrated from Sicily and the southern Italian provinces of Abruzzi, Campania, Apulia, Lucania, and Calabria between 1876 and 1930, the two forces are difficult to separate. Southern Italy and Sicily, invaded throughout recorded history in turn by the Phoenicians, Carthaginians, Greeks, Romans, Vandals, Goths, Austrians, Arabs, Normans, French, Spanish, and several northern Italian kings, were never politically unified or economically independent. In mountainous terrain such as the Abruzzi, malaria from the marshes prevented peasants from working the more fertile valleys, and centuries of war drove them to cling together behind walls on the barren hilltops — each village isolated from its neighbors.

By the late nineteenth century, the sharp Abruzzi hills, described as deeply wooded by classical writers, had become desolate and eroded after generations of peasants had cut firewood and let their animals overgraze. National unification had come late to Italy, and in the south, feudal social organization remained in force throughout the nineteenth century, with the signori owning the vast bulk of the land, and the contadini struggling along as tenant farmers. In the last quarter of the century, contadini income went down, population went up, and the cost of living doubled.[3]

No industrial base had developed in southern Italy, and a vast pool of unskilled and illiterate day laborers who could find work only during certain seasons grew up in even the smallest villages. Seasonal migration — the migrants were poetically called "birds of passage" — and permanent emigration benefited not only the individuals involved but the entire Italian economy, as money sent home from Italian laborers flowed through the villages and the working-class sections of Naples and Palermo. Of the total population of fourteen million in southern Italy and Sicily, more than one-third had left to work overseas by World War I.

Until 1900, Italian emigration abroad was directed primarily to South America, where the climate was more congenial, the languages easier to learn, and the culture slightly more familiar than in the countries farther north. It is interesting to note that Sicilian immigrants to South American cities, although they came from the same villages and often even the same families as immigrants to Chicago and New York, never developed the Black Hand, the Mafia, or the reputation for criminality that, to some degree, still haunts Italian-Americans today.

Buenos Aires and Rio de Janeiro did not have the capacity to absorb vast numbers of unskilled workers. The United States in the late nineteenth and early twentieth centuries needed cheap labor to build railroads and subways and to man the factories of the industrial Northeast. Irish immigration, the first great wave of unskilled labor, had peaked in 1851, and by the 1890s, the Irish were climbing out of the ditches onto the first rung of the social ladder. The desperate southern Italians were more than eager to replace them in the ditches. "The Irish have ceased building railroads and constructing public works," C.F. Parker wrote in the popular magazine *The Forum* in 1893. "The Italians have taken their place."[4]

News that there was unlimited work in the United States spread quickly through southern Italy, aided by the glowing reports of the padrones and steamship agents who went from village to village, signing up males between the ages of fourteen and forty-five. Unlike the Irish, Italian women never emigrated alone to work as domestic servants or factory workers; they came only as sisters, children, or wives. By 1900, the dream of America eclipsed all others, although some Italians continued to emigrate to Canada, Australia, and even northern Europe as well as South America. Despite evidence of ethnic discrimination so clear the most ignorant paesano could see it on arrival in the United States, the myth of opportunity for the next generation — free public schools, family businesses, scholarships to higher education — was a powerful incentive for the family-oriented southern Italian. Language, they knew, was the greatest barrier. But the chopped-up mountain dialects would have marked the southern villagers as strangers in Milan or Rome as well as in New York.

From the 1890s until the setting of immigration quotas in 1927, the United States exerted such a strong pull that whole villages were systematically emptied of the young and were sustained only by remittances from abroad. In 1910, even Benito Mussolini, then unemployed and broke, planned to seek his fortune in the United States. The future dictator escaped "America fever," but others did not, and they willingly endured the hellish steerage passage and a lifetime of hard labor as the price of a chance for their children, if not for themselves.

Vito Volpe walked with a cardboard suitcase down the mountain to take the train to Naples for the first time in 1902. All he would ever see of his country beyond his village was the Naples train station and the docks. With the address of his stepbrother in Yonkers in his pocket, Volpe joined perhaps a thousand contadini herded into the steerage compartment of a liner bound for New York.

Steerage on an ocean liner was the compartment nearest the steering gear, well below decks, where an old-fashioned wheel could be used to maneuver the ship if the automatic mechanism failed in a storm. By 1900, the worst horrors of the wooden "coffin ships" that had brought Potato Famine survivors to the United States were in the past, but a steerage voyage was still not without dangers. At the turn of the century, New York authorities tried to correct abuses by the steamship lines by fining captains $10 for every dead steerage passenger; but the officers often simply buried the immigrants at sea and altered the passenger lists.[5]

The trade in immigrants was so profitable that captains were willing to take chances; steerage passengers yielded more profit than any inanimate cargo the hold could carry. A steamship line could make $60,000 profit one way on steerage alone, sometimes carrying as many as fifteen hundred to two thousand immigrants a trip.[6] The padrones, the American contractors, and the immigrants themselves wanted the cheapest possible passage, and the passengers were in no position to complain once they arrived in the United States.

"The steerage never changes, neither its location nor its furnishings," Edward Steiner wrote in *On the Trail of the Immigrant* in 1906. "It lies over the stirring screws, sleeps to the staccato of trembling steel railings and hawsers. Narrow, steep and slippery stairways lead to it. Crowds everywhere, ill smelling bunks, uninviting washrooms — this is steerage. The odors of scattered orange peelings, tobacco, garlic, and disinfectants meeting but not blending. No lounge or chairs for comfort, and a continual babel of tongues — this is steerage."[7]

In 1902, when Vito Volpe made his first voyage to the United States, the typical steerage compartment was a converted upper cargo hold without portholes or any other ventilation, with tiers of metal bunks bolted to the bulkheads like the sleeping arrangements in World War II troopships. Sometimes men and women were separated by decks, with the children staying with the women, or the compartment was divided by blankets thrown across lines. Nothing muffled the noise of the engines through the iron hull, and the deck vibrated continually with the pounding of the waves, rolling in heavy seas. There was no provision for bathing, the latrines usually clogged from overuse in the first couple of days, and many passengers, who had never even seen a ship before, stayed sick for the entire voyage. For those who could eat, the food was typically barrels of salted herring and crackers. This was not only cheap, but the saltiness was supposed to reduce seasickness.

The memory most immigrants kept of the voyage was the seasickness. "I remember Mother told me she was sick the whole way — every day," Vito Volpe's nephew Samuel Benedetto said of his mother's voyage. "Steerage was the bottom of the ship. She was so sick other women had to look after the kids. It never failed, every time we went by the wharf on Atlantic Avenue where the ships used to dock, she'd tell us, 'That's where the ship arrived, thank God!' She never wanted to go back."

The voyage lasted from two to four weeks, and many of the immigrants lapsed into an apathetic state, remembering little afterward. On calm days, the steerage passengers might be allowed up onto the after-deck, where the first- and second-class passengers could look down on them, careful not to approach too close for fear of disease. From those encounters come the many black-and-white photographs of hollow-eyed peasant women in kerchiefs and dark-moustached men crouched on a bare deck, staring expressionless at the camera — the "Boat People" of their day. Often the scene is New York harbor, and the Statue of Liberty is visible ahead, with the immigrants' faces staring blankly toward it. Ahead for the first- and second-class passengers lay New York and home or hotels. For the immigrants, the destination was the Island of Tears.

Before 1875, the federal government left the regulation of immigration to the states. In New York, the most popular port of entry, an arrival center was maintained by the state at Castle Garden on Manhattan. As the "Garden" became swamped by the load of immigrants from eastern and southern Europe, the federal government built a processing and quarantine center at Ellis Island, staffing it with translators, immigration agents, and doctors, all in military-style Immigration and Naturalization Service (INS) uniforms. The uniforms and polished jackboots gave rise to the belief among terrified immigrants that the women were undressed and examined by soldiers.

From the lower decks, the steerage passengers watched as the first- and second-class passengers embarked by lighter to go through customs on the pier. The immigrants were brought en masse in barges to be processed through the Great Hall, tagged like baggage with the numbers of the ship's manifest, directed along twenty-two lines of inspection bordered with iron railings that twisted through the echoing hall. Any immigrant who aroused suspicion was marked with colored chalk on his or her tag and set apart in an iron cage "for all the world like a segregated animal," as Edward Corsi, an immigrant who later became a commissioner of the INS, described it. Stinking and numb after the weeks in the hold, most immigrants endured the process as docile as cattle, but often the tension and fear would cause outbreaks of uncontrollable weeping that spread through sections of the Great Hall. Many later remembered thinking of the day as the Last Judgment, when the damned would be returned and the elect allowed to enter the gates of earthly paradise.

In 1902, there were several hurdles to overcome as the endless lines pressed through the hall. First the tuberculosis doctor, then the specialist in "loathsome and contagious diseases" (even curable infections such as ringworm were deportable offenses), then the dread trachoma examination, the cause of most deportations. Often women were detained for trachoma because their eyes were sore from weeping. An interpreter questioned even the small children to check for mental retardation and to see whether any were deaf and dumb. After the physicals, interpreters took the immigrants to cubicles and tried to determine whether the applicants fell into the categories of polygamists, mental defectives, anarchists, or sexual deviants — a list almost identical to the one used by the INS today.

For southern Italians, the only real danger lay in the contract labor questions. Virtually all examiners turned a blind eye to this regulation, and it served to weed out only those contadini who were naive or honest enough to admit having been contracted for. "It sometimes happened that one member of such a group would produce a letter from a friend or relative within the United States to prove that work had been provided for him here. He would willingly sign an affidavit of this, thereby leading not only to his own deportation, but also that of his entire group," an INS officer recalled in 1907.[8]

Ellis Island had been built to accommodate five thousand immigrants at one time, but by 1902 as many as fifteen thousand were arriving in a single day. "I thought it was a stream that would never end," the same INS officer remembered. "Every twenty-four hours from three to five thousand people came before us, and I myself examined from four to five hundred a day. We were simply swamped by that human tide."[9] At the time of Volpe's immigration, the INS kept records of how much money each immigrant had on arrival, though lack of funds was not yet a basis for exclusion. In 1900, southern Italians were among the lowest ranking in terms of savings, $8.84 per person. The poorest were the Lithuanian Jews at $7.96 a head; the wealthiest were the Scots with $41.51. In the same

13

year, 62 percent of southern Italian men entering the United States were unable to sign their names.

Just five years later, Italian immigration would peak at more than a quarter million a year. Yet the door was already closing as the public debate that had begun in the 1880s between advocates of limited and unlimited immigration reached its climax.

The first restriction on immigration, passed in 1884, had excluded only one ethnic group, the Chinese. The Haymarket Riot in 1886, for which six immigrants were sentenced to death after a bomb explosion at an anarchist rally in Chicago, had brought calls to stem the tide of Italian and eastern European immigrants. Italians were frequently a target of labor opposition because they were used as strikebreakers. Before the quota system was introduced, the literacy test was seen as a means of excluding not only Italians but poor Jews as well. Literacy test legislation had already passed each house of Congress once when Vito Volpe arrived. The test would be made law fifteen years after he was admitted.

For Vito Volpe, the Ellis Island ordeal was soon over. There was a place to stay with the stepbrother whom he had never seen but who had found him a construction job. From New York, he traveled to stay with relatives in Wakefield, Massachusetts, and worked for a time in a rattan factory, saving his money.

By his second, and what would be his last, voyage across the Atlantic in 1905, Volpe's situation had changed greatly, although he probably carried the same battered suitcase and still traveled steerage. He was no longer a bird of passage. Virtually all Italian immigrants saved as much of their money as possible, but for many the goal was a new house in the village, a few acres for the family, or an addition to the old stone dwelling for his bride. Vito Volpe made clear in his letters (dictated to a more literate friend, then read aloud to his fiancée by the parish priest) that he had other plans.

After their marriage, Vito and Filomena stayed in the village long enough to help bring in the harvest. But by late fall they could delay no longer. Filomena was now pregnant, and a winter crossing in steerage would be too dangerous for her. They booked passage on the *Canopic,* a ship of the White Star Line bound for Boston. "The voyage was so terrible she never wanted to go back, like all the women," her daughter Grace Gonella would remember. "Even if they could afford it later, the memory of steerage was too strong."

On November 13, 1905, Vito and Filomena arrived in Boston's North End.

14

NOTES

1. Richard Gambino, *Blood of my Blood* (New York: Doubleday and Co., Inc., 1974), p. 62.

2. Ibid., p. 80.

3. Jane Namias, *First Generation: In the Words of Twentieth Century American Immigrants* (Boston: Beacon Press, 1978), p. 31.

4. Quoted in Robert Foerster, *The Italian Immigration of Our Times* (New York: Arno Press,1969), p. 358.

5. Terry Coleman, *Going to America* (New York: Random House, 1972), p. 241.

6. Ibid., p. 245.

7. Quoted in Willard A. Heaps, *The Story of Ellis Island* (New York: The Seabury Press, 1967), p. 38.

8. Edward Corsi, *In the Shadow of Liberty: the Chronicle of Ellis Island* (New York: Macmillan, 1935), p. 76.

9. Ibid., p. 73.

CHAPTER II

Bread and Shelter

I N APRIL 1982, a crew from the Perini Construction Company was excavating under the Harvard Square area of Cambridge for the subway's Red Line extension when one of the laborers found a buried time and wage book dated October 18, 1899. In a neat, copperplate hand, the timekeeper had listed the laborers who had worked on the first subway excavation nearly a hundred years before. On the first page, the names read: Sullivan, Ryan, Hennessey, Casey, Riordan. All received $2 a day. On the next page, just the word "Italian" or the letter "I" indicated the next twelve workers, who were paid $1.50 a day for the same job. Only one worker in the book was paid less, the water boy. He was black, and his name was spelled out precisely.[1]

A later generation of Italian-Americans would joke that their fathers came to the United States believing that the streets were paved with gold and found that the streets were not paved at all and that *they* would be required to pave them.

"They called us Dagos," Samuel Benedetto explained, "because the old-timers were digging at the bottom of the subway trench, and they would only see the sun at noon. When they thought it might be close to quitting time, they yelled up, 'Da day go?' And the Irish up above started to call them Dagos. I don't know if the story is true, but I know they were the ones at the bottom of the ditch."

The original impetus for Italian immigration had been the need for labor gangs to build the railroads, and even after they were built, Italians gravitated to the building trades. Some, like Vito Volpe, would eventually become skilled craftsmen; most would spend their lives at the bottom of the ditch. In its 1907 study of employment patterns, the U.S. Immigration Commission found that Italian immigrants made up 44 percent of all construction workers in the United States.

In 1906, the year Vito's and Filomena's first child, Grace, was born, Boston author Amy Wood wrote an article titled "The Italians in New England" for *New England Magazine.* Construction industry wages had, apparently, not increased at all in the twenty-four years since the Cambridge timekeeper had written his book. "What is left of his $1.50 or $2.00 a day, he stores away for the time when he can go back to Italy with a few hundred dollars," Wood wrote of the Italian migrant laborers, "and live in idle opulence for three or four years until his wealth is gone, and he is obliged to return again to accumulate a fortune."[2]

Wood, like many of her fellow New Englanders, was alarmed by the increasing Italian population of New England and cited the 1900 census report that 73 percent of all Italian-born Americans were located in New England, New York, and New Jersey. The fact that more than one-fifth of the New England immigrants were wives brought as permanent settlers gave authors such as Wood additional cause for concern. "Thoughtful minds see in the high yearly percentage of Italian immigration and in the well-known fecundity of the race, a cause for grave apprehension in its probable effect on future citizenship," she concluded.

Wood's prejudice was typical of the Yankee attitude toward immigrants. They had feared and exploited the Irish; now it was the Italians' turn. The increase in the New England Italian community continued, and in 1900, the report of the Massachusetts Commission on Immigration concluded that 28,785 Italian-born Americans lived in the state. By 1910, there were more than 85,000.[3]

Vito Volpe had saved enough money by 1907 to buy a house. With his wife and baby, he had already moved northeast of Boston to Revere, and in the fall, he bought his first American property, a two-story square wood frame house on Water Street in Wakefield, from a man named Joe McGinnis. Vito Volpe was the first Italian to move to what was then an Irish and black neighborhood, although other Italians were already living elsewhere in the town of about five thousand people.

Old photographs of Water Street show a rural scene with open fields, a swamp full of cattails, and an outhouse behind each building, but by the time the Volpes arrived, Wakefield had long ceased to be a farming community. Only ten miles north of Boston on a major rail line, Wakefield was a small factory town, with a few Yankee families scattered among the immigrants.

Antonio Mezzacappa, Professor Emeritus of Romance Languages at Northeastern University, lived in Wakefield from 1912 to 1920. "At least five or six other Italian families and my grandmother were already living in Wakefield well before 1900," he remembered. "The area, strangely, was more industrialized then than it is now, and much more accessible to other cities. We had excellent train service to Boston on the Boston and Maine, and many people commuted there or to Lawrence. The trolley went right along Water Street all the way to Boston through Malden, and the other way to Lynnfield and the Lynn industrial centers.

"The majority of the immigrants from Italy and Sicily worked at the Haywood Wakefield Company, which made rattan furniture, rugs, and a number of other things. I myself worked there after school making porch furniture. There was a factory that produced lead-lined water pipes near Crystal Lake where my father worked, the Evans Show Factory where many Sicilians worked, and a knitting mill.

"In terms of national origin, there were still some Yanks in the town but very few if any wealthy people. The Irish were gradually being displaced by the Italians, and soon Water Street and its side streets were all Italian, with several little grocery stores. The pattern of Italian settlement was for one person from a village to move there, and then others followed — not always relatives but often simply the younger generation of one part of a village. When my family arrived, there was already a nucleus from my hometown of Molise in the provice of Campobasso.

"There were two Italian churches in Wakefield, a Catholic chapel and an Italian Baptist church, which I attended. This was not the influence of America, by the way. There have always been Protestants in Italy, and so there were here, and they were tolerated by the other Italians. We were like the French. We were not fanatical about religion, and the men were often completely indifferent to it. The way that Wakefield was unusual for Italian towns was in that, even though most of the people were only factory workers, about thirty percent of the high school graduates went on to college. When I graduated, I went to Amherst, and in 1920 when my parents returned to Italy, I went to Harvard."

Although Vito Volpe was one of the first natives of Pescosansonesco to come to Wakefield, his cousins, and eventually his three stepbrothers, followed. By 1910, the town records show that all the Irish names on the deeds of houses near 96 Water Street, where the Volpes resided, had changed to Italian. The Irish and Yankees had coexisted peacefully with their black neighbors but fled when the Italians arrived. The black families remained, and their children were the only non-Italians who would play with the Italian children. Amalia Benedetto Robbins, Vito Volpe's niece, remembered asking for a black baby doll for her first toy. In the social order of the day, Yankees stood at the top, the Irish in the middle, and blacks and Italians at the bottom.

As more and more villagers arrived, Vito Volpe became not only the founder but the informal leader of the small community. "Vito was very well known among the Italians, a leader," Robbins remembered. "He spoke broken English, like all his generation, but in Italian he could make a powerful speech even though he had very little education. He was the kind of man who could turn around a vote at a meeting. He went to night school like many of the men, and he learned to read the Italian newspapers like *La Notizia*. Even though he was a strong person, he wasn't ashamed to ask the children what an English word meant or how to spell something after they were going to school — and he would always remember when you told him. He was taller than his sons when they were grown and looked very distinguished with thick white hair.

"He wasn't an educated man by today's standards, but you have to remember how little *anyone* knew. They were Italians, but they didn't know anything about the history of Rome or Venice, or their literature, or even their proper language. My own father couldn't read or write his name, and I remember he told me that when he got off the boat, God help him, he saw the statue of the cigar-store Indian and thought it was a saint and blessed himself. All they knew was that little village and the hard life. But Vito was never ashamed of being Italian. We used to joke that he was a member of every Italian-American organization that ever existed and president of many. He was proud to be an Italian, and he wanted the rest of us to be proud, too."

Although the immigrants soon found work in the construction trades, the business in New England was seasonal, then as now. Samuel Benedetto, Vito's nephew, remembered that his uncle, Domenic Benedetto, was the envy of his friends because of his steady job. Domenic Benedetto's service in World War I had earned him a place as the first Italian on the town payroll, and in every Italian parade he wore his old uniform and rode in front on horseback. "He was a town laborer," Samuel Benedetto explained. "Down in the ditch. But we thought he had it made because he got paid every week summer and winter and didn't have to look for work like the rest of us."

On December 8, 1908, the Volpe's first son was born in the house on Water Street. The relatives and friends who had come from Pescosan-sonesco called on them, bringing baby clothes and food and marveling at the size of the newborn — eleven pounds. Filomena asked to name the boy Giovanni, after her father, who was still living in Italy. But Vito insisted on an "American" name; the child was a United States citizen, although Vito and Filomena would not become naturalized until later. Reluctant to ask an American what the English equivalent of Giovanni was, Vito remembered hearing Irish construction workers called "John-ny" and decided that was close enough. He filled out the birth certificate with his best guess at the spelling (there is no letter "J" in Italian), and the result was "Gionne." Gionne was the second child born at the Water Street house; a baby girl had died in infancy. After Gionne, there were four brothers: Patrick, Richard, Henry, and Peter. Patrick, only fifteen months younger, was almost like a twin to Gionne. As the oldest son, Gionne shared a bed not only with a younger brother but a boarder as well. Until after he had married, he never slept alone.

The small house in Wakefield was as crowded as a home in an Abruzzese village, for there were always boarders. A young man would come to Wakefield and board with the family until he had saved enough money to marry. Often, instead of a wife, he would bring over from Italy a brother or a friend to be yet another boarder. The boarders sometimes stayed for years, practically becoming family members.

For the children growing up in the house on Water Street, each day was much the same as the one before. They rose early, for Vito worked at least a ten-hour day, traveling to jobs in Cambridge and Brookline by trolley. On the few snowy days when the trolleys were not running, Vito would walk the ten miles to Boston if there was work.

Breakfast was instant cocoa and hot water with a few drops of milk and a piece of bread. Gionne's first memories would be about the cold mornings he and Grace walked to school between the mountains of snow pushed up by the plows that cleared the trolley lines, and the snow packed down by rollers and sprinkled with ashes on the road. Before he left each morning, Vito put out the wood the children were to cut into firewood after school. Grace and Gionne attended the Lincoln School on Crescent Street, a half-hour walk from home. There they first heard English spoken, and Gionne became "John."

John's first year at the Lincoln School was hard. He could understand neither the teacher nor his "American" classmates. As he learned the language, the Americans teased him about his broken English; Grace would run and hide, but John would fight. At home, he kept his troubles to himself. Vito did not want to hear about fights in school; John should appreciate his opportunity to get an education. After a year, John was fluent in English, and his grades were good, but he still fought. One afternoon on the way home from school, another Italian boy stole his book. John promptly hit him with a stone, and the boy's head began to bleed. The boy's mother reported the incident to Vito. No excuses were accepted, and Vito took off his belt and administered the customary beating. Vito did not want his sons in trouble.

While Vito worked and the children were in school, Filomena remained at home. In the Pesco community, most of the women kept house, although a few worked in family-owned groceries. There was more than enough to do at home. All the family's clothes were homemade on her machine, her first purchase in the New World. At night, while the children slept, she sewed their clothes from old blankets, curtains, and cut-up adults' clothing by the light of the kerosene lamp.

After school, the older children helped her wash the kitchen floor, make beds, and run errands for the boarders. At the age of eight, John learned to make ravioli by cutting the dough with a saucer, shape gnocchi with his thumb, and heat the pizzele iron to the right temperature on top of the old Franklin stove.

In the summer, each family used the backyard for a vegetable garden where the children tended the tomatoes, eggplant, peppers, and zucchini; no Pesco family would have considered wasting space on grass. Even the rubbish pile furnished food, as the seeds from tomatoes and melons thrown out with the ashes sprouted into new plants. The Pesco children were forbidden to play ball or learn to swim in the nearby creek. Although the Water Street house was next to a swamp where the American children skated in winter and a hill where they went sledding, none of the Pesco families let their children join them.

"They never did those things when they were young, and they were afraid for us," Vito's niece Amalia Robbins recalled. "If you skated, you might fall in. If you went swimming, you would surely drown." Filomena's fears were reinforced when Grace and John, aged five and three, played beside the forbidden creek and John had to be rescued by a fruit peddler everyone knew as the "Banana Man." When the Banana Man arrived at her door with the boy slung over his shoulder, limp as a sack, she thought at first he was selling potatoes. Even on trips to Revere Beach, the

21

children only waded and splashed, while their American counterparts swam. When their mothers were not watching, they would hold hands in a circle, count to three, and bravely duck their heads under all the way.

In the winter, the whole family was in bed by eight o'clock, but in the summer, there were evening visits to relatives and friends. Sundays were the only holidays, and Vito would decide which relatives they would visit. The whole family went together, and the children played while the adults drank homemade wine or coffee.

In all the Pesco families, the father's authority was absolute and unquestioned, enforced with a leather belt — the buckle end reserved for serious offenses. "You have to remember that all that generation of men were tough people who had hard, crude lives," Volpe's daughter Grace Gonella later recalled. "It was the same way of life in all the families. Mother was the one with you all day, the one who was affectionate. Mother never hit us. She comforted us and tried to protect the boys and to intercede for them with Father. I was never beaten because I was a girl, but it was painful for me to see them punished. I remember that John once went sledding and hurt his face after Father had forbidden him to go. Mother put him in bed and told him to keep the covers over his face, but Father noticed, and he got the beating anyway."

Vito's stern moral code operated without reference to the Catholic Church. Like many Italian men of his generation, Vito was anticlerical. The priests, he believed, were in league with the landlords. He respected the Bible and the basic teachings of Christianity but took his politics from the old conflict between the pope and the Italian nationalists over the creation of an Italian state. Volpe, like the "progressive" men of his village, supported a national government and democratic principles. The pope had formally excommunicated any Italian who voted or ran for office, but few took the prohibition seriously.

In most Italian families, the church-state conflict played itself out only in a joking accommodation. The women went to church faithfully. The men appeared, stiff and uncomfortable, only at weddings, baptisms, and funerals. Between Vito and Filomena, in the early years of their marriage, the conflict was at times bitter. Filomena was a devout church-goer who kept statues of the saints and holy pictures in the home. Vito would permit John to be baptized only after several friends and relatives had interceded. Throughout the children's early years, Vito held firm against the Church.

As the Pesco community in Wakefield grew, Vito became increasingly involved in Italian organizations and politics, although he never ran for office himself. He had learned the trade of plastering, but this was a seasonal occupation, and unless a building was completely enclosed and heated, there was no work in the coldest months. Vito spent his winters organizing. Although he was a founder of the Malden lodge of the Sons of Italy, Vito's greatest efforts went into the Pescolano Society, a "mutual aid" society for the immigrants from Pesco. After five years, the society had five hundred to six hundred members, more than the entire population of Pesco at the time. Vito was elected president. The society built a function hall and was active in all for about twenty-five or thirty years.

The mutual aid societies were the first-generation Italians' response to life in the United States; nothing like them had existed in Italy. Invariably composed of people from the same village, the societies probably began in New York, where the *Societa Unione e Fratellanza Italiana* was founded in 1863, and spread to wherever immigrants settled. By the early 1900s, there were as many as fourteen hundred active in the United States.[4] The mutual aid societies never developed into larger organizations or political movements but mostly served the immigrants' need for a social life and recreation. Although organizations such as the Sons of Italy largely replaced the old societies, a few remain active even today as combination charities and men's clubs.

The main social events of the societies were then, as today, the feasts. On the feast day of the village's patron saint, the society's officers paraded the saint's image, draped with streamers to which donors pinned money for charity, through the streets behind the band. Vito always saw to it that his sons played in the band. After the parade, there was a picnic, and the air was full of the smell of onions, grilled sausages, and stuffed clams. At night, the saint stood against a baroque backdrop of colored lights, and there was dancing and finally fireworks.

Like other mutual aid societies, the Pescolano Society functioned as a life and health insurance company for members at a time when there was no Social Security or Workmen's Compensation. Members paid dues when they were working and received a small income in case of illness, along with death benefits. When the function hall was built, it provided space for informal night classes in English and basic literacy, preparing members for citizenship and providing a nucleus around which to organize political activity. During Vito's first years in Wakefield and Malden, the Italians who did become citizens had little success in organizing politically. The Irish, and the remaining Yankees, dominated politics in the small town. "Every time the Italians put up a candidate, the people already in the jobs would get an Italian from another village to run and split the vote," Volpe's nephew Samuel Benedetto remembered. For the succeeding generation, the situation would be different, and Benedetto himself would be elected a selectman in Wakefield. For the immigrants themselves, political office would be an impossible dream.

The goal of keeping the villagers together socially was more easily realized. All through John Volpe's childhood, the Pescolano Society kept up the community spirit with celebrations of the Italian feast days just as they were celebrated in their village in the Abruzzi. At carnival time, the children dressed in Abruzzese costumes while Vito played the clown on stilts. Each new immigrant from the village would be welcomed with a party at the hall by members who could play the mandolin, the guitar, or the accordion.

In 1912, Vito Volpe rented out the Water Street house and moved back to Revere, where there was work for plasterers building beach houses in the developing summer resort. The family, now including John's younger brother, Patrick, moved into a three-room apartment over a grocery store. Vito worked for a year as a plasterer's apprentice in Revere and then returned to Wakefield. Filomena began to work for her cousin Nicolo and his wife, Vincenza, who had opened a small grocery next door to the Volpes.

Filomena wanted to stay within the security of the Pesco neighborhood, but Vito was restless. For almost all the other immigrants from Pesco, the voyage from Italy would be the only great change in their lives. Secure within the exile group, they spoke the same dialect, ate the same food, and worked as day laborers just as they had in the Abruzzi. But Vito had the skills of a journeyman plasterer, and the towns south of Boston were in the midst of a construction boom. He took another chance, as he had when he left Italy. In 1916, he left the security of the community he had started in Wakefield and sold the house on Water Street, moving the family to the center of the town of Malden, several miles south of Wakefield and closer to Boston, into an apartment near the police station. Again, they were the first Italians on the street.

Vito's English was now good enough for him to converse with "Americans," and soon after he arrived, he befriended an old Scotsman named William Bryce, who lived alone in an old shack across the street. Bryce had been a plasterer for years and began to take Volpe on jobs with him around Malden. Bryce was the introduction Volpe needed to make contact with the many small Irish and Yankee contractors in town. Within three months, the two men began to subcontract as "Bryce and Volpe,

Plasterers." Bryce did the selling and estimating and functioned as the "inside man." Volpe, the "outside man," did more of the plastering.

To make commuting to Boston and Brookline easier, Volpe moved his family to Main Street near the trolley stop, and in the fall, John began the third grade at the nearby Centre School. The parochial school was just as close, but Vito did not even consider it. All the children would attend public school.

By 1919, Bryce and Volpe, Plasterers, was doing well enough for Vito to buy a house on Eastern Avenue for $1,500. The house was a sagging wood frame building, seventy-five years old, but gradually the Volpes added plumbing, electricity, and central heat. They planted the yard behind it with a vegetable garden and copying their American neighbors, added roses, irises, and lilac bushes. Like the Main Street apartment, the Eastern Avenue house was outside the Italian section of Malden, and the Volpes' neighbors were black, Oriental, and Jewish. As it is today, the street was mostly commercial. The only rural touch was a small brook running behind the house near the railroad tracks, but the water ran dark with the effluent from a dye plant upstream.

Malden in the 1920s was a small city of about sixty-one thousand, made up of factories and factory workers. Originally a stagecoach stop in the eighteenth century, by the 1850s Malden was already industrialized. The center of both the factories and the immigrant population who provided the manpower was the neighborhood of Edgeworth, the home of Converse Rubber Company, the Boston Rubber Shoe Company, knitting mills, mattress factories, and scores of small bakeries, markets, and coal companies.

The city then had eight wards, and Edgeworth (Ward 2) was the most populous. By 1920, the Italians were beginning to catch up to the Irish numerically, but not politically. Italians often were slow to become citizens because they lacked language skills and literacy (Vito Volpe did not become naturalized until 1920), and the political life of Edgeworth was dominated by the kind of politician later generations would call "colorful" — men like John J. Lucey. Lucey, an Irish immigrant alderman whose power base was a local branch of the Ancient Order of Hibernians (AOH), drove a wagon for the Locke Coal Company by day and after working hours appeared at political functions dressed in a derby and a sleek black coat with a velvet collar. Men like Lucey had the connections to get their constituents citizenship in short order. Lucey was alleged to have taken one Irish colleague up for his citizenship exam only to have the judge ask the man the name of the current president of the United States instead of the usual queries about George Washington and Abraham Lincoln. The prospective citizen gave the name of the president of the AOH club on Charles Street, and the judge, laughing, gave the man his papers.[5] Using the name of the president of the San Rocco Society probably would not have elicited such a favorable response.

Italians in Edgeworth got their citizenship later, usually through the Americanization schools that employers set up in the factory buildings after working hours so that immigrants could "get a better idea of true Americanism." The classes were geared primarily toward increasing work efficiency. A 1920 poster proclaimed: "When making enrollment, the points to consider are; I shall be able to: 1. read and write better 2. understand my foreman's directions better 3. do more efficient work." But for the first-generation Italians, this was the only education they would ever get, and they were thankful for the opportunity. A photo from the 1920s shows an Americanization class at Converse Rubber: the young workingmen sit at school desks looking solemn, their hands folded before them like small children, learning the Pledge of Allegiance.

Edgeworth in the 1920s was a mill town of narrow, unpaved streets and small, wooden houses. Wages were low, and it took at least two workers to support one Italian family. In the morning, the men walked to the rubber shoe factories, and the women, dressed in long skirts and aprons with scissors at the waist, walked to the knitting mills. Unmarried girls might commute to the candy factories in Cambridge and Somerville, but mothers had to work close to home. Even though virtually all the women worked, small children were never left unattended. "Italians are the only immigrant women who make no charge for tending to others' children," Robert Foerster wrote in *The Italian Immigration of Our Times.* Various forms of welfare and poor relief were available at that time, but in the Italian community, the stigma would have been too great to endure.

At noon, the mothers returned home from the mills for an hour to fix a hot lunch with the produce they bought fresh from pushcarts in the streets or at the factory gates. Meat was a rarity, but vegetables were plentiful; often five or six vegetables were served with the pasta at one meal. In summer, every inch of space around each home was put to use growing vegetables, and there was usually a grape arbor along the back fence. After work, the men sat under the arbor on benches drinking homemade wine or playing bocce on the packed earth.

"There was a sense of community you won't find today," Bill Mini, a Malden High School teacher who grew up in Edgeworth, remembered.

"If you had trouble with your wagon in the street, someone would help you. If you were sick, your Italian neighbor brought spaghetti. The Jews brought chicken soup. Doors were really never locked. I remember that the women would sit on the front porch nursing their babies, and we kids would pass by and say hello and never think that wasn't proper. We cut our own hair, patched clothes, fixed the soles of our shoes with cardboard or, if we were really affluent, with rubber soles from the ten-cent store. People couldn't afford coal in the furnace — coal was two weeks' pay — so they burned scrap lumber, battery casings, anything. If you got desperate, you burned the woodshed."

But the closeness of the ethnic neighborhoods had its dark side. Max Goldberg, now a Malden attorney, was a high school classmate of John Volpe's in Malden. He remembered the fights and the fierce territoriality of the same streets. "If you were going through a neighborhood where you didn't belong, you went with five or six other guys. You ended up on the wrong street, and you could be greeted with a hail of stones. I still have scars from the rock fights. We had boundary lines you didn't dare cross. There are isolated incidents of this kind of thing today, but nothing like the bigotry and prejudice that existed then."

The Volpe family still maintained close ties with the Wakefield cousins during the years that John was growing up in Malden, but as the children became more involved in school, and the father in building his own business, the distance grew. One of Grace Gonella's most vivid memories concerned the children's own expedition back to Wakefield on Memorial Day in 1918. John, then nine, saw the parade going down Main Street to the cemetery and persuaded the other children to follow the band. Pushing the baby in his carriage, they marched to the cemetery. Once there, John felt it would be just a short walk on to Wakefield and led them on a five-mile hike in the hot sun. At Wakefield Square, a former neighbor took the tired travelers and the wet baby in, fed them, and brought them back on the trolley to their frantic parents. Instead of a hero's welcome, the expedition's leader got the stiffest beating.

At eleven, John was already working with his father on weekends, learning to mix the plaster and carry a hod up a ladder. But his real interest had suddenly become school. "I remember we would all be playing, and John would be studying," John's cousin Amalia Robbins recalled. "We would tease him, but my mother would rush in and say, 'Let him alone — someday you'll wish you had studied.' The rest of us weren't interested in books." Here John was lucky, for Malden had a better public school system than the surrounding towns.

Morris Slonim, a former teacher and statistician for the Air Force, and a classmate of John Volpe's, remembered Malden High School's academic standards. "When I entered Harvard from Malden High, there were two courses on physics for freshmen. I had only taken one year of physics at Malden, and I asked the professor if I could take the harder course. He asked me where I had gone to high school. All the other Harvard students seemed to be from prep schools, and I figured he had never heard of Malden High. To my amazement, he asked me what I got from Johnny Hutchins. When I told him an A, he suggested I take the harder course. I was just as well prepared for Harvard as any boy from prep school."

Although the town was not wealthy, about half the high school's graduating class went on to college, and almost all followed the pattern of immigrant parents by working after school. For the Jewish immigrants in Malden, who then numbered about twelve thousand, education for the children was a goal to be realized at all costs. "Our parents came here for the opportunity," Max Goldberg explained. "We were supposed to make the most of it. We never questioned their ambitions for us. My father was an orphan who left Poland when he was thirteen to escape the pogroms. He had a credit clothing business in Boston, Goldberg Brothers. People put a five-dollar down payment on a suit and paid fifty cents a week on it. I was a big kid at thirteen, and he sent me out to South Boston and Charlestown to make the collections. The customers never gave me any trouble — they were all basically very honest but very poor.

"All the Jewish families had small businesses, and the only way they made ends meet was by working fifty or sixty hours a week and having the kids work. One thing I remember about John was meeting him downtown when he was at Wentworth, and he had plaster on his shoes. We knew we had this great chance for an education our parents had been denied, and we took it."

Harry Reinherz, another classmate, told a similar story. "My father came alone at eleven from Latvia. He stayed with relatives and worked for them until he was able to live alone. Neither he nor his brothers or sisters could read or write. He started out peddling door to door, just as people did in the old country. He carried staples like needles and thread, and samples of things like silverware. Then he got a horse and buggy and finally opened a men's clothing store in 1912. Our generation spoke Yiddish at home and picked up our English in the streets. All our families started out poor around 1900, but they started to make money after

28

World War I. By 1918, we had a Ford, and we could see then that we were going to make it."

In addition to his plastering jobs, Vito Volpe was working the night shift at a cardboard box factory, while Filomena worked at a knitting mill during the day. In the summer, John and Patrick met the produce trucks from Boston at 6 A.M., helped unload the vegetables, and worked until 6 P.M. for the local pushcart owners for fifty cents a day and whatever vegetables were left over. Throughout his school years, like most Italian boys, John would work off and on as a grocery store stock boy, a soda jerk, a meat cutter, and a laborer, earning about $4 a week for the family.

The fact that John, a first son, stayed in school was unusual. "The older kids would always leave school by fourteen," Bill Mini recalled. "My family was pretty typical. There were five kids, and both my parents worked. My older brother quit after the seventh grade to work, and my older sister quit after the fifth grade. Then there was enough money coming in so that the three youngest could finish high school. No one considered college then.

"Our parents had great respect, even awe, for education. If you went home and told your father the teacher hit you, you'd get another belt from him. The teacher was always right. But our parents couldn't speak the language, and they were ashamed to see the teacher. There were no guidance counselors; nobody ever told us we *could* go to college. So we went to work."

Even for a child, work in the summers and after school meant long hours and adult responsibilities. Children of fourteen worked the night shift at bakeries scrubbing pans or delivered milk on contract by horse and buggy until 3 A.M. Mini wrote years later of his days on his father's produce wagon:

"My father would park his horse and wagon outside Converse Rubber each day at 3:30. When the people would come out at 4:00, they would stop to buy their fruit and vegetables. I took care of the cuff book, and on pay day, which was Friday, the bills would be paid. After all the people had left the shop, we would pack our wagon and roam the streets of Edgeworth yelling 'Shala Borbala,' a name that the people of Edgeworth knew my father as. It was an Italian expression for one who carried everything in the market and sold it cheap.

"If we had anything left on the wagon by six or seven o'clock, we would put samples in a small basket and hit all the barrooms. This would usually finish off the load. Whatever was left went home to be consumed by the Mini family."[6]

Although Vito discouraged sports, the Volpe boys were given music lessons by a Calabrese musician named Domenic Sica. John learned to play the guitar at twelve and Pat the mandolin, and the two played at weddings and christenings or with a local group. At the time, the only Italian band in Boston was the Roma Band in the North End, so Vito decided to start another. Dubbed the Sons of Italy Band, the group practiced in the basement of the house on Eastern Avenue. The band eventually grew to about twenty-five members, with John on the bass drum and Patrick on the French horn. They played at the annual San Rocco festivals in Edgeworth, marching behind the little girls dressed up as angels, saints, and Sicilian peasants.

"All the people in the Jewish community knew the Volpes because of the father's business and the sons' music," John's classmate Harry Reinharz recalled. "They had the respect and goodwill of the neighborhood. They had everything but money."

At Malden High, John played in the school band, and he began to share the dream of the Jewish boys: college. Math was his favorite subject, and in the tenth grade, he enrolled in the college preparatory course, hoping to study engineering at MIT.

Many years later novelist Mario Puzo wrote in *The Fortunate Pilgrim* words that described well the dream of the young Volpe: "[A]s a child, the wildest dream had been to escape the fear of hunger, sickness, and the force of nature. The dream was to stay alive. No one dreamed further. But in America, wilder dreams were possible. . . . Bread and shelter were not enough."

For both father and son, the high school years were full of hope. Vito Volpe bought a used Dodge truck to replace the horse and wagon that had replaced his pushcart full of mason's supplies. Then came a Maxwell "touring car." John drove back to Wakefield with his guitar to serenade his cousin Jennie Benedetto, bring her chocolates, and have coffee and cookies with the family. Short and wiry, with thick black hair slicked back into a pompadour, John was popular with his classmates. Because of his hair and his temper, his nickname at school was "Firpo," after the Argentinian prizefighter known as the "Wild Bull of the Pampas."

John sometimes was quick to anger and could hold a grudge. When he sprained his wrist cranking up the family truck, he and Vito quarreled. Vito forbade him to use the truck for a month. John countered that he would *never* drive the truck again! For six months, John refused to drive, doing his errands on foot. Then he realized that he was only punishing himself and began to drive again.

"John used to come every day after school to my house and study algebra with me," Morris Slonim remembered. "And he must have been an unusual person because my parents were very Orthodox and usually didn't have Gentiles over. They thought well of him, and so did I. He was a nice kid, quiet, reliable — and later, when I heard he was in politics, I didn't believe it at first. He didn't seem the type. I remember when I was accepted at Harvard, all my relatives came over, but he was the only one of my classmates who came to the house to congratulate me."

For John, the congratulatory visit was both happy and painful. At the beginning of John's senior year, Vito Volpe's partner died. The partnership had been running into trouble because of Bryce's alcohol problems. Now Vito did not want to work with a stranger and could not run the business alone. He took John aside after school. "I think MIT can do without you," he said, simply. "I can't." There was no discussion. John switched from the college preparatory course to the technical.

On June 17, 1926, the family gave a party to celebrate the first high school graduation in the clan. This was cause for celebration at a time when few Italian children received diplomas. The Sons of Italy musicians played, and all the families he knew in Wakefield were there.

In September, while his friends from Malden High went to Northeastern, Boston University, and Harvard, Volpe signed up for evening blueprint-reading courses at a Boston technical school, Wentworth Institute, and "Volpe and Son" began operation.

NOTES

1. *The Boston Globe,* 6 April 1982.

2. Amy Wood, "The Italians in New England," *New England Magazine,* n.s. 35 (1906), p. 21.

3. *Report of the Commission on Immigration* (Boston: Committee of One Hundred for Massachusetts Immigration Legislation Pubs., 1914), p. 5.

4. Carl Wittke, *We Who Build America: The Saga of the Immigrant* (Cleveland: Case Western Reserve University Press, 1967), p. 447.

5. *Malden This Week,* 13 March 1980.

6. *Malden This Week,* 13 July 1980.

CHAPTER III

Volpe and Son

VOLPE AND SON was not a success. For a little more than a year, the Volpes worked on plastering jobs together, but the building boom of the early twenties had peaked. Vito, strong and heavyset in his youth, was aging now. And John had not inherited his father's endurance; small and light, he was not built for the grueling ten-hour days carrying a hod up the ladder, constantly inhaling plaster dust. But this was the only trade he knew. Soon there was not enough work for the two of them, and John hired out to another contractor, William P. LaSpina.

The summer of 1928 was to change John's life. When he first began to work for LaSpina for $75 a week (including estimating on weekends), his life seemed to have come to a standstill. College seemed an impossible dream. He was nineteen, still living at home, courting Jennie but without the means to support her, and attending night classes at Wentworth Institute. He worked hard at his studies but found it more and more difficult to absorb the course material after a full day on a construction job.

Bill LaSpina was an unusual boss. A kind and gentle man, LaSpina also was intensely religious. As John confided in him, LaSpina advised him to join a Catholic study group for young people in Edgeworth. John began to take instruction in the Catholic faith for the first time. John did not tell Vito initially, but when the time came for his First Communion, he found that his father had no objections. "You're old enough now to

choose for yourself," Vito told him. "After all," he added, "Christ w
over thirty when He was baptized." John received Holy Communion 1
the first time at the age of nineteen. LaSpina, like Vito Volpe, also w
interested in involving other Italian-Americans in community projec
John and LaSpina founded the Italian-American Citizens Club with
small clubhouse. At its height, the organization had about 150 to 2(
members and worked on voter registration and citizenship issues.

While he worked on a job at a Somerville apartment house th
summer, John met Dick Dwan, who was already a construction superi
tendent at the age of twenty-six. Impressed by Dwan's competence, Jol
asked how he had become superintendent so young. Dwan, a carpent
replied that he had gone full-time to Wentworth for two years and earn
a degree in architectural construction. Although this would mean spen
ing his savings and cutting his expenses to the bone, John resolved to go
Wentworth full-time beginning in September. There would, he realize
be no more evenings out with his friends, and his courtship of Jenn
would have to stop. One evening, he told her simply, "We can't continu
to go steady. Let's just be pals." Jennie was shocked but agreed. Sh
continued her nurse's training at Winchester Hospital and later at Bell
vue Hospital in New York.

Wentworth Institute was then a technical institute, not a degre
granting college, but the students were given a complete course in draf
ing, rudimentary engineering, and construction methods. Part of th
curriculum involved the class in building every section of a house i
basement shops.

Volpe graduated from Wentworth in June 1930, but by then th
Depression had put almost all building on hold, and only he and one othe
graduate received job offers. Volpe had to choose between working fo
Stone and Webster, an international engineering firm for $27.50 per week
or a local company, Frankini Construction, for $25. Reasoning that h
would get more varied experience with a smaller company, Volpe, un
knowingly, made the choice that would lead him to found his own com
pany. Stone and Webster remained sound during the Depression, and ha
he worked there, Volpe probably would never have considered leaving a
secure job to start his own business in the 1930s.

Frankini went under in two years. Volpe, starting as timekeeper on a
project at a junior high school in Somerville, had worked up to foreman
then superintendent. Trying to salvage the failing company, Volpe and his
supervisor, a recent MIT graduate named Romeo Bossi, worked sixteen-
hour days on the jobs through Saturday and did their estimating on

33

Sundays. Volpe was one of the last men working on Frankini's last job at Norfolk Prison, and then the company went into receivership.

John Volpe was twenty-four, out of work, without a college degree, and still living at home. Vito Volpe's prospects were similarly bleak. He had been a subcontractor on a development whose owner had overbuilt. Just before the crash of 1929, the new homes remained unsold. Of the twenty subcontractors, all but Vito declared bankruptcy. This Vito could not do. He went to each creditor, asking for time. Then, with his last savings, he bought a gas station in Malden and began the process of working to pay off his debts. John returned to selling door to door in Wakefield. He sold coal for the Blue Coal Company, along with shirts, dresses, and ladies' underwear. He tried not to become bitter. Many others were in a worse position than he was, he reasoned. He had a home and the support of his family. He had voted for Franklin Roosevelt and believed, as did most of his friends, that the Depression soon would end.

In March 1933, during the week of the national Bank Holiday, the cousin of an old friend, a bricklayer foreman named Fred Grande, dropped by the Eastern Avenue house to see whether John would be interested in bidding with him for a job to convert an old theater in Everett into a church. Each partner would have to come up with $500 to be bonded. Volpe promptly cashed in an insurance policy for $300 and borrowed another $200 from an uncle, and the two men were in business as Grande and Volpe. They did not get the church conversion job, but shortly afterward, Volpe figured out the successful bid for an addition to the heating plant of the Eastern Massachusetts Street Railway's car barn in West Lynn. The bid was for $1,287. Grande and Volpe were low bidders by $14.

Other small jobs followed, mostly public works, as Volpe, with virtually no overhead, was able to underbid established companies. The main obstacle he faced was bonding, but Volpe was able to get the loans from Malden Trust. The bank's officers remembered that Vito Volpe was the only subcontractor on the housing development job who did not declare bankruptcy, and they extended their confidence to his son.

On the first few jobs, Volpe worked at the sites, setting frames, pouring concrete, and shooting grades, but soon he was spending more time at his desk than at the job site. Volpe became the "inside man," making the phone calls, estimating, following up leads in the commercial journals, taking architects to lunch. To save on overhead, he used a desk in the front parlor of the Eastern Avenue house, gradually taking over more and more space in his parents' home. Grande, big, bluff, and occasionally

hot-tempered, was the field man who stayed long hours on the sites and socialized with the men — a hard worker. After the first several years in operation, Grande and Volpe specialized in "monumental" construction: schools, offices, police stations, and hospitals. The company did not build houses, except housing units on military bases, or bid on highway work. When work was slow, Grande moonlighted as a bricklayer for other companies, but Volpe never did plastering work again.

Within two years of his own company's founding, Volpe was also helping organize an association of building contractors to lobby at the state level for their own interests. For three years, Volpe served as secretary of the fledgling Building Contractors Association of Massachusetts, which later was affiliated with the national Associated General Contractors of America (AGC). Three years after he sent in his first bid for Grande and Volpe, Volpe was in Indiana representing the Massachusetts branch at the AGC's national convention.

In 1934, Volpe finally felt secure enough about his prospects to propose to Jennie after a long, and often frantic, courtship that had included night buses to New York City, where she was finishing her nurse's training at Bellevue Hospital. On one weekend visit, finding that Jennie had drawn weekend duty, John dressed as a doctor to be near her while she worked. But it was Jennie who had the last laugh; she was assigned to the syphilis ward. Volpe never tried the doctor routine again.

Once Jennie had her degree, she returned home to Wakefield, and on June 18, 1934, John and Jennie were married at St. Joseph's Church, John gaunt and tired after fifteen months' work getting the company started. After the grand Italian wedding reception, the couple drove away in the used 1926 Chevrolet John had bought for the business. They returned to their new home, an attic apartment in a single-family house in Malden, and Jennie began working nights at Winchester Hospital.

Shortly after John Volpe moved off Eastern Avenue, his business moved in permanently. Beside the front porch of the old house, he built an eight- by ten-foot concrete block addition, with a partition and just room enough for a desk and a chair. He hired his first secretary, Armita Palmerino. Vito Volpe sold his gas station, going to work instead for his son as watchman and general assistant.

"When I came to work there, John's parents and Peter were still living in the house," Palmerino, now Mrs. Peter Volpe, remembered. "The office itself was a tiny room added to the front where the yard had been. John's office was behind mine, and there was hardly room to shut the door; the estimators had to spread the blueprints out in the living room. I remember John would not waste a minute. Always on the go. 'I'm not in business for my health,' he'd say. Jennie was still nursing. Vito was helping, too, running errands, driving out to the sites. John was not much help on the site because he was not good mechanically. His mother was the homey type; she'd cook dinner for all of us at noon.

"Everything was done to build the business; all the energy of the family went into it. Later, when the company closed for the war and I went to work for another contractor, the other girls asked me, 'Don't you know how to stretch your work?' Nobody learned to stretch their work with John Volpe."

At first, all jobs came through public bidding, and most were small buildings. Gradually, Volpe cultivated friendships with architects and began to be an invited bidder. Although the jobs increased steadily in size, company profits did not always keep pace because John's relentless search for new business kept the office busy bidding on ever-larger jobs. If the bids did not win, the loss of time would gradually eat up the profits of completed jobs. A safer course would have been to continue bidding in the same price range from year to year, but John continued to gamble.

John's youngest brother, Peter, began to work nights for the business after graduating from high school, while he attended Wentworth. Peter began as a timekeeper, handyman, and payroll clerk and worked up to assistant engineer. "When I started out, Fred Grande was working outside; there were two superintendents, four or five foremen, maybe a total of ten people in management," Peter said. "John would almost never fire a good engineer; even if he did not have the work, he'd keep him busy estimating. When you're a small construction company, your managers *are* your capital, what you build on. The workers are hired by the hour, and the equipment is rented. He always had a knack for keeping that core of employees loyal — very few of them ever left except to start their own companies.

"When you're a small company like we were then, you have certain advantages. Your low overhead allows you to underbid the big companies on the public works jobs, and in the Depression, public works was the only business available. But there were a lot of small companies competing for those few jobs. For every job in construction you worked on, you knew there were at least four or five guys waiting to take your place. The problems for a small company come when you try to make the transition to multimillion-dollar jobs. Suddenly, your size is no longer an advantage but a drawback. You cannot absorb the losses if the job turns sour. One mistake at this point, and you're out."

A year after John and Jennie had set up housekeeping in the attic flat in Malden, they moved to somewhat larger quarters on Judson Street, and on April 22, 1936, their first child, Loretta Jean (later shortened to "Jean"), was born. That summer, despite his frantic schedule at the construction company, Volpe made his first run at public office.

In the early thirties, ethnic alliances were not as firmly fixed politically as they would become after World War II. Yankees (a term that by then included Scandinavian and German immigrants and their descendants) no longer predominated numerically in Massachusetts, but they were still a considerable force in the state legislature and still ran the Republican party. The Irish, by far the largest immigrant group, dominated the Democratic party. ("There are three political parties in Massachusetts," Boston's Richard Cardinal Cushing used to joke, "the Democrats, the Republicans, and the Italians.") In the larger cities, the Italians tended simply to follow the Democratic machine, but in smaller enclaves such as Medford and Malden, the Italians, eastern Europeans, and Jews sometimes ran on the Republican ticket to bypass the machines.

When John Volpe turned twenty-three in 1932, he voted for Franklin Roosevelt, like nearly everyone else in Edgeworth. When the promised economic miracles failed to appear, he began to be drawn more toward the opinions of Joseph Tauro, a local lawyer whose family came from the same part of Italy as the Volpes. Tauro, who was the Volpe family's lawyer, advised young Volpe that the Republican party offered more to a man interested in having his own business.

Although the city had voted solidly for Roosevelt, Malden was almost evenly divided between Republicans and Democrats before World War II. Max Goldberg, a Malden lawyer long active in politics, remembered that party loyalties in Malden were not as fixed as they were in Boston. If the competition in the primary looked too tough, a man might switch. Several of the Jewish politicians did.

"When we came from the cities, we were all Democrats," Goldberg recalled. "We were working people — we didn't know anything about capitalism. But after we'd come up in the world somewhat, or for personal reasons, people changed. Louis Glaser was a Republican state rep from Malden, later a judge. George Fingold was a Democrat on the common council, and he got beaten so badly in a state senatorial race he became a Republican. When I went to run for common council as a Democrat, I found I myself had been registered as a Republican at twenty-one."

In the spring of 1936, Joseph Tauro, then a leader in the Republican party in Malden, held an organizational meeting at his home on Highland

Avenue. As usual, the problem was how to get an Italian-American elected to the council or school committee. By this time, Italian-Americans constituted about 40 percent of the voters in Ward 2 but always sent three Irish-American representatives to the council, as the Italian-Americans invariably split the vote.

The Volpe home on Eastern Avenue, where John was still registered, was in Ward 1. Tauro and the others present convinced Volpe to run at-large for school committee, where the field was large, to test the waters. Volpe also was offered support from local Jewish leaders.

Being a representative on the Malden School Committee was an unpaid position, and like the Boston School Committee, it often was a steppingstone to higher political office. Since there were not many divisive issues, the election usually was a popularity contest. Volpe set out to campaign with his usual enthusiasm, sending out flyers and putting up posters. The Sons of Italy helped, but the lodge at that time was not well organized. The Italian-American Citizens Club that Volpe had founded with LaSpina was still operating, and members lent their time and effort. This was the extent of Volpe's base of support.

One of his Malden High classmates, Morris Slonim, remembered seeing the campaign posters: "I left Malden after college, and I remember on a visit home I was amazed to see 'Volpe for School Committee' posters and thinking it couldn't be the same guy. He was so studious, so basically shy, I couldn't imagine him out there shaking hands and making deals in back rooms. He didn't even smoke! I didn't really believe it until he ran for governor and I saw his picture, and then I knew it was him."

Within ten days of Volpe's announcement, another Italian declared for an at-large seat, just as had always happened when an Italian declared in Ward 2. Volpe's friends convinced the other candidate to withdraw. Still, Volpe finished fifth in a field of ten, just ahead of a Congregationalist minister. Only the top four were nominated.

"That cured him for a while," his brother Peter recalled. In fact, he would never run for local office again, but the interest in public service stayed with him, finding other outlets: the Sons of Italy, lobbying for the Associated General Contractors, charities, committees, fund drives. From then on, he rarely missed an opportunity to speak at a function, serve on a committee, testify before the legislature, or write to his representatives. If the Associated General Contractors opposed or favored a crucial piece of legislation and Volpe agreed, every legislator would receive a letter, and a copy of his answer would go into the files for next time.

Before World War II, most of Volpe's working hours were spent building his business. It was at this time that he hired the men who would become the core of the company: Salvatore Danca, an accountant and best man at his wedding, and Gosta ("Gus") Mortenson and Pasquale ("Patsy") di Milla, both carpenters who worked their way up to foreman, superintendent, and general superintendent.

Danca was one of Volpe's first regular employees. As teenagers at Malden High, the two had gone to boxing and wrestling matches at the old Malden Arena and double-dated at the amusement parks and the beaches of Nantasket and New Hampshire. Di Milla had worked as a carpenter with Volpe on his first job for Frankini Brothers in Somerville in 1930. He would stay with Volpe for more than forty years. Volpe also hired his former supervisor at Frankini Brothers, Romeo Bossi, a few years after Frankini went out of business.

For all his interest in the democratic process, Volpe's style of administration within his own company was anything but democratic. "John was always the boss," Fred Dobson, an engineer who came to work for the company after World War II, remembered. "He would talk to others, get their opinions, but he made all the decisions. Once made, they were not questioned. He did a certain amount of political and civic work at the office, but during the day he was always there, always knew what went on. Often, he'd go around the office and take us all out to lunch. When he was alone, he'd eat at the local diner, not some private club. He didn't harbor resentments. He never swore, which is pretty unusual in this business. But when he got through raking you over the coals, you got the message loud and clear."

As long as John Volpe was in charge, the style of administration remained strictly paternalistic. And there were benefits: profit sharing, lavishly catered Italian company picnics complete with bocce tournaments, bonuses, and gifts. Early on, Volpe began the practice of sending flowers, cookies, presents, and fruit on holidays, birthdays, and sick days. The gift lists grew longer as he drifted into public life. He was generous but expected others to be generous in return.

From 1935 to 1942, the dollar value of the jobs rose steadily, though most were still won by public bidding — the hard way. A school in Wrentham for $81,000 in 1935. The town hall in Stoneham for $145,000 in 1938. A hangar for the U.S. Navy in Squantum for $203,000 in 1940.

In the fall of 1939 came the transition to the first million-dollar job, a post office garage in South Boston. When he got the news that his was the low bid, Volpe took the train to Washington to see the chief engineer of the federal Public Works Administration (PWA). The engineer, sizing up the twenty-nine-year-old Volpe, asked why Volpe senior had not come. "I am the Volpe of Grande and Volpe," John replied. "You look very, very young," the engineer answered, and proceeded to fill him in on the potential problems with the job.

South Boston, where the postal garage was located, had once been a peninsula ending in a fort called Castle Island. The land close to Boston around the annex had been a maze of old wooden wharves, channels, and stone jetties, gradually filled in as the brick warehouses around South Station were built for the textile industry. Volpe's crew had drilled samples, but no one knew what was really down there. In addition, the schedule specified that much of the work would have to be done in winter. Anticipating a sour job, most of the established contractors had avoided bidding on it. The word went out that Grande and Volpe were headed for bankruptcy.

But Grande and Volpe were able to pull it off, using a new, faster dehydrating process for concrete from a company in Pennsylvania. Two years later, Volpe presented the finished building to the federal inspectors. The postal garage job was a turning point in Volpe's personal fortunes. The business was still not incorporated, and the two men owned it as a personal partnership. With the profits, Volpe allowed himself the first taste of an affluent way of life — a new garrison colonial house in Winchester, near the hospital where Jennie had worked, and a 1938 Oldsmobile, their first new car. In February 1940, he took Jennie and three-year-old Jean by ship to Cape Hatteras, North Carolina, then to Savannah, Georgia, and finally by car to Miami. It was the family's first vacation.

The next winter, the family went off to Florida again, this time with one of Jennie's sisters. After the years of struggling in the house on Eastern Avenue, the sudden days of freedom on the road, the comfortable car, and time alone with his small family far from Malden seemed almost a fantasy. Stopping at a motel in St. Petersburg one afternoon, the four of them strolled over to a band concert in the park at the edge of the sea. The night was warm, and Jean fell asleep. As the band played the national anthem in the tropical sunset, John stood with the rest of the audience, remembering all the times he had played that tune with the Verdi Band at the Italian feasts, and tears came to his eyes. Edgeworth seemed very far away. He was only thirty-two and had achieved more than even Vito, with all his dreams of America, had thought possible. And yet he was seeing for the first time just how big the country was outside the Italian ghetto and beginning to understand how much further there was to go. What Vito had seen as the end might be only the beginning.

40

CHAPTER IV

"Competence Brings Respect"

BY 1939, THE OLD HOUSE on Eastern Avenue stood behind a new facade: a wall of multicolored brick and glass blocks, with tiny windows on the first floor. Office space had taken over both the first floor and the several additions that filled what had been the backyard. The secretaries joked that with one more addition, they'd be sitting on the railroad tracks. The firm was now one of the larger construction companies in the area, doing million-dollar jobs, and yet Vito and Filomena still lived upstairs.

The street itself had changed little since the Volpes bought the house, other than to become slightly more commercial. Harold Askenazi, their next-door neighbor, had moved away but remodeled his house into his business, Malden Glass. The diner and the gas station across the street were still there, and the radiator shop next door had been there long before the Volpes came.

For a year, John and Jennie had been living in Winchester, a suburb of large lawns, Victorian houses, a lake, and a country club. Instead of freight, the train carried husbands to North Station and then the financial district. Not many Italians had made it yet to Winchester, but there was a Sons of Italy lodge, which Volpe joined. One of the Volpes' first new friends was Dr. Angelo Maietta, who had a family practice at Winchester Hospital, where Jennie had worked.

Although Maietta was born in Medford, studied at the Middlesex College of Medicine in Waltham, and never left the small towns north of Boston, he cherished a romantic view of Italy and Italian culture at a time when many Italian-Americans were trying to leave their language and culture behind as they moved from the old neighborhoods. It was not an easy time to proclaim pride in an Italian heritage. The middle thirties had seen an upsurge in publicity about the Mafia, "public enemies," shoot-outs, and FBI heroes such as Melvin Purvis.

Although he was already well established and did not need the con-tacts to build his practice, "Ange" Maietta was the driving force behind the Winchester lodge (number 1580) of the Sons of Italy. As the two men became friends, Maietta began to introduce Volpe to a more glamorous concept of Italian civilization than he had absorbed at home and in Edgeworth at the saints' feasts under the colored lightbulbs. Maietta talked of the Italy of grand opera, baroque palazzi, Renaissance princes, Roman ruins, poets, and emperors. This was heady stuff for a man who spent his days calculating the amount of concrete needed for a school basement.

While Volpe was assistant venerable at the Winchester lodge, Maietta decided to rewrite the initiation ritual, changing it from a simple swear-ing-in ceremony to a performance more like the rituals of the Freemasons and the Knights of Columbus. But unlike the rituals of other fraternal organizations, the Sons of Italy's ceremonies were not held in secret. Maietta's secular ritual was performed for the first time at the Winchester Town Hall and included participating lodges from the neighboring towns of Medford, Woburn, Melrose, and Malden.

The new initiation ceremonies were performed on Sunday after-noons by the Winchester ritualistic team, featuring Maietta himself as herald and Volpe as installing officer. Resplendent in long red, white, and blue gowns with silk-lined hoods and emerald green sashes, the men of the ritualistic team paraded into the lodge with their arms crossed, left over right, to a piano rendition of their anthem, "Sons of Italy in America" — words by Dr. Maietta to the tune of "O Tannenbaum." At the front of the lodge stood an altar draped with red, white, and blue bunting and a single candle. On each side and to the rear of the hall stood three officers with boxes representing liberty, equality, and fraternity, with electric lighting inside that could be turned on during appropriate parts of the ceremony.

After a long recital of the accomplishments of Italian-Americans from Amerigo Vespucci to the present, Maietta concluded: "Awaken, therefore, O Sons of Italy in America! Cast aside the shackles of lethargy and become alive to the glorious heritage bequeathed to you by our illustrious ancestors. Awaken, I say, to live again and again, both by word and by deed, their noble achievements and be ever proud and ever worthy of being Americans of Italian extraction. Harken once again to the inspiring words of the oath of initiation, which states in part, that I believe in retaining the most affectionate regard for the rich cultural patrimony of the land of my forefathers."

After the first initiation of about a hundred men and women, requests from other lodges came in, and soon the "degree team," as it became known, was traveling all over Massachusetts and as far as Pennsylvania and New Jersey — including the national office in Philadelphia — to install new members and officers. Until after World War II, Winchester had the only degree team in the United States, and Volpe and Maietta made friends in the Massachusetts lodges and elsewhere. Often the lodge officers were town officials and politicians who would remember Volpe later.

Although both Maietta and Volpe were Republicans, their only political effort at the Winchester lodge was to lobby for a state law funding teaching of the Italian language in Massachusetts public high schools if fifteen students could be found to sign up. The law eventually was enacted but was not often implemented because few students signed up. For years in his speeches to members of Sons of Italy lodges and other Italian-American organizations, Volpe included a plea to register their children for the classes. Yet at that time, his own fluency in the language was fading. He and Maietta always spoke English to each other. Neither man had ever seen Italy, for by the time they could afford to go, Italy had become a fascist state. All the Sons of Italy ceremonies they wrote were in English.

With the coming of war in 1941, the construction business was finally emerging from the Depression. Grande and Volpe built a hangar for the Navy in Squantum, a USO club for the Army in Lowell, barracks for the Navy in Hingham and Braintree, gun mounts for the Army, and finally, a 250-unit military dependents' housing project in Bath, Maine. In March 1942, John Volpe, Junior, was born. Now thirty-three years old, with two children and contracts for vital defense work, John Volpe stood no chance of being drafted. But construction workers and engineers alike began to leave the company to go into uniform.

The business faced internal problems as well. Tensions had developed between Volpe and Fred Grande, and they worsened as the company expanded. In 1941, the two agreed to split the assets and go their separate ways. Some of Grande's relatives had been in the business, and they left with him.

With the war in full swing, the Volpe Construction Company was doing nothing but defense work, yet Volpe himself was restless as more and more of his friends volunteered or were drafted. He had been too young for World War I. The fact that the United States was at war with the homeland presented few problems, for Mussolini was never popular with Italians in America. What held Volpe back was his family. Jennie knew nothing about construction and had two young children to raise. Vito was growing old, and Peter was too young to run the business. Patrick had not gone into the construction industry. Without John Volpe and Frank Marcucella, the MIT graduate engineer who was now helping him run the company, the business could soon become worthless. As he traveled with the degree team urging Italian-Americans to combine a sentimental feeling for Italian culture with patriotic duty to America, he became increasingly uneasy.

The turning point came when Ange Maietta volunteered for the Army Medical Corps. Volpe debated about which branch of the service he should join. Later, he would joke that his motivation was his building experience — the Navy's officers' barracks were more comfortable than the Army's. There was only one drawback to going in the Navy: Volpe had never learned to swim, and no one made it out of Naval Officers Candidate School without passing the deep-end test.

In late 1942, about halfway through the company's last job, the military housing project in Bath, Maine, Volpe volunteered for the Seabees, hoping to become a roving construction supervisor, building installations across the Pacific as the Navy advanced toward Japan. He also mentioned his ability to speak Italian as a qualification for duty in Europe, but like his Italian-American friends, he found the services uninterested in that particular skill. Despite his obvious experience, Volpe could not qualify as a lieutenant commander because he did not have a college degree, so he accepted a commission in January 1943 as lieutenant jg (junior grade). His brothers Peter and Richard followed him into the Seabees. Patrick Volpe received an appointment with the regular Navy. Even Vito volunteered for civilian duty with the Coast Guard.

Before John left, Jennie insisted that after the completion of the Bath project all the assets of the company would be liquidated and put into the bank for the family. Thinking that there would be an enormous demand for housing once the war was over, Volpe wanted to buy twenty or thirty two-family homes as an investment, but Jennie refused. Who would collect the rents and manage the properties? They compromised on two houses, and shortly after he left, one of them was partly destroyed by fire.

In February 1943, Lieutenant jg Volpe was not flying into tropical sunsets over the Pacific but riding a crowded train south to Virginia into his first experience with legal segregation. He went through basic training at Camp Allen, in Norfolk, then six more weeks of boot camp at Camp Peary, not far from Williamsburg. One of his first assignments at Camp Peary was policing the barracks. Policing, he discovered, did not mean guard duty. "After being the president of my own company, I found myself all of a sudden collecting bits and pieces of refuse on the base," he wrote to a friend. "It's really a comedown."

But worse was coming. In April, after basic training, Volpe's newly organized battalion was sent overseas. Volpe was assigned to stay at Camp Peary and train black sailors in a separate unit for work in construction battalions.

The conditions for draftees were such that even the Navy described them as "far from ideal." Camp Peary was taking in as many as a hundred black men a month. Yet the Navy placed black sailors only as cooks and mess workers, so the excess trainees simply accumulated in boot camp. Some men had been in boot camp for more than a year. Conditions were not only separate but patently unequal. The white sailors had the drill hall six nights a week, the blacks one. Whites had weekend passes, movies, and permission to go to town, while the blacks were confined to the base. A further source of tension was the fact that virtually all the drill instructors were white southerners. Each time a white drill instructor stepped over the line between discipline and abuse, racial tensions flared.

Volpe remembered the way Italians had been looked down on during his own childhood. The prejudices the other white officers took for granted unsettled him. The United States was fighting a war to bring freedom to oppressed people and yet was oppressing its own soldiers.

Volpe convinced his superiors to build a new area with its own drill hall for the black sailors. He decided that the first step toward lessening racial tensions would be to train black drill instructors (DIs). He reasoned that black recruits would be better treated and would be more likely to accept discipline from one of their own. But he soon discovered that most of the men would never pass the exams for DI because they were illiterate. He set up a basic literacy class, teaching it himself. The men proved to be unskilled mechanically as well, but Volpe rounded up enough recruits with construction backgrounds to start teaching carpentry, plumbing, and masonry in hopes of getting blacks placed into regular construction battalions. He had his men paint a sign — "Competence Brings Respect" — and hang it in the drill hall.

Of his first class of sixty black sailors, forty-eight graduated to become DIs. Remembering the band started years earlier by his father, Volpe formed his own unit marching band. Blacks working as plumbers might be viewed with suspicion, but a black brass band met with the complete approval of the white officers, and even the base captain used to drop by on Saturday mornings to watch the band march and drill. But the process was slow, and Volpe was alone in trying to buck the system for his sailors. "Only his unceasing tact and diplomacy averted several near riots among the colored personnel under his command," his commanding officer wrote after Volpe had served there a year.

In June 1944, almost a year after his arrival, Volpe came down with "cat fever" — gastritis and exhaustion — and was hospitalized and sent on home leave. When he was able to return to his unit, he found that twenty-five officers had been assigned to his old job. From then until his next assignment, he was the unit's military advisor, no longer on the firing line. Before he left, he had the satisfaction of seeing sailors he had trained forming a black stevedore battalion for duty in the Pacific (led by white officers who had been construction foremen before the war), as he had requested.

After his men had been assigned to other posts, Volpe was interviewed by a lieutenant commander at the Bureau of Naval Personnel who was looking for his own replacement. Still hoping to get to the Pacific, Volpe was sent to Washington for supposedly temporary duty interviewing Civil Engineer Corps officer candidates, although he himself did not have an engineering degree. Like temporary buildings and temporary taxes, temporary jobs in Washington often become permanent. Volpe interviewed candidates for exciting jobs in the Pacific and Europe, but each time he applied for one himself, his commanding officer advised waiting. After several months, Volpe gave in to the inevitable, sold the house in Winchester, and brought his family to Arlington. When the war ended, he was still at a desk at the Bureau of Naval Personnel.

Volpe was released to inactive duty in February 1946, and he and his family moved in with Jennie's parents in Wakefield. He reopened the Volpe Company in March and a week later was awarded a $600,000 contract to build a Catholic girls' school, Marycliffe Academy, in Winchester. One of his subcontractors wrote him the same month: "You did a very noble thing in giving up your business to enter the Navy while some of the others stayed home and made some money."

Now he was making money again. This time, building up a business was easier than it had been at the start of Grande and Volpe. By April, there were contracts for two Catholic schools and a church in Revere. His new general manager was Frank Marcucella, who had joined the company in 1942 and then served as an officer in the Seabees.

Housing was the area most affected by the building boom that was in progress, but schools, hospitals, and other public buildings were going up, too. In early 1947, Volpe learned from an architect that Beth Israel Hospital in Boston was planning a $4 million addition. This was a private job, and contractors would bid by invitation only. Beth Israel was just the kind of job Volpe had been looking for since the post office garage: a monumental brick and concrete job that would lead to more hospital and university contracts, for the Boston area was rapidly becoming the educational and medical center of the Northeast. But bidding on such a large job could absorb all the energies of his staff for weeks. Volpe was still sole proprietor, and if the job went sour, the capital he had accumulated before the war would be wiped out.

While thinking it over, Volpe took the architect he knew best to lunch and asked him bluntly if an Italian-American had a chance bidding on a job for a Jewish hospital. The architect talked to the trustees and assured him that he did. That was enough for Volpe, and he began the estimating. The contract was to be on a cost plus fixed fee basis. It was customary, if the contractor was able to bring it in below cost, to split the difference between the contractor and the client. But Volpe sweetened the deal by offering the hospital 75 percent of the savings. He won the bid and committed all the company's resources to the project.

One morning, when Volpe was visiting his superintendent, Gus Mortenson, on the sixth floor of the eight-story addition, they heard screams from below. The two men ran to a window and saw a man lying flat on his back on the hoisting tower platform at ground level. There had never been an accident before on their hoisting operation. Luckily, this one was not fatal; instead of falling all the way, the workman had tumbled onto the platform and ridden down the shaft on the hoisting tower. This incident galvanized Volpe into efforts to improve safety procedures. In the late forties and early fifties, the construction business had the highest rate of injuries per worker of any industry — higher even than firefighting or mining. Volpe proceeded to set up a system of cash bonuses for superintendents and foremen with the best safety records, as well as publicity with banners, flags, and signs advertising accident-free days.

Not long after the Beth Israel job, Volpe addressed the National

Safety Congress in Chicago. His speech was titled "One Hundred Ways to Save a Buck." In addition to talking about the humanitarian aspects of accident prevention, Volpe quickly got down to the bottom line for contractors: A safe job record resulted in lower insurance costs, and bids could easily be won or lost on the difference. Volpe brought in the Beth Israel job well under estimated cost in 1952. The hospital, under their agreement, saved almost $400,000.

While working on the Beth Israel job, Volpe also began a $13 million project at Loring Air Force Base in Limestone, Maine. At that time, the home office had about twenty-five employees, all of whom were expected to do whatever was needed, shifting from outside field engineer to estimator to project manager with the demands of the work.

In the summer of 1950, with Beth Israel and Limestone well underway, John and Jennie made their first trip to Italy, a Holy Year pilgrimage led by Archbishop Cushing of Boston. Volpe had just begun to get involved with one of the archbishop's pet charities, the Don Orione Home in East Boston. The previous year, the archbishop had invited priests from the Italian order of the Sons of the Divine Providence to Boston to set up a retirement home for elderly Italian immigrants who had barely learned to speak English and had not adopted American culture. Volpe had helped the first priests and nuns through the immigration process.

After their trip to Assisi, the Volpes left the tour, borrowing a car and driver from Don Piccinini, the procurator general of the Don Orione Fathers in Rome, and set out for Pescosansonesco. The fathers had not warned Volpe that his chauffeur was a retired race car driver. As the two-lane macadam dwindled into a steep dirt track, the driver, eager to impress his guests, took the switchbacks at maximum speed, sometimes on two wheels, ignoring the Volpes' pleas to slow down.

John and Jennie had heard their parents describe the steep mountains but had not really believed them. They found that Pesco stood on the shoulder of one of the highest mountains in Italy. The village itself was much smaller than they had imagined — about a thousand people then, mostly elderly, living in stone houses with dirt floors. Almost all the young villagers had gone to Milan or overseas to work. Fifty years before, a landslide had pushed a fourth of the town into the valley, stopping just at the church, and none of the damage had been repaired. There was no restaurant or hotel, and they found only elderly relatives; most of their cousins had gone abroad to find work. Volpe could understand now why his parents had seen no future there.

After the tour and a brief stopover in Paris, Volpe returned to Boston with the idea of setting up a branch in Italy to bid on public works projects financed by the United States and to train southern Italians in modern construction methods. The company also was looking at other areas of the United States for expansion; construction was a cyclical industry, and diversifying would lessen the impact of a downturn. Washington seemed the most likely market for public buildings, and the company began to plan an office there. The Washington branch opened in 1953.

At the same time the company was undergoing expansion, more and more of Volpe's time off the job was being spent on public service and charity work. As is often the case, public speaking and leadership in volunteer work led to thoughts of political office. With his company well established, Volpe was one of the first Italian-Americans to become prominent in the business community. Ethnic pride was a strong factor. Like Vito, he was eager to show what an Italian could do. But there were other motivations as well. Anyone running a construction firm saw first-hand evidence of corruption in state and local government. Volpe had quickly learned which subcontractors and which jobs to avoid, but he was not content simply with keeping his own business clean. He felt the same pull to action as he had in Camp Peary, the same desire to step in and set things right. He could speak out on issues, but change could come only from within the political system. Frank Marcucella, the company's vice president, began to take over more of the day-to-day operation of the company. Volpe also had a new assistant.

Helen Ross was a graduate of Portia Law School (now New England School of Law) in Boston but had never practiced law since her graduation in 1928. Women lawyers were not readily accepted then, and though a Yankee and a descendant of Betsy Ross, she came from a working-class family with no political or business connections. A brisk, no-nonsense woman with curly black hair, invariably dressed in dark suits, Ross had been working as a secretary for Sawyer Construction until Volpe was forced to expand his staff during the Beth Israel job.

Ross liked the construction business and was looking for a growing company. She quickly sized up her new boss: "I thought he could go on and really be big, make his company into one of the national corporations," she remembered. "At first I was cynical about the religion business. Before I met him, I'd heard about his charity work. I'd heard people say, 'He's God's little brother,' so I thought, there has to be an angle. I'm a Protestant, and he never mentioned his religion to me, but I found after years of working closely with him that he lived his religion, a very unusual thing, especially in politics.

"And that family was crucial to him. Vito was still working there, though they did not live upstairs anymore, and the love between them was obvious. You could see that he cared not only for his wife and children but the whole extended family, and the work with Italian charities came from that. But there was another side to him. He was hungry for recognition, hungry for political power. Anyone who gets elected has to be. He went at it with the same drive, the same Type A-plus personality, that he went at making money."

Ross's title was "personal and confidential secretary," and she soon became Volpe's speech writer, advisor, scheduling and advance person, and political helper. Although he had money now, Volpe faced long odds within the Massachusetts Republican party structure, which was tightly controlled by Harvard-educated Yankees. Volpe was not only ethnically an outsider, but he had not had the years of writing essays, reading the classics, and running for class monitor that the Brahmin politicians had enjoyed in prep schools and Ivy League colleges. While the Cabots and the Lodges had been honing their rhetoric on the debating team, Volpe was selling ladies' underwear door to door in Edgeworth.

Short, thin, nervously smiling, Volpe initially was a poor speaker. He was honest, and made no pretense at hiding his ambitions, in a political party where office-seekers were supposed to be motivated solely by a sense of public duty. And he had a grating habit of referring to himself in the third person, even in private conversation — "John Volpe can," "John Volpe thinks." Within the company, his employees overlooked his mannerisms because they saw, up close, his good points. In charity work and civic organizations, he impressed because he got the job done. But total strangers were more difficult to win over.

Although Volpe had been doing legwork for the Republican party before the war, he got his first break in May 1951. The party was then controlled by Massachusetts Republican Committeeman Sinclair Weeks, a wealthy Yankee industrialist from Newton. Weeks saw the need for letting in more "ethnics" at the state level. Instead of appointing one or two Yankees as his deputy state chairmen, Weeks selected four relative newcomers: an Irishman, a French-Canadian, a non-Brahmin Yankee, and an Italian. Edwin L. Olander, thirty-four, had been a school committeeman and mayor of Northampton in western Massachusetts and was now in the building materials business. Robert Boudreau of Marlboro had been an FBI agent and president of the Franco-American Civic League of Massachusetts. James J. Gaffney had been captain of the Harvard football team, a lieutenant colonel in the Army, and Lowell District

Republican Finance Committee chairman before the age of thirty-five. The fourth man was Volpe.

Deputy state chairman was not just an honorary position, and Volpe soon found himself stumping the state; organizing Republican town, ward, and regional committees; and speaking at debates, lodge events, and civic associations. Ross did his scheduling and wrote his first speeches, adding new words with pronunciation given in parentheses to increase his vocabulary. At first he balked, telling her to remove the offending words because he did not talk that way. Ross would argue that he *ought* to talk that way and gave him the definitions. Gradually, both his grammar and accent began to sound more Winchester and less Edgeworth.

There were other forces behind Volpe's ambition to hold political office. After he had been asked to serve as deputy chairman, but before he had accepted, an incident at home made the decision for him. One afternoon, coming home from the office early to dress for a dinner meeting, Volpe found his daughter, Jean, then in high school, absorbed in the televised Kefauver hearings on racketeering. He sat down with her in the living room and watched. "Daddy," she asked after a while, "are all the people in government really connected to the underworld?"

Volpe assured her that they were not, that he knew many honest people in government. Neither of them said the word "Italian," but it hung in Volpe's mind. What kind of country am I going to leave for my children? he thought. And what have I done for my country to repay what I gained? All he had done so far, he concluded, was serve in the Navy. That did not seem enough.

After a year as deputy chairman, Volpe decided to seek statewide office, if one became available. In 1952, the Republicans had lost the last two statewide elections. The Democratic governor, Paul E. Dever, was seeking a third term, and the Democrats still held all six of the state's constitutional offices. Henry Cabot Lodge, Jr., was seeking a fourth term as U.S. senator against then-Congressman John F. Kennedy. Although the Democrats seemed well entrenched, voters were turning to the right on the national level. Eisenhower's campaign was getting underway. Richard Nixon was making headlines on the Senate Unamerican Activities Committee, and Congress had just overridden President Truman's veto of the McCarran Act forbidding employment of communists in defense work and barring anyone who belonged to a communist organization from entering the country.

By the spring of 1952, the acknowledged Republican favorite and Weeks's choice to oppose Dever for governor was Representative Christian A. Herter, Eisenhower's campaign manager for Massachusetts. But in the Massachusetts legislature, the opposition to Dever had been spearheaded for the previous two years by Sumner Whittier, a young state senator representing Everett, Malden, and Melrose. Whittier was a Yankee and a descendant of poet John Greenleaf Whittier and Charles Sumner, the abolitionist Massachusetts senator. But Sumner Whittier had never been one of the insiders who ran the party. Born in a three-decker in Everett, near Malden, Whittier detested the term "swamp Yankee" that the press applied to non-Brahmin WASPs and dubbed himself the "three-decker Republican." He worked his way through Boston University (where he was voted most handsome man in his class) and won election (in a district that was 70 percent Italian-American) to the Everett Common Council, the Everett Board of Aldermen, the Massachusetts House, and the state Senate. Once in the Senate, Whittier made a career of attacking "Dever-stating" taxes, as well as the Dever budget, the Employment Security Unit, the Port Authority, the state Department of Conservation, and William Callahan of the Department of Public Works, the "Maharajah of Macadam."

Whittier was a favorite of the State House press corps, and when he decided to run for governor in 1952, he carried with him the support of *The Boston Herald,* the state's largest conservative newspaper, but not necessarily that of the party leadership. Weeks would wait and see.

For several years, Massachusetts had not held state preprimary conventions, and the 1952 convention to be held in Worcester was "unofficial." It also was to be preceded by eight preconvention rallies in different parts of the state. When Volpe decided to declare for lieutenant governor in June, he faced two formidable obstacles. Another Italian-American, Alfred B. Cenedella, a Milford lawyer who had been Worcester County district attorney for sixteen years, declared for the same office shortly after Volpe. And yet another Italian-American, Roy C. Papalia of Watertown, declared for state treasurer. The Republican party chiefs might decide that the time was right for one Italian-American on the ticket; two would be unlikely.

After Volpe's announcement, Whittier asked him to lunch to size him up. "The discussion was friendly; we went over to the Parker House," Whittier remembered. "I ordered pork chops or whatever, and Volpe ordered two soft-boiled eggs. I asked him what was the matter, and he told me his stomach was acting up. I could tell he was sharp, but my impression at that time was that he had only run for office once, and he did not have his feet wet yet. I thought, 'If he's nervous now, he'll have a rough time when the campaign really heats up.' "

But Volpe had the advantage of his wealth and his organizational ability. During the campaign, Volpe kept in touch with his office by car phone; the staff would try to get him back to look over the final estimates for flaws, but he spent the rest of his time on the campaign. Before each of the eight preprimary rallies, the Volpe campaign staff put on an elaborate cocktail buffet for delegates. Whittier himself showed up at several, shook hands with Volpe, and ate the free food.

Before the first rally, in the White Eagle Hall in Northampton, Whittier had switched from the gubernatorial to the lieutenant governor's race. Christian Herter, now running virtually unopposed, proved to be an unexciting speaker. The only contest to watch was Whittier-Volpe-Cenedella. Whittier, angrily waving a comic book the Democrats had used to attack the last Republican nominee, won over the Young Turks of the party. Volpe told the audience he was an "honest businessman on the Republican ticket" who "understood the problems of labor and management." But it was Cenedella who captured most of the audience. With ringing, old-fashioned rhetoric, he tore into the tax-and-spend policies of the Democrats, dragged in communism, and brought the audience to its feet. In the last three rallies, however, Cenedella made the mistake of attacking Whittier personally as a Yankee. This Yankee had been elected from Italian wards, and Cenedella's support faded.

When the sixteen hundred delegates arrived in Worcester Municipal Hall on a steamy June 28, Whittier almost lost it all. Without his approval, the delegates who had supported his attacks on Dever in the state Senate launched a floor fight in his name against Herter for the gubernatorial nomination. Demonstrations for Whittier broke out on the floor, cheered by his friends in the press gallery, as Whittier hurried to the hall from his hotel.

When the convention began, Volpe was clearly ahead of Cenedella but well behind Whittier. If an upset came off in the gubernatorial race, he would walk away with the nomination to the second spot. He sat toward the back, with Ross and his campaign workers, while the hall echoed with "We want Whittier!" Although it was not yet noon, the huge blowers at the doors could not dissipate the heat, and the sweating delegates fanned themselves with the campaign literature that also covered the floor.

Whittier walked through the front door, down the length of the main aisle, to the cheers of the delegates and the spectators, still seeming uncertain. He talked to some of the men on the platform. Finally, he stood at the microphone and said tensely, "I am not running for governor, but it is for the delegates to decide."

It still was not over. Twice Senator Leverett Saltonstall, who was presiding, was asked if delegates could still vote to nominate Whittier as governor. He replied that they could, and the hall was hushed as the count began. In the end, it was Herter 813, Whittier 343, and Henry Sears 36. Whittier was then officially nominated for lieutenant governor. When Cenedella's name was called for lieutenant governor, he withdrew. Then Volpe bowed out, for the sake of party unity. Whittier was nominated by acclamation.

In his acceptance speech, Whittier called the slate the "Miracle of Worcester." The Republicans had finally nominated a ticket of "several different racial strains." They had produced what passed for a racially balanced ticket in 1952 — two Yankees, one Italian-American, and an Irish-American. In November, Herter narrowly defeated Dever, but Roy C. Papalia was beaten by the man the Democrats had nominated for state treasurer, Foster Furcolo. Their Italian-American had beaten the Republicans' Italian-American.

In Winchester, there was no time for Volpe to mull over his defeat. On July 1, his new house on Mystic Lake was finished. Volpe had planned a one-story contemporary, but Jennie dreamed of a Georgian colonial house with a circular portico and tall white columns. During the design phase, Volpe tried to compromise, as he would with a client. But Jennie had waited a long time for her dream house, and there were no concessions. On July 3, they moved into a neoclassical mansion with six two-story columns at the front. The next day, with furniture still arriving, Volpe packed his bags and took the train to Chicago as an alternate delegate to the Republican National Convention.

In Chicago, Volpe and the other Massachusetts regulars supported Eisenhower against Taft. When he returned on the victory train to Boston, Volpe immediately threw himself into campaigning for the Eisenhower-Lodge-Herter ticket. With the Italian-born wife of Connecticut Governor John Lodge, Volpe went from meeting to meeting, town to town. After they made their pitch, Volpe often would play the guitar, and Francesca Lodge, wearing a bright red, white, and blue dress with a green sash, would dance a spirited tarantella. When word got out through the party faithful that some entertainment besides the usual speeches was available, the crowds grew.

Once the election was over, and Herter and Eisenhower were in office, Volpe flew to Italy in December to open an office in Rome. Anthony Benedetto, Jennie's brother, took over the direction of the new business. Their first contract was a provincial road in Calabria.

During the past two to three years, Volpe had been renewing his ties with Italy, and recapturing his fluency in the Italian language, through his work with the Don Orione Home. When the Don Orione Fathers had first arrived in Boston, a women's club, the Faro Club of Boston, had held spaghetti dinners and raffles to raise money for two old wooden houses on Orient Heights in East Boston. The houses needed plastering, repairs, and painting, and Father Rocco Crescenzi approached Volpe for help. The next Saturday, Volpe and his younger brother Pat were in a run-down wooden house in East Boston trying to show Father Rocco how to mix the mortar and carry the hod so they could patch the ceilings. Pat Volpe had not done any plastering for fifteen years, nor John for thirty. The job was further complicated by the fact that neither Father Rocco, nor any of the other priests and nuns, spoke English. Volpe had not spoken Italian regularly since childhood.

Father Rocco proved a good apprentice, and Volpe soon discovered that the priest also was an electrician. Just before his first Christmas in America, Father Rocco astonished the Volpes and the neighbors in East Boston by setting up a five-foot-high Neapolitan crèche complete with electric lights, a running waterfall, and a miniature river.

When the Massachusetts Sons of Italy voted in 1951 to raise the money for a new Don Orione Home, Volpe was the natural choice for chairman. The Sons of Italy approached him. Volpe refused. Then Vito asked. At last Cardinal Cushing invited him to the cardinal's official residence in Brighton and put it to him. This time he acquiesced. The first campaign, helped by Vincent Brogna, then associate justice of the Massachusetts supreme court, as treasurer, brought in almost $300,000. There were few big donors, for the Italian community in Massachusetts had few millionaires.

Volpe did not regret the time he had spent on the Don Orione Home, for less than a month after he returned from Italy, Vito died. His staunch anticlericalism had moderated, and three months before his death, he had begun to receive the sacraments again. Volpe decided to donate a chapel in the new Don Orione Home in Vito's memory.

Less than a month after Vito's death, Governor Herter called Volpe into his office. Herter needed to replace the "Maharajah of Macadam" with a manager who had experience in construction, and he asked Volpe to serve. Volpe declined; he was needed at his company. Volpe advised hiring Boston Department of Public Works (DPW) Commissioner George Hyland, who had served as deputy state DPW commissioner when Boston Mayor Maurice Tobin became governor. The Republican leadership would not accept a Democrat in such a crucial position, however. Again, Herter called in Volpe. "I'll have to think a while before I propose another candidate," Volpe told him. "No," Herter replied, "I already have one. It's you."

The DPW commissioner's salary was $15,000 a year. Volpe was earning many times that amount in business, and he was just starting to enjoy the good life in his home on Mystic Lake. The appointment would be temporary — only for a year. Volpe finally agreed.

In April 1953, shortly after he had taken office, Volpe and the other members of the Don Orione Home board made a spiritual retreat with the Don Orione Fathers to a Trappist monastery in Spencer, Massachusetts. The retreat lasted three days, and during it the men followed the strict rules of the order, including no talking except to pray. The retreatants rose at 3:30 A.M. to kneel with the monks in an unheated chapel for morning prayers.

By day, Volpe watched the monks working in the fields. He thought of his ancestors planting their fields in Italy and of his own parents tending their garden in Malden. During John's childhood, Vito had been the moral anchor, the father whose advice he had followed without question. Now that support was gone. In his own daily life, there was little time for privacy or reflection. Even while traveling, he had a driver who kept him on schedule as he went from business appointment to political meeting to charity function. At home, there were the demands of a wife and two teenage children.

Volpe had seen many men his own age already fall prey to political corruption, alcoholism, alienation from their wives and children. He searched for something specific to bind himself to the values he wished to sustain and settled at last on receiving the sacraments every morning, no matter what his schedule. "If these guys can get up at three-thirty every morning and not talk every day of their lives," he told Father Rocco, "the least I can do is go to Mass every day."

Just before Volpe assumed his DPW post and put Frank Marcucella in charge of his company, the final alterations were made at Eastern Avenue. Now widowed, Filomena Volpe was living with her daughter in a house Volpe had built for her and Vito. Crews put up brick walls around the Eastern Avenue building. Then in one day, they demolished and extracted the roof beams of the old wood and stucco house with a crane and roofed over the new building. The Volpe Company was closed only one day, then reopened. The last vestiges of the old house were gone.

CHAPTER V

Commissioner Volpe

V OLPE MOVED INTO the DPW commissioner's office on February 26, 1953. Although he had never worked for the government as a civilian, by this time he had accumulated considerable managerial and administrative experience. In the Navy, he had supervised as many as four thousand men. Although his company had started out as a small business, during the height of the Limestone job, more than three thousand workers had been on his payroll, roughly the same number as the work force at the DPW.

There were two crucial differences. Until shortly after the Limestone job, Volpe had either owned his business in partnership or outright as personal property; any worker who did not produce could be let go. Even after the company became a corporation, Volpe owned a 95 percent interest. At the DPW, practically every employee was under civil service protection. Both in the Navy and in his own company, Volpe had built his organizational structures to suit his own managerial style. In the DPW, he stepped into a system created by one of the state's most powerful political figures, William Callahan.

Under Callahan, the DPW had become much more than a road-building agency; it encompassed a Byzantine network of personal loyalties, favors, obligations, and family relationships built up within the state legislature from the early 1920s through the terms of several speakers of the house, governors, and political appointees. It was common knowledge that, while elected officials came and went at the whim of the electorate, Bill Callahan stayed. His motto, often quoted in committee rooms, was: "He gets things done." Callahan did get things done, but the price could be high.

Callahan was born in Stoughton, Massachusetts, the son of a shoe factory superintendent. After high school, he went to work as bookkeeper, then treasurer of a small marine dredging company. He was forty-two years old when he entered public life, becoming commissioner in 1924. What might in more prosperous times have been a minor position in state government brought Callahan immense authority during the Depression. At a time when one-third to one-half of all workers in the state were unemployed, Callahan could deliver steady jobs — work any unskilled man qualified for. All he needed in return were appropriations from the legislature. For the state's contractors, Callahan's public works often were the only projects available to bid on.

By the late 1930s, Callahan had put supporters and relatives of a good percentage of the legislature on the payroll in various ways. "Highway inspectors" drove around in state cars looking for potholes. Private citizens rented trucks, station wagons, and even power saws and lawn mowers to the department. Newspapermen were put on the job as "traffic consultants" to ensure a favorable press.

Although Callahan had many friends on Beacon Hill, he inevitably made enemies as well. One was Christian Herter, who when serving on the House Ways and Means Committee, accused Callahan of padding payrolls. In 1937, Governor Charles F. Hurley tried to force Callahan's resignation but was stymied by Callahan's supporters on the Governor's Council. In 1939, Republican Governor Leverett Saltonstall appointed a special commission and held public hearings aimed at discrediting Callahan and removing him from office, charging him with fourteen cases of "squandering public funds."

Callahan did not submit meekly. He rallied his supporters on the Governor's Council and floated rumors that, if forced to resign, he would run for governor himself. When the Governor's Council at last voted to remove Callahan based on charges that he had awarded contracts without inviting bids, paid for unnecessary consulting services, and built unneeded bridges, Saltonstall sent his personal bodyguard from the state police to take possession of the commissioner's office on Nashua Street. Saltonstall made the mistake of appointing an architect with no political experience to undertake the department's reorganization and recommend reforms. His efforts produced little change.

Two years later, Callahan returned to his old office, reappointed by the new Democratic governor, Paul Dever, to preside over the state's postwar building boom. By 1951, Callahan controlled what had become the largest department in the state, with $250 million in highway funds, and was being referred to by Republican legislators and the Republican press as "God," "Frankenstein," and the "Highway Czar." By this time, Callahan looked the part of the quintessential political fixer — heavyset, with a face like the bust of a Roman senator under one of the later emperors. In 1952, Dever appointed him to an eight-year term as chairman of the new Massachusetts Turnpike Authority, as well as chairman of Boston's Government Center Commission, bringing the total of public funds at his disposal to more than a billion dollars. The new tunnel from Boston to Logan Airport was named the Callahan Tunnel, in honor of his only son, who had died in World War II in France.

Although his term did not expire until 1955, Callahan chose not to fight Herter as he had Saltonstall. He resigned quietly a month after Herter's inauguration, but he kept his positions as Massachusetts Turnpike Authority chairman and Government Center Commission chairman. Volpe occupied his office without the help of a state trooper.

Although Volpe inherited virtually all of Callahan's staff, the former commissioner did nothing to impede Volpe's reforms. Only once did the two men clash — at a meeting of the New England Road Builders' Association in May 1953. After Volpe told the audience they would no longer be told where to buy their cement or arrange their bonding, Callahan leaped to his feet, tore open his collar, and speaking with difficulty because of cancer surgery, defended his record. After that encounter, Callahan retreated to his position on the Turnpike Authority, which he held until his death in 1964.

Volpe had been appointed to the DPW to clean house. "I feel that the appointment of Mr. Volpe will mean a lifting of the iron curtain on the Public Works Department," Lieutenant Governor Whittier commented. To accomplish this, Volpe himself would have to appear to be — and, in fact, to be — outside the old system. His association with the Volpe Company immediately caused problems. The Volpe Company had never built highways, except access roads on housing complexes and military bases, but to avoid the appearance of conflict of interest, Volpe ordered Marcucella to cease bidding not only on state business but also on local and federal jobs unless bid work was already in progress. He continued to draw a small salary from the company and donated much of the $15,000 a year commissioner's salary to charity. Within a few days, Volpe discovered that the DPW secretaries were unwilling to put in the long hours he was used to and brought Helen Ross in as his personal assistant. "When I started mailing his checks to the charities, I suggested he give me his salary and donate mine to charity," Ross recalled.

Volpe remembered, "The first time I went to dinner at my mother-in-law's house in Wakefield after I was appointed, she asked me if she had to call me 'Commissioner' now, or could she still call me John? After we got that cleared up, in walked my brother-in-law, looking very pleased with himself. He mentioned casually that he was renting three trucks to the DPW, and now he guessed he'd be renting some more. I tried to think of a way to break it to him, and finally I said that, unfortunately, there wouldn't be any more trucks leased because no relative of mine was going to get a dime out of this. In fact, I'd have to cancel the ones he was already leasing. If a reporter ever found out that I was doing that, I'd lose all my credibility. He didn't speak to me again for six months!"

Volpe plunged into a sixteen-hour-a-day schedule to learn all that he could about the workings of the department. Two weeks after his appointment, a *Boston Globe* reporter followed him through a typical day: starting with Lenten Mass at 6:45, through a long day at the Nashua Street office, to a speech in English at a Catholic school, a meeting in Italian with a priest at the Home for Aged Italians, and a commemorative service for Don Orione in East Boston. The day ended after midnight.

Although the press and various investigative committees had focused on bid manipulating as the principal source of corruption and Volpe expected to find this was the department's main problem, this aspect proved relatively easy to deal with. Under a state law, all contracts of more than $1,000 had to be won through open bidding. Contracts sometimes were split into under-$1,000 segments, but this practice proved easy for auditors to spot. Only an experienced contractor could detect the more subtle methods. One involved having the engineer draw up specifications well above minimum standards. If a road needed only an eight-inch gravel base, the DPW specs would call for twelve inches. Then the favored contractor would be tipped off and become low bidder, and the job would still pass inspection.

A few months after Volpe took office, Herter sent Whittier to see how he was doing. "I found he had straightened out the contractors," Whittier recalled. "There was one revolt when several of the asphalt suppliers threatened him with making it impossible to buy in the state unless he paid more. But he called them on it and got ready to buy from out of state. They take their cue from the man at the top; if he's honest and willing to take the heat, he can cut down on a lot of the funny stuff. But as soon as he leaves, a lot of people are ready to go back to business as before."

Personnel problems were harder to deal with. In 1953, the notion that a good percentage of the work force, from the engineers down to the men painting the white lines, were political appointees bothered neither Volpe nor Herter. They did, however, see a distinction between what was considered "legitimate" and corrupt patronage. Legitimate patronage, as Volpe saw it, was the appointment of upper level administrators favorable to the new governor's policies, plus the allocation of a reasonable number of unskilled positions, such as summer jobs cutting grass. "Nonlegitimate" patronage was giving out no-work or no-show jobs.

To spot no-shows, Volpe began taking home time sheets for small projects. On street repair crews, the DPW would hire twice the number of temporary police officers necessary to direct traffic. Half the crew would work one week and sign the others in, then the next week they would reverse the order. Supervisors would take a DPW car home for the weekend, check some stoplights on the way to church, and bill the state. Another potential abuse built into the system was in the hiring of "junior engineers." During World War II, private construction had almost stopped, and few men were receiving engineering degrees. With the postwar boom, graduates were not attracted to the lower paying state jobs, and the DPW was forced to hire untrained men with the proviso that they get their degrees later. Some went on to night school and qualified, but others remained on the payroll at an engineer's salary for years as "juniors." Outside consultants frequently were hired for jobs the staff could do as well.

Volpe set about the job of reforming the DPW with the same zeal with which he had undertaken his first Navy job — and with similar results: a shake-up for the bureaucracy and exhaustion for himself. He tackled personnel first. "The personnel situation is sad," he told a group of friends at a testimonial given by the Associated General Contractors of Massachusetts in April 1953. "They're not all lazy, incompetent, or crooked. A great many are competent. Morale has dropped because in some instances employees have not been properly guided." Volpe had no doubt that he was the man to guide them.

At first, he met with passive resistance and the attitude that the system would simply wait him out. As he dug his heels in deeper, department heads began to object. "Every time I said I wanted something changed, Bill Tuttle, the chief engineer, would tell me, 'Commissioner, that isn't the way we've done it for thirty years,' " Volpe remembered. "One day, I couldn't take it anymore. I told him, 'I'm a Christian man, and I shouldn't say this, but damn it, if you tell me that one more time I might be tempted to throw you out that window!' " Tuttle took the hint and said no more about it. Callahan offered Tuttle a job at the Turnpike Authority, and he left the DPW shortly thereafter.

The appointment of Tuttle's replacement caused the only public questioning of Volpe's integrity during his tenure at the DPW. The Volpe Company had been in the process of bidding on a school job in Beverly just before Volpe was appointed to the DPW. As low bidders, they were awarded the contract. During his meetings with the Beverly School Committee, Volpe met and was impressed by Gordon Gray, a civil engineer on the town's building committee. After Tuttle's resignation, he offered Gray the job as DPW chief engineer. Several newspapers carried a syndicated column accusing Volpe of appointing Gray as a reward for the contract, an allegation impossible to prove. Herter advised letting it ride, and soon Gray was taking over the day-to-day operation of the department, leaving Volpe to work on policy changes.

Barely five months after Volpe had taken office, the first, and worst, of several natural disasters of the early fifties struck Massachusetts. On June 10, in the wake of an afternoon thunderstorm, a tornado touched down near the Worcester/Shrewsbury line, demolishing two brick housing projects, ripping up several manufacturing plants, and destroying most of Assumption College.

As soon as the news came over the police radio at DPW headquarters, Volpe and his driver headed for Worcester on Route 9. Moments after they had crossed Lake Quinsigamond on the outskirts of Worcester, they saw a young teenage boy screaming hysterically and waving them down. After the boy could speak, he told them that his mother had sent him to the store for a loaf of bread. When he returned, his house and his whole family were gone. There was nothing standing on the street but smashed timbers and rubble. Using his car radio, Volpe got in touch with the Worcester police and waited until someone came to take charge of the boy. The experience left Volpe shaken. He had fought World War II from a Navy base and a desk in Virginia and had never seen a loss like that before. That boy could have been my own son, he thought, and thanked God for having been spared.

The DPW joined the massive cleanup efforts as the National Guard and the Red Cross were called to Worcester. President Eisenhower flew over the area to inspect the damage in the *Columbine* and approved a half million dollars in federal disaster relief. The final toll for the afternoon was 123 dead and 8,000 homeless.

The summers of 1954 and 1955 also brought hurricanes and floods. Cottages were swept away on Cape Cod, trees were downed and power lines knocked out, and the Merrimack River flooded as high as the steps of Lowell City Hall, but none of these storms came close to the Worcester tornado in the amount of human suffering they caused.

By the summer of 1954, the pressure of the DPW reforms had eased, and there were no more complaints from disgruntled contractors. As a state employee, Volpe did not participate in the 1954 gubernatorial campaign. At the June convention, the Republicans renominated Herter and Whittier. Herter's original victory over Dever had been a surprise, with a majority of only 14,500 votes, but he was reelected by a majority of more than 75,000. Although there were no changes in the executive branch, the Democrats gained control of the House, making it more difficult for Herter to push through his legislative programs.

In addition to housecleaning his department, from early 1955 on, Volpe faced the job of implementing the biggest road-building plan in the state's history. It was a long overdue task. In 1946, when cars suddenly became available after sixteen years of pent-up demand, the city of Boston began to develop gridlock. During the Christmas shopping season in the late 1940s and early 1950s, delivery trucks could take as long as an hour to go three miles from a warehouse in South Boston to Jordan Marsh or Filene's downtown. A taxi ride from North Station to South Station was a half-hour trip, though the stations are only a mile apart.

The original master highway plan for greater Boston had been developed under Governor Bradford's administration in 1948 and was one of the first city master plans in the nation. The Bradford solution called for two beltways: Route 128, the outer belt, and an Inner Belt surrounding Boston, with eight connecting routes radiating from downtown through the neighborhoods toward the beltways like the spokes of a wheel. Bradford, a Republican, did not have the necessary two-thirds vote in the state legislature, and his bond issue failed to pass. Once Dever was elected, the bond issue went through, and Callahan began to build Route 128, which would become "America's Technology Highway," and the section of the Inner Belt now called the Central Artery and the Southeast Expressway. The artery and expressway as they are now constitute only one-third of Bradford's original plan.

As Bradford's engineers envisioned it, the Central Artery in Boston was to function as a giant overpass, allowing a driver to avoid crowded intersections and to enter and exit close to shopping areas, Massachusetts Bay Transportation Authority (MBTA) subway stations, and local landmarks. Exit and entrance ramps were designed at close intervals, with extremely short approaches, to avoid land-taking in crowded neighborhoods. The artery was designed for a speed of 35 miles per hour, with a 25-mile-per-hour ramp speed.

After it was opened in late 1955, the Central Artery did serve its intended purpose. At first. Early photos show only a few cars in each lane, and a driver could zip from South Station to North Station in five minutes. No one in the DPW imagined in his wildest fantasies that the road would be used for daily commuting from as far away as Scituate in the south or Marblehead in the north, or that more than one in three Bostonians would own an automobile.

The Southeast Expressway was envisioned as a truck route and a means to shorten long-distance trips between towns. In a 1956 speech, Volpe described the master plan's glowing future: "A driver can get on one of the new roads at the New Hampshire line, sail right through Boston over the Central Artery, hook up with the Southeast Expressway, and keep right along the entire Cape without stopping once for a light," Volpe declared with more than a trace of happiness in his voice.

In less than ten years, that fantasy trip would become a motorist's nightmare. The state's highway planners did not foresee the abandonment of the old trolley and commuter rail systems or the drop in population within the city of Boston. No one envisioned the seductive power of those new highways to pull commuters out of the old neighborhoods and into the subdivisions.

While Volpe was still serving as DPW commissioner, a presidential commission headed by General Lucius Clay was developing a unified national highway program. Since the mid-1930s, the Bureau of Public Roads had been cranking out designs for an interstate system, which were shelved by Presidents Roosevelt and Truman. Eisenhower made an abrupt turnaround. In his first "State of the Union" speech in 1953, Eisenhower made the building of new schools and new roads his first two priorities. "During World War II, I had seen the superlative German *Autobahnen* — national highways crossing that country and offering the possibility, often lacking in the United States, to drive with speed and safety at the same time," Eisenhower wrote in his memoirs. "I recognized then that the United States was behind in highway construction. In the middle 1950s, I did not want to fall still further behind."

At the time Clay's commission was studying the problem, scant attention was paid to any other transportation issues. The idea of nation-alizing the railroads — the solution European countries had adopted — was too radical even to be considered by either the administration or Congress. Direct subsidies to private rail companies were dismissed as contrary to the goals of a free-enterprise economy. Indirect subsidies to auto manufacturers, trucking companies, and the construction industry were seen as acceptable, however, because they stimulated related busi-nesses. To many Republicans, the railroads were still tainted with their exploitive image from the days of trust and utility monopolies.

An improved highway system also was touted as a means of reducing the skyrocketing number of traffic accidents, especially in rural areas. In the early fifties, rural highways often were unlit and narrow, cars were built with powerful V-8 engines, and sharp curves often were marked with white crosses commemorating accident victims. To Volpe, who had cru-saded for safety in the construction industry, a campaign to design safer highways was an appealing cause.

There also were defense considerations, the justification for almost all federal programs in the fifties. Educational improvement programs were justified by the need to catch up with the Russians. Foreign aid was needed to win allies in the struggle against communism. An improved highway system would be used for two purposes: to evacuate civilians from urban areas in the event of enemy attack and to move military personnel and equipment. "Our roads ought to be avenues of escape for persons living in big cities threatened by aerial attack or natural disaster," Eisenhower wrote. "But I know that if a crisis occurred, our obsolescent highways, too small for the flood of traffic of an entire city's population going one way, would turn into traps of death and destruction."[1] Yet at the same time, he proposed that along the new highways, millions of motor-ists would read signs that stated: "In the event of an enemy attack, this road will be closed." The project Eisenhower proposed is still called the National System of Interstate and Defense Highways.

On February 22, 1955, the Clay commission sent its recommenda-tions to Congress. The original cost was pegged at $101 billion, of which the federal government would finance $31 billion and the states the rest. The bill passed the Senate in 1955 but failed in the House by a margin of 123 to 292. Sinclair Weeks, the Republican State Committee chairman who had launched Volpe on his political career, was now secretary of commerce, having refused Eisenhower's other offer to be chairman of the Republican party. The implementation of this plan would come under the Bureau of Public Roads, then part of the Commerce Department. Weeks,

Volpe, and the chairman of the New York State Thruway commission, Bertram Tallamy, lobbied intensively for the bill. Like Volpe, Tallamy was in the midst of pushing his own legislature to fund a massive state road-building program. The bill's failure was due to disagreements over the funding methods, not the concept.

Volpe was one of six men appointed to redraft the plan. When the bill was reintroduced in the following session, the administration sweetened the deal to 90 percent federal funding, to be raised from taxes on gasoline, tires, and commercial vehicles. In 1956, the Democratic version of the bill, sponsored by Albert Gore, was enacted into law. The Federal Highway and Defense Act of 1956 proposed the building of forty-two thousand miles of limited-access four- to eight-lane roads linking major cities, to be finished by 1970 at a cost of $27.5 billion. This was to be the biggest single construction project the United States had undertaken.

Anticipating that some form of the highway bill would pass, the Bureau of Public Roads engineers began to design the interstate system in 1955. When the bureau sent Volpe the first draft, he noticed that part of the Massachusetts section was exactly where Route 128 was located, though no route labels were used on the map. By late 1955, two-thirds of Route 128 had already been built, with 50 percent federal funding and the other 50 percent state money. Because Massachusetts had gone ahead with its road plans, the Commonwealth would benefit much less than other states from the new funding.

Realizing that if he approved the draft, Massachusetts would be locked into the 50 percent federal funding instead of the 90 percent for Route 128, Volpe called the bureau to ask for a meeting before the draft was finalized and had his own engineers draw up a proposed second highway where industry could expand after the Route 128 area was full. This outer belt would link the dying mill towns of Lawrence and Lowell to Marlboro and the industrial area around Worcester. Officials from the bureau delayed. At last, the only available time for a meeting before the deadline was Christmas evening. Volpe and Governor Herter agreed.

On December 25, Herter, Volpe, and Francis DuPont, special assistant to President Eisenhower and former commissioner of the Bureau of Public Roads, met at the Ritz in Boston. They went over the plans for a giant half-circle, now Route 495, from Amesbury near the New Hampshire border, west almost to Worcester, and south to Buzzards Bay on Cape Cod. DuPont agreed to back the plan. The project would cost more than half a billion dollars to build, 90 percent of which would be federally funded. Herter and Volpe wished each other Merry Christmas on Arlington Street and went their separate ways, pleased to have gotten a massive public works project for the state. Only later did they realize that they had laid the groundwork for the revival of the Lowell-Lawrence area and the reindustrialization of southern New Hampshire.

Throughout his tenure at the DPW, Volpe kept his hand in Republican politics and Italian-American charitable causes. He was a frequent speaker before groups such as the Italian-American World War Veterans, Italian-American civic associations, and church societies. He made a point of returning to Italy with Jennie and the children at least once a year and gradually built up friendships in the hierarchy of the Vatican. Like other conservatives of his time, Volpe began to view the Catholic Church, rather than the liberal democratic state, as the strongest bulwark against communism within Italy, at a time when the Italian Communist party was the largest in Europe.

As one of the few Italian-Americans who had achieved political power and wealth, Volpe was welcomed at the highest levels in Italy. On his visit to organize a branch of his construction company in early 1952, Volpe conferred privately with Pope Pius XII and Premier Alcide DeGasperi on relations between the United States and Italy. Although he held no public office then, on returning he held a press conference to bring DeGasperi's greetings and his own opinion that the "strong religious convictions of the Italian people will keep their country safe from communistic dominance." This was a viewpoint that meshed well with mainstream Republican political thought at home.

Volpe's only point of disagreement with his party's policies on Italy was over the issue of immigration. The McCarran Act had severely cut the quota from Italy at a time when the country was barely recovering from World War II and had an enormous unemployment problem in the south, while at the same time the American economy was booming. To Volpe, it seemed natural to open the gates. Instead, U.S. policy tended more and more toward cutting off the flow of unskilled workers from all but a few countries.

In the summer of 1955, Boston Mayor John B. Hynes asked Volpe to cochair Boston's part of the State Department's new People to People program. Boston would be host to a delegation from Rome in a Salute to Rome for a week in November. In a press release for the event, Secretary of State John Foster Dulles's office boldly set out the celebration's purpose: "to counteract the $3,500,000 program by which Russia tries to prove to the world that American capitalists are a gadget-loving bunch of barbarians." In the context of the times, the rhetoric was mild. At the same time as Volpe was hosting a delegation from Rome, Soviet Prime Minister Bulganin and First Secretary Khrushchev were on a publicity tour of India, Burma, and Pakistan, stridently selling their own solutions for underdevelopment, denouncing Anglo-Saxon militarism, and entering into trade agreements.

For a week beginning November 22, the Roman delegation headed by Mayor Salvatore Rebecchini toured Boston's cultural institutions and schools, met local politicians, and was entertained and photographed. Volpe was master of ceremonies at the main banquet but saved his most emotional speech for the students at Boston College: "Whether you are the son of an immigrant or a son of the American Revolution, you are engaged in the struggle of decent men throughout the free world to triumph over the evil ideology of communism. In a word: you are fighting the final war which can lead to eternal peace among men of good will."

The salute had its lighter moments, too. On impulse, shortly after the delegation arrived, Volpe asked Rebecchini if he would like to see the lightweight championship fight between Tony DiMarco from Massachusetts and the defender, Carmen Basilio. Rebecchini, a scholarly engineer and university professor, was not a boxing fan, but he was game. "After all," he told Volpe, "the Italians can't lose." Unrecognized in the smoke and darkness, the two men watched Basilio successfully defend his title at Boston Garden. "He was a little nervous at first," Volpe recalled, "but by the time things were going, the mayor got pretty excited. He loved it."

Nineteen fifty-six marked the year the interstate highway program was finally implemented. As DPW commissioner, Volpe took on the task of lobbying for adequate state funding to match the federal money. By June, however, he had fallen ill with a viral infection, been hospitalized for exhaustion, and been ordered by his doctor to work only a few hours a day for the next several weeks.

Gordon Gray ran the department, and for a few weeks Herter took charge of the lobbying. By July, two bills were under consideration. The first proposal, originating in the Democratic Ways and Means Committee, called for an $80 million bond issue and the authority to issue short-term notes up to $120 million to meet federal matching funds. An alternate bill, authored by Republican House minority leader Charles Gibbons of Stoneham, called for a straight $200 million bond issue financed by an increase in the gasoline tax and another $100 million for future construction to run for four years without legislative action. Herter and Volpe both lobbied for the Republican bill. Also by July, Volpe was publicly announcing his intention to resign the DPW post to return to his business once the bond issue passed.

He reminded Herter that he had originally intended to stay only a year and had accepted the appointment with the understanding that he could not complete the term of office. Yet leaving the administration was a loss to Volpe. He had become close friends with Herter, spending time at his summer home by the sea in Manchester, learning the ins and outs of state government and the Republican party.

Although Herter had been portrayed in the press as the quintessential Boston Brahmin, he was, like Volpe, an outsider. Herter's family came from New York, and he was born and raised in Paris, where his parents were expatriate artists. He had graduated from Harvard, married a Standard Oil heiress, and planned to become an architect, but he joined the Foreign Service instead, later becoming an assistant secretary under Herbert Hoover when Hoover was secretary of commerce. After dabbling in publishing in Boston, Herter ran for the state legislature from the Back Bay area, moving up after twelve years to speaker of the House and then serving ten years in the U.S. Congress.

Tall and aristocratic looking, Herter was often reserved and rarely a moving speaker. He was most effective as a compromiser and peacemaker. He suffered from arthritis of the hip joints, a condition that made campaigning difficult and became increasingly hard to conceal. During his reelection campaign, Volpe met Herter as they were both leaving a fund raiser at the function room on the top floor of the Parker House. A short flight of stairs led from the function room to the elevators, and Herter, by the end of a long day, was in too much pain to walk down. Volpe, who was nearly a foot shorter than the candidate, and an aide managed to hold him up under the arms and maneuver him down the steps. To Volpe, the sacrifices in time and money he was making for public life suddenly seemed small in comparison with Herter's.

The 1956 state election was a political disaster for the Republicans. Herter had been appointed secretary of state by Eisenhower to replace John Foster Dulles. Whittier, who had then served two terms as lieutenant governor, easily won the nomination for governor. Charles Gibbons, a conservative self-made businessman from Stoneham who had been elected speaker in 1953, was nominated for lieutenant governor. George Fingold, a lawyer from the West End and Malden, was nominated for attorney general.

After former governor Paul Dever declined to seek the nomination, State Treasurer Foster Furcolo took the lead in the Democratic race. Furcolo, a Yale graduate and the son of an Italian-American doctor, had served two terms in Congress when the Massachusetts legislature named him state treasurer in 1952 to fill a vacancy and to add variety to the "all-green" ticket. Furcolo was something of a political maverick, regarded as unpredictable by the regulars. In 1953, he was invited to be keynote speaker at a convention of the Massachusetts chapter of the liberal Americans for Democratic Action (ADA). He took the podium and told the stunned audience that the most patriotic thing the ADA could do for the Democratic party was disband. From then on, he tried to walk a fine line between the political middle and the McCarthy supporters in the state. In June 1956, Furcolo became the first Italian-American nominated for governor of Massachusetts, and by September the polls were running against Whittier. In the general election, the Democrats swept every constitutional office except that of attorney general. Furcolo was sworn in as the state's first governor of Italian descent.

In early October 1956, Volpe submitted his resignation from the DPW, along with a detailed "account of my stewardship." In Washington, Secretary of Commerce Weeks asked Volpe to serve as the first federal highway administrator. When Volpe refused, Weeks asked him to hold the post for six months until someone else could be found. Volpe finally agreed to this after he learned his replacement would be New York's Bertram Tallamy, who could leave New York in six months after his work with the New York State Thruway was complete. Ten days after his last day at the DPW office on Nashua Street, Volpe was standing with his mother, wife, and children, Helen Ross, and Joseph Tauro in the White House, being sworn in by President Eisenhower.

After his three years at the Massachusetts DPW, Volpe knew most of the top personnel at the Bureau of Public Roads (BPR) and had a good idea of what they did. The previous year, he'd been elected vice president for Region 1 of the American Association of State Highway Officials and knew many of the state highway department heads. The job was not unfamiliar, but Washington was.

Volpe's first executive decision was to bring Helen Ross down as his secretary. He found that the new office was not in a high-status location but in the old General Service Administration Building four blocks from the White House. Housing proved to be a more serious problem. Jean was then a junior at Trinity College, a private Catholic girls' school in Washington, and Volpe thought his new job would provide an opportunity to spend some extra time with her before she graduated and was on her own. Jack was at boarding school. Jennie would fly down for weekends when he could not return to Winchester, and he and Jean would live together in an apartment. The housing situation in Washington proved to be tight, but

Volpe finally located an apartment on Connecticut Avenue uptown, near the Roma Restaurant, and Jean kept house for the two of them for the remainder of his time there.

Volpe saw his mission at the BPR as similar to the task he had undertaken at the DPW: getting more work done with the same manpower. A newspaper reporter at the time called Volpe a "human pile driver," packing down the organization. The new federal highway plan would nearly quadruple the volume of work at the bureau, and officials there expected to double or triple the work force. Volpe thought otherwise.

The slack, he felt, was in the local and regional offices. During his tenure at the Massachusetts DPW, Volpe had often wondered what the fourteen or fifteen people in the Massachusetts district office did. Now he decided to find out. After some digging, he discovered that less than 50 percent of all highway projects were approved or disallowed at the regional and local levels. The offices were simply passing work along to Washington. At a meeting with the regional administrators, Volpe laid it on the line. Decision-making would take place at the district and regional levels. The workload would increase but not the number of employees. In the end, the bureau added only two hundred new employees nationally (the bureau then employed about six thousand people). The two hundred new employees were to be used in reviewing land-takings.

After the initial confrontations, Volpe's tenure as highway administrator ran smoothly. Tallamy met with Volpe at least once a month to familiarize himself with the departments. There were almost no objections to the first land-takings, as the first highways built were intercity, running through farmland, woods, and deserts. The more politically troublesome routes through city voters' backyards would come later. Tallamy was able to finish up in New York a month earlier than anticipated, and after four and a half months, Volpe was able to step down. On January 13, 1957, more than a thousand guests turned out for his testimonial dinner. Although it was common then for the proceeds to go to the outgoing politician being honored, the money was donated to the Don Orione Home. Volpe did receive two gifts: a gold and onyx rosary and a set of golf clubs.

Before Volpe left Washington, he was asked to see the head of the White House staff, Sherman Adams. After a few preliminaries, Adams came straight to the point. "The Boss thinks you'd be a good assistant secretary of defense," he told Volpe.

"If I wanted to stay in Washington, I would have stayed in highways," Volpe replied.

Adams considered that, then asked if there were any other position for which he might be willing to interrupt his career. Volpe thought back to the Salute to Rome and his meeting with then Ambassador to Italy Clare Boothe Luce. Luce had been appointed in 1953 and had just given her notice. He asked Adams for the appointment. Adams would have to clear it with John Foster Dulles. At that time, the State Department followed a policy of not sending diplomatic representatives to their countries of ethnic origin.

Dulles's reply was negative, though he offered any of the five or six other embassies then open. Volpe declined; he had no desire to be a career diplomat. He would make his political career back in Massachusetts.

Before he met with Adams, Volpe had requested a last meeting with the president. He presented his final report in the Oval Office and mentioned that one day he might be running for public office. Did the Boss have any advice?

Eisenhower considered the question. "You build highways," Eisenhower told him, "so you know where the center line is. You can go up to thirty-five percent to the right or to the left of that center line, and you'll be all right. More than that, and you'll land in the gutter."

NOTES

1. Dwight D. Eisenhower, *Mandate for Change 1953–1956* (New York: Doubleday and Co., Inc., 1963), p. 502.

CHAPTER VI

Vote the Man

H OW NICE IT IS to be back in private life!" the forty-eight-year-old Volpe wrote to a Massachusetts state representative in February 1957. The same letter went out to eight other House members. Volpe was writing to them about a bill to regulate public bidding on brickwork. Back at his Malden office, he was keeping track of every piece of legislation affecting the construction industry and calling or writing every legislator he knew when important votes were coming up. Helen Ross had moved back to her old home in Melrose and was still his private secretary. Peter Volpe had become treasurer of the company in 1956.

The business had done reasonably well in Volpe's absence. Six months after his return from Washington, the Volpe Company opened two more branch offices: one in Dallas and another in Miami. Business grew somewhat more slowly in the Texas and Florida areas than it had in Washington, but within eighteen months, their contracts included a shopping center in Houston, an addition to a hospital in Hollywood, Florida, and a Veterans Administration hospital in Gainesville, Florida.

In May, Volpe became a member of the Associated General Contractors (AGC) committee raising money to build a national headquarters in Washington. And there was work on the Don Orione Home and Madonna Shrine. In June, the Sons of Italy's Grand Lodge of Massachusetts named Volpe "Man of the Year." He had served the order for ten years as grand financial secretary and as grand orator. Their honoree the previous year had been Boston's Archbishop Cushing.

Slowly, inevitably, Volpe's "private life" grew more and more public. He accepted many speaking engagements and always found something to say about the new federal highway system, religion, or moral education — sometimes even a combination of all three. "I have pointed out to you that federal highway aid is there for the states if they ask for it — but the government will not go to the states and request that they take it," Volpe told his audience at a Communion breakfast. "The same is true of God's aid to us. It is there for the asking, but we must ask for it." After a full day at the Malden office, two or three nights a week Volpe would nap in the back of a company station wagon while his driver took him to his speaking engagements.

March 1958 marked the Volpe Company's twenty-fifth anniversary, and the staff celebrated by dedicating a new wing (with a blessing by Auxiliary Bishop Jeremiah F. Minihan) and an open house. The list of political figures who dropped by was impressive: Senators Leverett Saltonstall and John F. Kennedy; Boston's Mayor Hynes; United Nations Ambassador Henry Cabot Lodge; and even Volpe's replacement at the DPW, Anthony DiNatale. In the national organization of the AGC, Volpe had advanced to be first vice president and so would be eligible to become president of the organization the following year. Publicly, he was committed only to his business and the construction industry.

In the summer of 1958, Salvatore Rebecchini was reelected mayor of Rome and was able to return Boston's 1955 salute. Jean graduated from Trinity College in June, John's school year at St. Sebastian's prep school ended at the same time, and Volpe arranged to take the whole family to Rome for the salute, along with Helen Ross to keep track of the details. Volpe and Mayor Hynes were cochairmen of the delegation. The family took a flat in Rome, while the rest of the Boston delegation stayed in hotels. They enjoyed ten days of banquets, tours, and receptions.

After a formal dinner at Castel Santangelo, Volpe and his friend Leo Barbo, the owner of Barbo's Furniture, went out onto the balcony at the top floor of the castle to look over the imperial city. It was a feast day, and the dome of St. Peter's was bathed in floodlights. The night sky was full of summer stars. For a long time, the two businessmen stood silent at the marble balustrade, awed by the scene. Finally, Volpe spoke. He told Barbo that he would like to come back to Rome someday as ambassador from the United States. Barbo nodded; nothing seemed impossible now.

As the rest of the Bostonians returned home, the Volpes took off in a rented Fiat for Elba and Lake Garda. Then they drove across the Alps to

Switzerland and France, and down the coast of Spain. After a month's traveling, Jack and Jean flew home from Madrid to stay with relatives in Boston, while Jennie and John continued on to Gibraltar, boarding the Italian liner SS *Augustus* for a cruise back to the United States.

Six weeks after her parents returned from Italy, Jean married Ensign Roger Rotondi, a recent graduate of Annapolis, at St. Mary's Church in Winchester. More than two hundred guests celebrated at an Italian buffet at the Everett Avenue home on Mystic Lake and danced to traditional Italian and contemporary American music until sunset.

Volpe had not intended to get involved in politics that year, but by September a bizarre turn of events thrust him briefly into the race for governor. In 1956, just before Volpe's resignation from the DPW, the Democrats had regained the governorship and swept all statewide offices except that of attorney general. Foster Furcolo had embarked on his gubernatorial term full of promise, with heavy support from suburban voters, although he was regarded by the party insiders as a maverick. In his inaugural speech, he spent two hours further alienating the regulars, condemning "business as usual" on Beacon Hill and promising an end to all deals and payoffs. Further, he promised an all-out assault on the deficit, which could mean only one thing: raising taxes. "We have inherited the worst financial mess in the history of the Commonwealth," Furcolo said, laying it on the line. "And with it we of necessity have inherited the greatest taxes. Our inheritance is taxes, more inherited taxes, and still more taxes. The Commonwealth has been living high, not paying its bills, and putting up a good front on credit. The day of reckoning is here."[1]

Furcolo was not exaggerating. Massachusetts, like every other state, had been caught by the costs of the baby boom and the move to the suburbs. Nationally, state and local spending had tripled from 1945 to 1956 to nearly $50 billion a year, but Massachusetts had been slow to raise taxes, still relying on the outdated property tax. In 1957, the state debt was more than $1 billion, the largest per capita in the United States, and a $40 million deficit was anticipated for 1958.[2]

Furcolo's solution, the sales tax, met with massive resistance in the legislature. The sales tax was scarcely more palatable to the public. At the 1958 Republican convention, the Old Guard unreservedly threw their support behind a non-Yankee candidate, Attorney General George Fingold, rather than former House Minority Leader Charles Gibbons or Christian Herter, Jr., who was then a governor's councilor. Fingold was nominated by acclamation.

One of the first Jewish politicians to rise to a leadership position in

Massachusetts Republican circles, Fingold was born in Boston's West End and grew up in Malden, attending Malden High at the same time as Volpe. His father was an immigrant Russian shoe factory worker. "I haven't had the Ivy League opportunities of the governor," Fingold declared after he had received the nomination. "I am a product of Boston's streets and a night law school."[3]

Fingold first came to public attention in 1948, when as an assistant attorney general, he was given the job of cleaning up corruption in Revere, a blue-collar oceanfront town whose principal industries were, and are, dog and horse racing, an amusement park, and a beach accessible by subway to Boston's old neighborhoods. Fingold set up his headquarters at the Metropolitan District Commission (MDC) police station because the Revere police would not let him have space in their station, and he proceeded to gather enough evidence to indict a majority of the Revere City Council. The charges did not stick, but Fingold became popular with the press. He was first elected attorney general in 1952, by the largest vote ever recorded in the state, and was reelected in 1954. In 1956, he was the only Republican to survive the Democratic sweep.

A pudgy, quick-witted prosecuting attorney who chain-smoked fat cigars, Fingold was a compulsive worker who stayed on the job as attorney general after his nomination for governor. In July, he collapsed in his office and was hospitalized for a "viral infection." His aides assured the press and public he would be on the campaign trail by Labor Day. On August 30, Fingold kicked off his campaign against Furcolo with a rally at the Sons of Italy Hall in East Boston. It was a hot night, the hall was packed, and Fingold gave a rousing speech denouncing Democratic tax-and-spend policies. The crowd loved him. The next day, a Sunday, Fingold was reading the newspaper in his backyard in Concord when he suffered a stroke and died instantly. The "virus" had in fact been coronary artery disease. Two weeks before the primary and two months before the general election, with a good shot at defeating Furcolo, the Republicans were leaderless.

The Fingold family had kept his illness not only from the press but from Republican insiders as well. No plans had been made to replace him. Senator Saltonstall came from his summer home in Maine to preside over an inconclusive meeting of the party leadership. There was no way that Fingold's name could be removed from paper ballots or machines in time for the September 9 primary; the Republicans would be forced to use stickers or write-ins.

State chairman "Chick" McLean called an emergency session of the entire Republican State Committee on September 2 at the Parker House. Of the hundred committeemen and women, ninety-eight showed up to vote in a crowded function room on the second floor. Saltonstall supported Christian Herter, Jr. Gibbons, who had lost to Fingold at the convention, was eager for the nomination, but several party leaders worried that his nomination might be struck down as unconstitutional by the Democratic secretary of state. Gibbons was already on the ballot to replace Republican State Senator Charles Ferguson of Lexington, who was retiring. Section 46, Chapter 53 of the Massachusetts Constitution reads: "No person shall be a candidate for nomination for more than one office."

Volpe began to receive phone calls before the Parker House meeting. Was he in the running for the nomination? He had been back from Washington only a year and a half and had spent part of the summer in Europe. Caught completely off guard, he was unsure what action to take. Fingold had not been a close personal friend, but Volpe had contributed to his campaigns and had fully expected him to win at least one term. Volpe decided to stay with his business a while longer. He probably would accept, he told the press, if handed the nomination. But he made no attempt to seek it and was conspicuously absent from the crowds at the Parker House, working at his Malden office instead.

As the Republican State Committee met, six names were placed in nomination: Gibbons, Volpe, Elmer Nelson, Christian Herter, Jr. (the convention endorsee for lieutenant governor), Congressman Lawrence Curtis, and Mayor Howard Whitmore of Newton. On the first ballot, Volpe led with 37 votes, Gibbons was next with 24, and Herter trailed with 15. Under rules previously agreed on, the bottom three were dropped. Volpe received a phone call from one of the committeemen. If you come here now, he said, the nomination is yours. Volpe stayed in Malden. On the second ballot, he was still ahead with 43 votes, Gibbons 35, and Herter 21. On the last ballot, Herter was dropped, and Gibbons won 59 to 39. "Chick" McLean led the victor, arms raised, out of the caucus room to greet the press. In the frenzied atmosphere of the Parker House lobby, a rumor began to circulate that Volpe would be persuaded to run against incumbent Senator John F. Kennedy. This he quickly denied.[4]

Charlie Gibbons, the new nominee, was not a Brahmin but one of the Main Street men who formed the core of the party. He boasted of a distinction unique in Massachusetts politics — having been born, like Lincoln, in a log cabin. Gibbons grew up in the hills of Kentucky and had not even seen Massachusetts until 1925, when he left the Navy and married a girl from Malden. Through the 1930s and 1940s, he built up a modest business, the Mercury Messenger Company, and worked his way up in local politics through the town of Stoneham and into the Massachusetts House leadership. A team player in the House, Gibbons had little statewide appeal and almost no time to get a campaign underway. After a brief wrangle over the constitutional question, Gibbons was nominated by sticker. Volpe and Herter each received several hundred unsolicited write-in votes. In November, Gibbons was soundly defeated by Furcolo.

In January 1958, Volpe had been elected president of the Greater Boston Chamber of Commerce, the first Italian-American to hold this office. Throughout 1959, he led a membership drive that included a five-week campaign by four hundred volunteer chamber salesmen. The theme of the speeches he made as chamber president usually was transportation or cutting Boston's rising property tax rate. He crusaded for the building of the rest of the Inner Belt expressway through Boston, Cambridge, and Somerville to take the pressure off the Central Artery and raise land values in what was becoming a depressed area. Some of his other proposals were turning the Massachusetts Transit Authority (MTA) over to the Port Authority to reduce corruption and mismanagement, instituting an auto tax to defray the MTA deficit, and putting Massachusetts toll roads into the interstate system as Maine and New Hampshire were doing. Predictably, Callahan resented this invasion of his turf. "Volpe is trying to confuse the public by planning dream highways," he told a reporter in May 1958. "If John A. Volpe would only announce what office he is a candidate for, as a leading Republican, the air would be cleared."[5]

By the fall of 1959, Volpe was involved in politics again. Although Furcolo himself was known as an honest governor, rumors of deals among some of his subordinates in the Governor's Council began to spread through the State House. Volpe was approached directly by his old friend, Meyer Pressman, a state representative from the immigrant town of Chelsea. Pressman was a Democrat, but in his first race, he had been nominated by both parties and had friends on both sides of the aisle. He respected Volpe's work and decided to give him a little advice. By then, the only public scandal involving Furcolo's administration had been a state Senate probe of the DPW rental policies under Anthony DiNatale, the commissioner Furcolo had appointed. Volpe had been called to testify, too, but the Republican-controlled committee could not make anything stick. Pressman thought more serious charges would surface but not until 1962 or 1963. The chances were that nothing would be public in 1960, when Furcolo was expected to leave the governorship and run against Leverett Saltonstall for the U.S. Senate. But Pressman believed that by 1964, some of the irregularities would be public, and an Italian-American candidate might find the voters unwilling to support him, no matter how honest he appeared to be.

At the same time as Volpe was considering Pressman's advice, he was, as first vice president, expected to be elected president of the AGC at the convention in San Francisco in March of the following year. In January, the managing director of the AGC heard that Volpe was considering entering the Massachusetts governor's race and called to urge him on. Massachusetts was not the only state where contractors were held in suspicion, and to have a contractor elected governor would help their public image immensely. He could still serve as president of the AGC later on, and the new first vice president would be willing to fill in as needed.

From some of the Massachusetts party regulars, advice was less than encouraging. The only election Volpe had actually won was for town meeting member in Winchester just before he left to serve in the Navy. He was advised to run for the Massachusetts House, then wait his turn. "You have to start at the bottom of the ladder," people told him. Volpe would reply that he had already started at the bottom of the ladder carrying a hod. And once was enough.

At the same time, the press was treating Volpe as a possible successor to U.S. Senator Leverett Saltonstall if the senator decided not to seek a fourth term. On January 29, 1960, Volpe announced that he probably would seek the governorship but wanted to survey the field for five or six weeks to make sure he had substantial delegate support.

By early February, Volpe had polled the eighteen hundred prospective delegates and discovered that more than 50 percent of them were still uncommitted to any of the four contestants. He was ready, but his most serious opposition came at home. Jack was finishing high school at La-Salle Military Academy in New York State, Jean was living with her husband and baby girl in Newport, Rhode Island, and Jennie had settled comfortably into private life with her circle of friends in Winchester. She had seen the sixteen-hour days at the DPW and objected to the run for governor. Why should her husband exhaust himself trying to reform the DPW, she reasoned, when the next commissioner might bring it back to the old ways? John, the idealist, would tell her that if honest men did nothing, government would be left to the dishonest.

One evening, Volpe screwed up his courage to tell Jennie that he was probably running. She began to cry. Politics in the state was so dirty, she said. The other candidates and the press would try to smear him, and all his work would be for nothing. But by the end of the next night, she was resigned to the fact. "The last thing my mother told me before I was married was 'it's your job to make your husband happy,' " she told him. "If this is what makes you happy, you go ahead. I'll help all I can — but don't expect me to make any speeches."

With the opposition from the house on Everett Avenue won over, Volpe considered his opponents in the Republican party. The strongest was Howard Whitmore, Jr., of Newton. Whitmore, like Sinclair Weeks, had built his political base in the prosperous Boston suburb of Newton, gaining statewide attention from opposing Callahan's plans to build the Massachusetts Turnpike through his town. In 1960, Whitmore was chairman of the House Ways and Means Committee and was one of the more powerful Republicans in the state.

State Senator Philip A. Graham and State Representative Frank Giles had been in the running for several months, although they had not officially announced until January. Giles, from Methuen, had replaced Charlie Gibbons as House minority leader and was claiming a majority of Fingold's supporters. Graham was wooing the same group, with less success. Running last was Christian Herter, Jr., who had gone to Washington for a short time to work for his father, who was then secretary of state. Republican State Committee Chairman "Chick" McLean was being scrupulously neutral, leaving the contest wide open.

Volpe, as an outsider, could not hope to win enough delegate support from party regulars alone and had been in politics long enough to know that elections were not won solely through the established party organizations. He set about building his own organization, one that would enable him to meet most of the delegates through a series of mealtime meetings in each state senatorial district. Meticulous organization and scheduling were vital because it would have been physically impossible for a candidate to meet all the delegates on their home ground. The criteria for delegate selection were determined by geography and gubernatorial vote, which weighted small towns and rural areas more heavily than metropolitan Boston. One of Volpe's first priorities was to set up a campaign structure and organizational chart, just as if he were running a business.

For campaign director, Volpe picked former Republican State Committee Chairman Elmer Nelson. Nelson was not a college graduate, but he knew the small towns and the rural areas where Republican delegate strength lay. The senior Joe Tauro helped in setting up the structure. The next step was to choose a county chairman from each county in the state. Each county chairman would recommend a chairman for each state senatorial district, who in turn would choose city or town chairmen.

Volpe met with each chairman and laid out his responsibilities. The official announcement of his candidacy was made in February.

Volpe's work in charitable organizations began to pay off as he started to build a statewide organization. He could check with friends in Sons of Italy lodges to see who was sympathetic in a small town. Friends from the Greater Boston Chamber of Commerce were eager to see a self-made businessman try his hand at managing the state. Over the years, Volpe had made many friends in Catholic lay organizations, among the clergy, and through the Knights of Columbus, and he had just been made a knight of Malta, one of the highest lay honors the Vatican could bestow. The Volpe campaign had no official headquarters before the convention, but the structure that would later be fleshed out in the final campaign was already in place.

Using his new organization, Volpe could meet every uncommitted delegate; the committed would not come to his receptions. It was in the preconvention stage that both his organizational experience and his personal wealth were crucial. Volpe could afford the luxury of holding cocktail receptions, paying a few staffers, and paying his own considerable travel expenses without devoting time to fund-raising. After the convention, if he won the nomination, he knew that funds would come from traditional Republican sources.

In March, Volpe flew to San Francisco for the AGC convention. In his acceptance speech after his election as president, he tore into congressional critics of the federal highway program. The House Subcommittee on Public Works was then investigating reports of waste and inefficiency. "Highways won't be built in hearing rooms," Volpe told his audience, and he went on to argue that some problems were to be expected in a program bigger than the building of forty Panama canals.

In April, there was a brief flurry of rumors that Sumner Whittier, who had been serving as head of the Veterans Administration in Washington, would enter the race for governor again. In May, more than a month before the convention was scheduled to open, Volpe announced to the press that enough of the 1,408 elected delegates were pledged to ensure him a first-ballot victory. He did, in fact, have enough pledges to cover a first-ballot victory, but just barely. By the week before the convention, the combined totals of the other three candidates would still be enough to block him on the first ballot, and it was not unknown for one delegate to pledge his support for two or even three candidates at the same time. Most of the other recent Republican conventions had been decided long before they opened, and the professionals were not sure what might happen in a wide-open race. The consensus among the pros was that if Volpe did not win on the first ballot, he would lose the bandwagon effect, and new coalitions would emerge on the second.

Just before the convention opened in Worcester, Volpe set out some of his proposals. He suggested a complete financial reorganization of the Commonwealth. Volpe also supported three constitutional changes to make administration more efficient: a four-year gubernatorial term, the short ballot (only governor, lieutenant governor, and attorney general on the ballot, with the rest appointed), and a limitation on state bond issues for capital improvements.

An early heat wave struck Worcester as the convention opened on June 11, and neither the convention hall nor much of the hotel was air-conditioned. "It was hot as the hinges of hell," Ross remembered. She checked and rechecked lists of delegates, typed press releases, and rewrote speeches in the Volpe hospitality suite of the Bancroft Hotel until the early morning hours on her first day. At 2:30 A.M., an exhausted Volpe came into the suite to bring Ross a sandwich. The political movers and shakers had turned in, but Ross was still at work. "I forgot to get you a room at the hotel," he told her, sheepishly. "I'm sorry." Ross said she could sleep in a chair, not to worry. But when the door shut behind him, the tension of the long campaign took its toll, and she cried. "I'd never let him know that. Or any of the other politicians. No man was big enough to make me cry."

The pain was forgotten the next day as the hoopla began. In an open horse race, candidates pulled out all the stops. Convention hats: South American sombreros for Giles, blue straw boaters for Whitmore, varicol-ored crew hats for Volpe, and yellow straw hats for Graham. Bands: Volpe's serenaded the delegates with "Oh, Johnny," Giles hired the Green Knights of Lawrence to play "My Buddy," Whitmore led his supporters through the hall with "Boola Boola," and Graham's floor demonstration was headed by a Scottish bagpipe band with his committed delegates jigging along behind.

Toward the end of the roll call on the first ballot, Volpe was only three votes short of the top. The crowd exploded, yelling, "We want Volpe!" After the roll call was finished, as the candidate himself emerged from a room behind the stage, the delegates invaded the platform, seized him, and carried him on their shoulders to the podium, then boosted Jennie up too. John and Jennie hugged and kissed each other and tried to speak, but the noise went on while the newsreel lights played over them. After the sergeants at arms had cleared the platform and the delegates were back in their seats, Giles, Graham, and Whitmore announced their withdrawal. The nomination was unanimous after all.

Augustus Means, a North Shore gentleman farmer and cousin of Henry Cabot Lodge, won the nomination for lieutenant governor. George Michaels, a Jewish lawyer from Newton, received the endorsement for attorney general, and Edward Brooke from Boston was nominated for secretary of state, becoming the first black man to run on a major party ticket in Massachusetts at a time when there were fewer than one hundred thousand blacks living in the state. Walter J. Trybulski, the former mayor of the western Massachusetts town of Chicopee, was the nominee for state treasurer. As in 1952, the convention had produced what was touted as a "United Nations" slate. No other Republican came forward to challenge Volpe in the primary.

The Democratic convention, held just a week later in the Boston Arena, a run-down hall in the South End of Boston used for circuses and fights, was a godsend for the Republicans. At times, the proceedings seemed indistinguishable from the arena's usual entertainment. Only two party leaders, Joseph Ward and Robert Murphy, had been contacting delegates before the convention started, and, sensing weakness, several other leading Democrats decided to get into the gubernatorial contest. Despite some overt antagonism between the Irish and Italian-American factions, Furcolo was easily nominated to challenge Saltonstall for the Senate seat.

Ward, with the help of House Speaker John Thompson (known as "The Iron Duke," or simply "Duke" to his friends), had done his homework and won easily on the first ballot. But a bloodbath worse than any of the prizefights held in the old arena soon followed. A few days after Ward's nomination, Murphy went to the press charging that the "leadership was power-drunk, the ward-heelers hungry for votes. Votes went to the highest bidder with total disregard of the consequences and cost to the taxpayer."[6] Within a few weeks of Ward's endorsement, no fewer than seven other Democrats had announced their intention to challenge him in the September primary.

The Democratic party in Massachusetts at that time lacked any internal discipline, and challenges to endorsees were common. From 1952 to 1962, the convention nominees for statewide office were opposed in the primary 62 percent of the time. Even for Massachusetts Democrats, however, the 1960 primary boasted an enormous field of candidates. But Joe Ward marshaled his forces, to the tune of his campaign theme song "Go Forward with Joe Ward!" (sung to a combination of "O Tannenbaum" and the "Holy Cross Alma Mater"). Ward himself was a flowery speaker but an unexciting campaigner. Often described as "colorless," Ward was a loyal party regular and main line Democrat. A graduate of

Holy Cross and Boston University Law School, he served in the House representing Fitchburg from 1948 to 1956. In 1953, he led a group demanding an investigation of Harvard President James Bryant Conant, Eisenhower's high commissioner to Germany, for possible communist links. In his law practice, he served as counsel to the Massachusetts Retail Liquor Dealers. In 1956, Ward received the convention endorsement for attorney general but was beaten in the primary by House Speaker John McCormack's nephew, Eddie. In 1958, Ward finally achieved statewide office when the incumbent for secretary of state died and the legislature appointed him to the vacancy. It was therefore Ward's responsibility in 1960 to prepare all the ballots and decide whose name should appear on more or less visible locations.

None of Ward's seven opponents in the primary was a political lightweight, and all were capable of inflicting various degrees of damage on Ward as frontrunner. The strongest was Robert Murphy from Malden, who was then serving his second term as lieutenant governor. Somewhat more liberal than Ward, Murphy was known as "Mr. Integrity" for his work against corruption in the Massachusetts House. Francis ("Sweepstakes") Kelly was a Boston city councilor who had built a statewide reputation advocating a state lottery. John Francis Kennedy, who had won election as state treasurer on name recognition alone, had taken to the field again, now that the other JFK was running at the top of the ballot for president. Endicott ("Chub") Peabody, the Democratic party's only Brahmin politician and a member of the Governor's Council, was hoping to benefit from a split among the Irish, who would be voting for Murphy, Kelly, and Kennedy. And two Italian-Americans, Boston city councilor Gabriel Piemonte and Alfred Magaletta, a real estate developer, also entered the race.

Volpe's strategy was to ignore all his potential Democratic rivals and concentrate on building and refining his own organization. Although it was customary for candidates to lie low until Labor Day, Volpe spent the summer stumping the state, with the exception of a trip to Chicago for the Republican National Convention in July to second Henry Cabot Lodge's nomination as vice president. Although Elmer Nelson continued to run the nuts and bolts operation of Volpe's campaign, James Gaffney, who had served as one of the "Four Horsemen" deputy state committee chairmen under Sinclair Weeks, was named state coordinator, and the other two "Horsemen" soon joined him in the campaign. Joe Tauro stayed on after the primary, and Sal Danca became campaign treasurer. Whitmore also gave much more than token support, donating his own primary campaign files and running Volpe's speakers bureau. Both Giles and Graham did some speaking for the party nominee as well.

Not long before the convention, Volpe also had recruited the man who became his most effective county chairman, Albert P. ("Toots") Manzi. Manzi and his two brothers owned a meat market and a grocery in an Italian neighborhood of Worcester. While his brothers ran the family business, "Toots" indulged his passion for local politics. He and Volpe had first met when they both supported Lodge. Manzi had many friends in the Worcester lodge of the Sons of Italy, a genius for organization, and a knack for planning down to the last detail. He held court behind the meat counter in his store or at a diner across the street, keeping tabs on the Worcester County vote. One week before the convention, Manzi came to Volpe with his estimate of the delegate vote for Worcester County. When the count was in, Manzi had missed by one vote — an extra one for Volpe.

Although the Democrats were fighting bitterly in the primary race the greatly outnumbered Republicans always faced an uphill fight. Worse yet, at the very top of the Democratic ticket in Massachusetts was Senator John F. Kennedy, the first Catholic nominated for president by a national party. Before the first television debate on September 26, Richard Nixon and his party seemed to have a good shot at the presidency, but he was certainly not going to carry his opponent's home state.

Volpe's staff drew up a campaign strategy based on the idea of a lone candidate waging a crusade against corruption and inefficiency. He had cleaned house for Herter in the DPW; now he would clean house for the whole state. The campaign slogan was "Vote the Man, Vote Volpe." Unless he was speaking to an exclusively Republican crowd, party affiliation was never mentioned.

The issues he chose were the standard ones for Massachusetts at the time: taxes, corruption, and waste in government. In his speeches, he presented himself as a businessman (the last time the state had elected a businessman as governor was in 1928, he reminded his audiences) with experience in budgeting, purchasing, and accounting, who would run the state like a business. Using the corporate model, he even proposed the creation of a complaint department, where taxpayers could resolve their problems with the Registry of Motor Vehicles or the Massachusetts Transit Authority, like the customer complaint department in a store.

Volpe's writers did not have to dig very hard to come up with examples of state governmental mismanagement. The DPW had just released a study by the well-known Stone and Webster Engineering firm that detailed waste and inefficiency. Volpe was quick to point out that many of the DPW's problems started when the department slid back into its old ways after he left, and that several of the reforms the report recommended had already gone into effect during his tenure, then were discontinued.

One of the more popular examples of DPW waste was the "$46 booklet," an anecdote Volpe recounted, holding up the offending booklet, in almost every speech he made from June to November. The DPW had hired a consultant to write a feasibility study for a proposed Adams Parkway through the South Shore suburbs of Boston. Instead of estimating traffic flow and costs, the author had simply recounted the history of famous people who had lived between the South Shore communities of Quincy and Plymouth. Only five hundred copies were printed, yielding a net cost of $46 per copy.

In the spring of 1960, the state legislature also had held hearings on mismanagement in the Metropolitan District Commission (MDC), the state agency that controlled the water supply, parkland, and beaches of eighty-two cities and towns, including Boston. The investigations revealed the bizarre activities of Boston city auctioneer "Mucker" McGrath as he bought and resold land between the city and the MDC through straws.

Such scandals had been the stuff of Boston's journalism for decades, yet in 1960 the voters seemed to be paying more attention to the voices for reform than in the past. One explanation was that many of the voters had moved up through education into white-collar jobs and out of the ghettos. All the core northern cities in the United States lost population after World War II, but Boston was the most seriously affected, having lost one-eighth of its people between 1950 and 1960. Boston's suburbs now held its voting strength, and the new suburbanites in garrison colonials were not favorably impressed by the antics of men with nicknames such as "Knocko," "Sonny," and "Mucker." The new voters wanted good schools, low taxes, and decent highways, not lovable rogues who sang at weddings, made deals under the table, and gave their supporters Christmas turkeys, loads of coal, and pick-and-shovel jobs.

Nationally, both Nixon and Kennedy were courting the burgeoning suburban vote. True to his campaign promise to visit all forty-eight continental states, Nixon arrived in Massachusetts in late September, just after the first television debate. Nixon and Volpe had met in 1952, when Volpe as Republican deputy state chairman had arranged a rally and motorcade in East Boston that drew more than four thousand people, and Nixon had been impressed. Now the two men had dinner alone at the Copley Plaza before a fund-raiser held at the Commonwealth Armory that evening in Boston. Nixon asked Volpe what he thought of the debate. Volpe, concerned that Nixon might not be getting honest feedback from his staff, told him bluntly that he had looked tired and pale, as if he had spent too long preparing, and that whoever did his makeup had done a terrible job. Nixon, unused to such candor, paused and then remarked that when you lose the first round, you fight harder to catch up. Volpe did not disagree, but he remembered one of Dr. Maietta's aphorisms from the Sons of Italy ritual: "First impressions are lasting ones." He doubted now that Nixon could win.

As Nixon and Volpe paraded to the head table that evening, Senator Saltonstall's wife, Alice, caught Volpe's attention. "Your wife did a great job speaking for you last night," Mrs. Saltonstall told him as he went by. Jennie, who had promised to do anything *but* make speeches, had come through. Volpe thought about it during the long evening. But on the ride home, he never mentioned it, for fear she might change her mind and never make another.

She made many more. By the middle of the campaign, she was on the road, too, though her first priority was, as always, home and family. Jack was working in the campaign, putting up signs and distributing literature, during his vacation between high school and Boston College. Jennie still did her own cooking and shopping, and she baby-sat for their first grandchild, Joy, when Jean visited. The home on Everett Avenue was Volpe's refuge from business and politics, and Jennie never failed to keep it ready. He played a little golf, a reporter wrote during the campaign, "but his hobby is his home."

Although the campaign began officially in August at a Taunton clambake, Volpe had campaigned without a break all summer, honing his basic speeches, "pressing the flesh," giving the public the "million-dollar smile." In September, Ward won his primary and set his own campaign in motion. For Ward, getting press attention was difficult. The media were focusing on the presidential race and on Khrushchev's month-long visit to the United Nations. Nearly all the major newspapers were Republican, and several endorsed Volpe. Volpe's Horatio Alger story generated considerable press appeal as his campaign workers brought it to public attention. "I take my hat off to any man who started work as a hod carrier and worked up the ladder to aspire to the governorship of the state," was a typical comment.[7]

Five weeks before the election, the Volpe campaign staff got the news from a television station that Ward had bought four half-hour slots in prime time between October 12 and October 25. They assumed the ads would be the usual "talking head" shots of the candidate giving his pitch.

87

On the evening Ward's first commercial was to be aired, Volpe settled in with his staff at the Tremont Street headquarters to watch.

Instead of the usual cozy scene at home that politicians then favored as a backdrop, Ward stood, stern and dressed in a dark suit, in a mock courtroom. At a table beside him were four lawyers, introduced as "a distinguished panel of attorneys": Paul Counihan, an Irish-American; William Homans, a Yankee; Joseph De Guglielmo, the Italian-American former mayor of Cambridge; and Jackson Holtz, a Jew. (Homans dropped off the panel after the first segment.) A gavel rapped, and a voice offstage intoned: "The people versus political contractor Volpe."

Silence fell over the campaign headquarters. Volpe's first emotion was anger at the one Italian-American who sat on the panel. Then shock. From the first hard years in the business, he had struggled *not* to be a "political contractor." There were few real secrets in Massachusetts politics. Everyone in the contracting business knew who the real political contractors were. The political insiders knew. But how was an ordinary voter to know? Volpe thought of Jennie and her misgivings about politics. How can they hurt me when I have nothing to hide? he had asked her. Now her worst fears had been realized.

Acting as both judge and prosecutor, Ward presented his "evidence," copies of letters from the DPW files on cards for close-up shots. His charge was the old one that Gordon Gray had been hired as chief engineer as a payoff for awarding the Beverly Junior High job to the Volpe Company. As he closed the show, Ward announced that more charges were coming, each more serious than this. As the picture faded, the staff members were urging Volpe to answer, to fight back. Phones were already ringing with calls from the newspapers, but Volpe was reluctant to jump in. Clearly Ward wanted him to respond. Then there would be more charges, and another response. Ward would be constantly the aggressor, Volpe always on the defensive. Accepting Ward's offer to debate would be futile, he realized. Ward was a skilled trial lawyer and Volpe a business-man who had never been inside a courtroom. He told the reporters "no comment," let the staff draw up their recommendations, and went home.

The next morning, he continued the campaign as if nothing had happened. Yet it *had* happened. It was always at the back of his mind now, the accusation all the more powerful for being completely untrue. An exaggeration of some error in judgment would have been, Volpe thought, easier to take, could be explained. When you lost your integrity, you lost everything.

As he continued campaigning, Volpe considered his options. Gaffney and others in the inner circle felt that the charges were hurting him. But letters and telegrams arrived at the campaign office offering support, and the crowds he met were still friendly. None of the people he saw on the campaign trail asked about the accusations. As the segments of the "trial" continued, local newspapers began picking up the story, favoring Volpe. The *Lynn Daily Item* printed a front page story rebutting the Beverly school contract charge. At the same time, Ward's campaign was paying for a full-page ad with an FBI "most wanted criminal" format, featuring a profile shot of Volpe wearing an unflattering grin and the caption: "Do YOU recognize this man?" Among the "crimes" listed in this ad was the accusation that Volpe supported a sales tax and an auto tax on commuters in areas served by the MTA.

The fourth and final segment of the "trial" featured the allegation that the DPW built an access road to the North Shore Shopping Center in Peabody to accommodate the Volpe Company, although the company won the contract with Allied Stores, the parent company of Jordan Marsh, only after Volpe had returned to private business. Immediately after the segment aired, the president of Allied Stores and other business-men featured in the trial came to Volpe's defense. None of them had been asked to do so.

The Volpe campaign then bought a half-hour segment on all three Boston television channels and one in Springfield. On October 25, Volpe sat alone at a desk and faced the cameras. He was not used to television, yet he felt oddly at ease, for at last he could defend himself publicly. "I appear before you tonight," he began, "alone with my conscience and with the truth." One by one, he refuted each charge, but made none against Ward except to say that his attacks had been unfair. But he did refer to remarks made about Ward by fellow Democrats, including a claim by Endicott "Chub" Peabody that Ward, as Secretary of State, had printed ballots with his name slightly taller and darker than those of his Democratic opponents. After Volpe's presentation, there were no further charges by Ward.

Two weeks later, Volpe was in a suite at the Somerset Hotel, watching the election returns come in. In 1960, Boston voted by machine, but "outstate," where the Republicans' greatest strength lay, still used paper ballots. Boston's results always came in quickly. There was always an almost religious atmosphere when the police closed a Boston precinct at 8 P.M. Poll workers, the men and women who stood just beyond the legal limit in front of a school or library holding a sign and handing out cards to their neighbors, gathered inside holding letters from the candidate's head-quarters authorizing them to hear the results. They stood in silence just outside a wooden temporary barrier the height of a Communion rail, as each machine was locked and sealed, then rushed to their homes or the nearest pay phone.

When Boston's vote was in, Ward had carried the city by only 51,000 votes. The experts calculated he needed a majority of 80,000 to 100,000 coming out of Boston to offset statewide Republican strength. Volpe's supporters downstairs in the ballroom were already celebrating victory, but Volpe waited upstairs until suburban returns had made the election absolutely certain.

At 11:30, he and Jennie finally ventured downstairs, into a rerun of the tumultuous scene at the Worcester convention. When Volpe appeared at the rear of the hall, the band struck up "For He's a Jolly Good Fellow," and instantly he and Jennie were mobbed, the crowd so frantic that extra police had to be called in. Protesting and laughing at the same time, Volpe was carried aloft the length of the hall and hoisted up to the speaker's platform. His sister, Grace, and brothers, Peter and Patrick, were already there, as was Filomena, beaming, with tears in her eyes. On their joint birthday in December, she would be eighty years old.

"I shall dedicate all of my energy to the great task of restoring confidence in the Commonwealth of Massachusetts and its rightful place of leadership," Volpe announced. "I will eliminate corruption and scandal."

After three hours' sleep, Volpe was calling members of his staff early the next morning. The final total gave him a 138,000-vote lead over Ward, although the Democrats had won every other statewide office. With his friends Ernest Nigro and Sal Danca, Volpe walked to the Workers' Chapel on Arch Street and attended Mass. Outside, as he emerged, the press was waiting. He flashed them his "million-dollar smile" and told them, "I'm full of energy and ready to go."

NOTES

1. Alan F. Westin, ed., *The Uses of Power: Seven Cases in American Politics* (New York: Harcourt, Brace and World, Inc., 1962), p. 358.

2. Ibid., p. 362.

3. *The Boston Globe,* 28 August 1958.

4. *Boston Herald-Traveler,* 3 September 1958.

5. *Boston Herald-Traveler,* 21 May 1958.

6. Murray B. Levin, *The Compleat Politician: Political Strategy in Massachusetts* (Indianapolis: Bobbs-Merrill Co., 1962), p. 98.

7. Ibid., p. 129.

CHAPTER VII

The Lonely Man of Beacon Hill

I N THE WANING DAYS of 1960, as Volpe assembled his transition team and drew up the plans for his inauguration, the state he was soon to govern found itself in transition as well. The first years of the sixties marked a turning point for Massachusetts. The old industrial base of textile and shoe factories manned by immigrant labor had eroded as the corporate owners sought nonunionized workers and low taxes in the South and overseas. At the same time, the national economy was beginning to shift toward a service base, and Massachusetts had always been a service center for banks, insurance companies, universities, and hospitals. In addition, the arms race was fueling the growth of America's Technology Highway, Route 128.

Yet Boston itself, the state's largest city as well as its capital, was physically unchanged since the Depression. From 1950 to 1960, Boston lost 13 percent of its population, and property values were falling.[1] "If the old things in Boston are too heavy and plushy, the new either hasn't been born or is appallingly shabby and poor," Elizabeth Hardwick wrote in *Harper's* in December 1959.[2]

Almost no new buildings had been constructed since the 1920s, the downtown shopping district was moribund, and the blight of the South End was creeping inexorably toward Beacon Hill through the Back Bay, where brownstone mansions were turning one by one into rooming houses. "But the people who worked on State Street sat at their rolltop desks and thought everything was all right," former Mayor John Collins remembered, "because it was the same today as it was yesterday."[3]

Even the most sacrosanct of Old Boston's landmarks, Boston Common, was being temporarily despoiled to build an underground parking garage. Girders braced one wing of the old State House, and planks propped up Saint-Gaudens's monument to Colonel Robert Gould Shaw and his black Union army regiment, inspiring Robert Lowell to write the grim "For the Union Dead": "One morning last March, I pressed against the new barbed and galvanized/ Fence on the Boston Common. Behind the cage,/ yellow dinosaur steamshovels were grunting as they cropped up tons of mush and grass/ to gouge their underworld garage."[4]

For Volpe, watching the muddy construction job, even right on the Common, was no more disconcerting than the sight of blood to a surgeon. He knew that the ground would heal. But the rumors of corruption surrounding the building of the garage disturbed him. Now Volpe himself was the titular head of state, no longer just a voice calling for reform. He would make things change.

In Boston, the process of physical renewal had already begun. Mayor John Collins owed little to established political interests, having defeated State Senate President John E. Powers by more than ten percentage points. He had lined up federal funding for the Government Center project that was to tear down the old honky-tonk bars of Scollay Square and create an enormous plaza for city, state, and federal offices; had developed a plan for the New Boston; and had hired a young urban planner name Ed Logue, who had organized New Haven, Connecticut's, urban renewal.

Volpe's plans were not about changes in brick and mortar but changing attitudes — the attitudes not only of men and women who worked for or did business with the state but also of the people the state served. On New Year's Day, 1961, a *Boston Globe* writer headlined his editorial "No Governor Ever Faced Tougher Task Than Volpe."

January 5, 1961, was a clear day, warm by Boston standards. In the Governor's Council chambers, Furcolo handed over the ritual objects of state: a big silver key that once unlocked the doors of the executive chambers and a small brown Bible presented by Civil War General Ben Butler after he could find no copy of the Scriptures in the governor's office. Inside, Butler had pasted a sobering admonition for future Massachusetts politicians: "But I say unto you, love your enemies, bless them that curse you, do good to them that hate you, and pray for them which despitefully use you."

Furcolo, who had spent a hectic morning making last-minute appointments, had to perform one final, painful gubernatorial duty. At the moment a new Massachusetts governor is sworn in, the outgoing governor must make the "lone walk" out the front door of the State House and down the front steps. The capitol police kept anyone else off the steps for those moments, and the press always attended. For Furcolo, the crowd on the sidewalk was small, and some of his supporters cried as they encouraged him, for he had been defeated in the primary in his race for the Senate. His political career was over. As the guns on Boston Common boomed out the twenty-one gun salute for Volpe, Furcolo got into the car waiting for him on Beacon Street and rode away.

A committee of the members of both the Massachusetts House and Senate came to escort Volpe to the dais of the House, with the sergeant at arms in his silk hat and armed with a staff leading the way. Cardinal Cushing gave the invocation, and Senate President John E. Powers administered the oath of office. Volpe felt well rested and looked tanned and fit after a short Florida vacation. He had given a great deal of thought to his inaugural address. Although it was milder in tone than other governors' recent inaugural speeches, there was no policy in it that Volpe was not fully prepared to carry out.

Volpe's first priority was legislation proposing a standard code of ethics for all public officials in Massachusetts. Until this bill could become law, he urged all elected officials to divest themselves of any interests that might conflict with their duties. Getting down to specifics, Volpe announced an immediate hiring freeze on all state employees and the firing of all temporary appointees who were not productive. For his legislative program, he planned to restructure the MDC, the DPW, and the MTA. His goals in the area of transportation were adoption of a no-fix computerized ticket system, construction of the Inner Belt, and compulsory auto insurance. Referring specifically to Boston's high tax rate as a cause of urban decay, he planned to introduce legislation to distribute the tax burden more fairly between cities and suburbs, never a popular idea on Beacon Hill, where rural and suburban voters outweighed the urban delegations.

Unlike Furcolo before him, Volpe did not harangue his listeners or openly condemn "the game as it is played on Beacon Hill." He followed the Navy adage: Criticize in private, praise in public. Volpe was the Old Man aboard ship, and he would need respect and cooperation if his reforms were to have any chance of success.

Furcolo had suspended the old custom of a grand inaugural ball as part of his austerity package. Volpe reinstituted the ball, the reception, and the other public ceremonials that had become part of the Commonwealth's tradition, and enjoyed them all hugely. The ball, held in the First Corps Cadet Armory, was military in theme, and many of the male guests were resplendent in dress uniforms, ranging from the knee britches of the Lexington Minutemen to modern dress blues. Jennie, now used to being in public during the campaign, was at ease with the press and charming to the guests. For years, she had designed hats and painted pictures for members of the family, and now her talents were suddenly on display. She wore to the inaugural reception a mink and velvet hat she had designed and made herself. At the ball, she appeared in an opulent beaded blue silk gown fashioned by a local designer, Fiandaca, and carried red roses. Volpe's mother, too, won over the press and public with her pride in her son. Jean and her husband came from Newport for the occasion, though she had just given birth to her first son in December. Only Vito was not there to share their joy, but he was rarely absent from Volpe's thoughts.

Just four days after he had taken the oath, Volpe stood on the dais again, speaking to an even more crowded chamber. President-elect Kennedy flew to Boston on January 8, spent the night in his old apartment on Bowdoin Street, and attended a meeting of the Harvard Board of Overseers the following morning. Volpe, Thompson, and Powers had jointly invited the future president to address a special joint session at 5:30, as a farewell to his home state. Kennedy had agreed to give a short address.

Although Powers, as presiding officer, had the privilege of introducing the president, he let Volpe have the honor instead. Outside the State House, a crowd of more than five thousand waited for a glimpse of the presidential limousine. Kennedy was rarely in Boston, for he usually flew in directly to Hyannis. Few of the crowd actually saw the president as he exited the limousine behind the old State House building. The Secret Service controlled his movements now, and Kennedy, chronically late to political events, was running on time.

"Since the Pilgrims found their way to our shores, Massachusetts has produced men who have shown the way in building, under God, a great nation and government on the cornerstones of freedom, opportunity, and equality," Volpe said as he introduced the president-elect. "Always a leader in the course of human welfare, Massachusetts continues to do that, again producing a native son to lead our nation, and guide and build our destinies."[5]

Kennedy took the podium and delivered what would later be called his "City on a Hill" speech. Referring to himself as "this son of Massachusetts," Kennedy also alluded to the state's long history. He quoted from John Winthrop's diary written on the *Arabella* 331 years before: "We must always consider that we shall be as a city upon a hill — the eyes of all people are upon us."

The heart of his speech concerned the state's future, not its illustrious past. He asked the legislators to consider how they would answer three questions. Were they men of courage, with the strength to "resist public pressure as well as private greed"? Were they men of integrity, "whom neither financial gain nor political ambition could ever divert from the fulfillment of our sacred trust"? And were they men of dedication, "compromised by no private obligation or aim"?

"The enduring qualities of Massachusetts," he concluded, "the common threads woven by the Pilgrim and the Puritan, the fisherman and the farmer, the Yankee and the immigrant — will not be and could not be forgotten in the nation's Executive Mansion."[6]

On January 19, Volpe flew with Jennie to attend the inaugural festivities in Washington. Inauguration Day was bitterly cold, and a snowstorm had paralyzed traffic in the city. But the inaugural parade went on, and the Volpes bundled up to ride in the open limousine. As governor of the president's home state, Volpe rode in the first car of the procession of governors. While the cars moved into position in the freezing wind, Volpe asked Jennie to stand up with him as they reached the reviewing stand and give Jack and Jackie a military salute. Jennie, ever tolerant, agreed, and they both executed snappy salutes as the Kennedys waved back.

The speech and the salute were preludes to a good relationship between Volpe and the Kennedy White House, despite their ideological differences. The White House correspondence files for the Kennedy administration show a cordial relationship between the Republican governor and the Democratic president. During and after the Eisenhower years, Volpe was always invited to state dinners whenever the honoree was Italian, but only Kennedy seated Volpe at the head table on these occasions.

After the inauguration, Volpe, the Governor's Council, and the Great and General Court had to come down from the heights of the "City on a Hill" and begin the process of hammering out a budget, appointing a staff, and bargaining over the new governor's legislative package. This was a job complicated by two factors: Volpe's minority position as the sole Republican elected official ("the lonely man of Beacon Hill," as editorial writers dubbed him) and the structure of the state constitution.

At a time when reformers and political scientists were advocating stronger executive powers on the national level, and Kennedy was sounding the themes of leadership, vigor, and activism, the political system of his own home state was a mass of checks and balances even Madison might have found daunting. The basic governmental structure was rooted in colonial opposition to royal governors and was designed to curb monarchial power. The ceremonial trappings of a long tradition and the perks of office — the elegant corner office, the private elevator, the limousines and helicopters and state police guard — made the governor seem to be a man of enormous power. Yet authority was not centered in the executive branch.

The principal holdover from pre-Revolutionary times was the eight-member Governor's Council, which held the power to confirm or deny more than eight hundred positions and appointments by the governor. The divided executive, which had been abandoned as unworkable in the early days of the federal constitution, was another anachronism. In Massachusetts, each constitutional officer ran separately; the governor and lieutenant governor were frequently of different political parties, as was the case with Volpe and McLaughlin. Even when they were from the same party, the two tended to be rivals; the system was an open invitation for the lieutenant governor to spend the entire term undermining the governor, who probably would be his electoral opponent. The two-year term constituted another obstacle to change. Massachusetts governors spent their first year in office feeling their way through the labyrinth of legislative committees and their second year running for reelection.

A second layer of checks and balances was created during the long struggle between the Yankees and the Irish for control of the state's political institutions. Like the glaciers that scoured New England, leaving giant boulders behind, the Yankee politicians left a legacy of roadblocks to power as they retreated, first from control of the cities, then the governorship, and at last the Great and General Court. The first place the Irish gained a foothold was Boston, where they outnumbered the Yankees by the mid-nineteenth century. The state government had responded to this perceived threat by removing most of the city's powers to levy taxes, with the exception of the property tax. In 1960, a tax on Boston hotel rooms, for example, was paid to the state and redistributed to the city by the legislature. Even the Boston police commissioner was then appointed by the governor, not the city's mayor. The legislature also had created a watchdog agency, the Boston Finance Commission (FinCom) to investigate and root out corruption in only one city.

Another legacy of the Yankee-Irish struggle was the creation of authorities and commissions whose executives' terms did not coincide with that of the governor. Instead of putting a state water and sewer department under the DPW, the legislature had created the Metropolitan District Commission (MDC), with powers not only to build water treatment plants but to run Boston's beaches and even police some of Boston's streets with its own cruisers operating from MDC police stations. A problem such as the pollution of Boston Harbor involved dozens of authorities, commissions, and city, town, and state agencies and departments. When problems like that arose, governors found that their only recourse was to create yet another agency, one they could staff with their own appointees. When Volpe took office, he found that 177 different agencies, boards, officials, and commissions reported directly to him, including the Board of Registration of Barbers, the Milk Board, and the agency that licensed carnivals, fight promoters, and private detectives. Yet as a manager, he knew that no executive can properly supervise more than twelve to fifteen employees at one time. In practice, these boards and commissions had become completely autonomous, functioning year after year without supervision.

Well before he took office, Volpe had assembled his team. Of the approximately forty thousand state employees at that time, no more than fifty to a hundred people could be appointed by the governor. Ideally, Volpe would have preferred to appoint managers whose experience was in private industry, for his theory at that time was that government could be run as efficiently as a business given the right leaders. But reality dictated that without help from people with legislative experience, his bills would go nowhere. Volpe was not only the lone Republican among the constitutional officers, but his party was outnumbered about two to one in both the Senate and the House. The heads of most departments, commissions, and agencies were Democrats, as were all eight governor's councilors.

For his top post, commissioner of administration and finance, Volpe named Charles Gibbons, who had served in the Massachusetts House as both speaker and minority leader. James Gaffney had been on a leave of absence from his job with a textile firm in Lawrence for the campaign, and now he left it permanently to become chief secretary of the staff. His experience in business had been in labor relations, and he was to prove invaluable in settling the MTA strike that came in April. State Senator Frank Lappin, the new legislative liaison, was a man Volpe did not know at all before he interviewed him, but he had been highly recommended both by the Senate President John E. Powers and Republican legislative leaders. G. Joseph Tauro, an attorney and Judge Tauro's son, became the executive legal counsel. And the indefatigable Helen Ross installed herself in the office next to Volpe's as personal and confidential secretary. It was also the custom for each governor to select a predecessors' portrait to hang over the mantelpiece in the corner office. For his first term, Volpe selected the picture of his friend and mentor, Christian Herter.

Volpe decided to start dealing with the legislators face to face, both in the office and socially. Once a week he would invite ten or fifteen House or Senate members to his office for coffee and donuts, "to show them I didn't have horns on, even though I was a Republican." The legislators did not know Volpe as they had Whittier or Gibbons, but some had dealt with him in his years at the DPW.

One legislator who remembered him was "the Iron Duke." When Volpe was DPW commissioner and Thompson not yet speaker, the state representative had come to the DPW with a constituent's problem. A Ludlow man's property had been taken by eminent domain, and the owner felt the compensation he had received was too low. Could Volpe help? Callahan had set up a five-member board to go over the appraisers' estimates and had never overruled them. When Volpe saw that the board members were all prominent realtors whose judgment he respected, he too left them alone. Volpe explained this as tactfully as he could to Thompson. "I suppose if I were a Republican, you could do it," Thompson snapped.

"If you were my brother, I wouldn't do it," Volpe replied. Then Thompson apologized. Not long afterward, he came to see Volpe again about another land-taking. This time, the owner needed an extension on vacating his home, as he had not yet found another place to live. Volpe verified that the extension would not slow down the construction schedule and granted it. The governor and the speaker had already taken each other's measure.

In addition to the office coffee sessions, Volpe held receptions at his home for the legislators and their wives. Massachusetts did not have a governor's mansion (a lack that Volpe later tried to remedy), and entertaining on this scale was almost unheard of. After one of the parties, a legislator's wife from South Boston buttonholed Volpe just before leaving. "My husband has been in the House for more than twenty years," she told him, "and you are the first governor who ever invited us to your home!"

With the campaign behind them, Jennie settled into the duties of a governor's wife, while Jack was living in a dorm at Boston College in Chestnut Hill, and Jean was a busy Navy officer's wife. In February, Jean and her husband planned to drive from Newport, Rhode Island, to San

Diego, where he was to be stationed. Joy, then nineteen months old, was still staying at the Winchester house, and the Volpes worried that the long trip would be too hard with two babies. Lincoln Day solved the problem. Volpe was scheduled to make two Lincoln Day speeches, one in California and one in Pittsburgh, and brought Joy along on the plane. Joy was good-natured and made no fuss about staying with the county Republican chairman's wife while Grandfather addressed the Allegheny County Republicans in Pittsburgh. On the long cross-country flight, the stewardess tried to take the baby to change her, but the governor handled matters himself until they were both safe in California. "Governor Volpe set new records in the fields of Lincoln orating and baby-sitting," *The Boston Traveler* reported.[7]

With Joy and her mother now in California, Jennie asked her husband what more she could do to help. Volpe had decided that he should visit all the hospitals run by the state at least once. The state then ran two kinds of hospital, public health and mental. He suggested that she choose one kind and he the other. Jennie, with her background in public health nursing, chose the public health hospitals, and she visited and reported on each one.

Volpe had had some contact with the state mental health system when he did small jobs at the Fernald State School and the Boston State Hospital in Mattapan in the 1930s. He had been horrified at what he saw then: locked wards, overcrowding, patients lying in their own waste, untrained staff, and underpaid doctors who often spoke little English. He could not help but be moved by the patients' suffering, but there had been nothing he could do about it then.

As governor, Volpe visited every mental health facility in the state and found conditions little changed, although new drugs were becoming available that would allow psychotic and severely depressed patients to be released with proper follow-up. He began, with John E. Powers, a campaign to close the giant mental health hospitals and substitute smaller, more humane community outpatient facilities and group homes. He also began putting together ideas to finance research and the training of more mental health workers through state-supported psychiatric fellowships.

Volpe's first legislative priorities were a general streamlining of existing structures and a citizens' crime commission that would not be susceptible to pressures by the legislature. He also tried to restructure the MTA, DPW, and MDC. Almost a month before his inauguration, Volpe's transition team unveiled a reorganization plan for the MTA, following some of the recommendations made by a just-completed $6 million independent study. The MTA, which was then running a $22 million deficit, was governed by a three-member board of trustees (which Herter had reduced from five) and administered by Thomas McLernon, a New York transit expert with an eleven-year contract.

The new plan proposed a governing board consisting of officials from the fourteen cities and towns served by the MTA and a moratorium on growth until the system's financial problems could be sorted out. Guessing that austerity programs would be in store for them, the Carmen's Union began to threaten a strike even before Volpe took office, although the contract was not up for renewal for another two months. On January 31, a "virus" swept the MTA workers, resulting in a ten-hour wildcat strike and massive transportation tie-ups.

In February, Volpe persuaded MTA management to give the workers a twenty-three-cent-an-hour raise over three years and announced that he was prepared to take "immediate action" (but did not say what that action might be) in the event of a strike. Although MTA workers were not considered essential personnel, Volpe believed their threat might have consequences similar to the disorders and riots that followed the 1919 Boston Police Strike. Certainly, the burden would fall most heavily on poorer workers who did not have cars and who depended on their weekly pay for survival. Negotiations, with Gaffney and Tauro representing Volpe, dragged on through March, when Powers attacked the MTA reorganization bill. Then the House Committee on Metropolitan Affairs scuttled the bill.

In spite of this, on March 31, a Saturday, the carmen struck over the matter of wages and other issues. The strike had the effect of shutting down the entire system. Volpe had threatened, and now was determined, to play hardball. Although his efforts at reform had been unsuccessful, the legislature, feeling the pressure of thousands of stranded constituents, passed emergency legislation allowing the state to seize the MTA for a forty-five-day period. Volpe named General Otis Whitney to run the system and obtained a temporary injunction against the strikers, and began the process of mobilizing the National Guard.

Now Gaffney was to prove invaluable; his job in Lawrence had been to deal with labor relations. Still, the negotiations were tense, and often bitter, as the two sides tried to come to an agreement to prevent another walkout from taking place when the system returned to the MTA general manager's control. A deal was finally struck. But McLernon, as they shook hands, told the Carmen's Union negotiator, "You won this round, but we'll get you next time." The Carmen's Union negotiator, furious at

100

the remark, told McLernon that now all bets were off. The strike went on.

The following night, Volpe escorted Jennie to a formal dinner to honor Cadillac dealer Peter Fuller. Instead of making a speech, Volpe spent the dinner hour at a pay phone in the lobby, checking on the union meeting and the state police headquarters where the National Guard generals were staying. Throughout the evening, Volpe dashed back and forth, still in his business suit, from head table to phone booth. "He's trying to get Charlie back on the MTA!" one of the speakers joked, referring to the popular Kingston Trio song about the Boston subway system. Late at night, Volpe and the union and management representatives adjourned to his State House office for more talks, until at last he invited reporters in to tell them the strike was settled. "Take the rest of the night off," he told the MTA chairman. Jennie was sitting patiently in the outer lobby, still wearing her formal gown. Volpe breezed out of his office. "Feel like going home, Jen?" he asked, grinning. She only nodded. The first crisis was over.

The strike had been settled, but neither of Volpe's two attempts to change the structure of the MTA met with any success. Neither did his efforts to restructure the DPW. At the heart of the DPW question was the tenure of Commissioner Jack Ricciardi, a Furcolo appointee whose five-year contract would take him well beyond Volpe's term of office. As early as Volpe's first week in office, he had sparred with Ricciardi over the Inner Belt. Volpe wanted to build a highway between Weston and Boston with federal funds to link up with the proposed Inner Belt, so that the Massachusetts Turnpike would lead directly into Boston. Ricciardi asserted that Callahan's Turnpike Authority should build it. As the issue was still in dispute, time was passing, and the road was not being built. It was also widely believed that the DPW, under Ricciardi, had hired a Boston accounting firm to review DPW records from Volpe's tenure to search for irregularities in land damage claims, and that any "evidence" was to be used in the Ward "trial" — but none was found.

Volpe's DPW bill would have replaced the system of three commissioners (one commissioner and two associates, one for the Division of Highways and the other for Waterways) with a one-man executive. This would have been the most drastic change in the department in its long history. As far back as 1893, when roads were built by the Massachusetts Highway Commission for horse and buggy traffic, there had been three commissioners, and the 1960 arrangement of power dated back to 1927. The reform package also included other changes, such as transferring the Division of Beaches back to the Department of Natural Resources, where it had been before Herter.

The bill never got off the ground. Powers, who had cooperated with Volpe on other reform issues, would not back it. Volpe would not give way until January 1962, when he and Ricciardi finally worked out a compromise. Volpe agreed to hire more DPW staff to work on new federal highway projects, while Ricciardi pledged his support on the Inner Belt and to help remove local veto power over the project that had been granted Boston, Cambridge, and Somerville.

Powers did support Volpe's bid to restructure the MDC. Powers had been chairman of the Senate committee investigating the MDC, and his discoveries of financial irregularities were later confirmed by a grand jury probe. In February, Powers threw his weight behind Volpe's nomination of Vincent P. O'Brien, editor of the *Lynn Daily Item* (the paper that had devoted a front page to refuting Ward's charges in the "trial") as associate MDC commissioner to fill the seat of one of the three commissioners whose term had expired. O'Brien was a career newspaperman who had served as Henry Cabot Lodge's press secretary in the 1960 vice presidential campaign, and Volpe reasoned that an experienced reporter could spot corruption. He could not foresee that O'Brien would be the central figure in the Boston Common Garage scandal in a few years, after having both spotted corruption and then taken full advantage of it.

Volpe's true feelings about the MDC were that the agency was not needed at all. The state police could take care of its law enforcement functions; the DPW could handle the water and sewer functions; beaches and parks could come under the Department of Natural Resources. Even for an optimist like Volpe, however, abolishing an entire agency seemed too radical a step. He tried to make the MDC more responsible to the fifteen cities and towns it then served by abolishing the appointed five-member commission and replacing it with a board of city and town officials to elect a seven-member executive committee. The governor would still appoint a paid director, but many legislators feared that reform would oust MDC Chairman "Mr. Integrity" Bob Murphy, the former lieutenant governor. After the House Committee on Metropolitan Affairs unanimously rejected it, the full House defeated the measure 145 to 66.

By the summer of 1961, all three major reform bills had failed, and there seemed little support in the legislature for Volpe's concept of a citizens' crime commission that would be totally independent of the legislative process. Legislators feared that such a commission would amount to a witch hunt of Republicans investigating Democratic officeholders; after all, most officeholders *were* Democrats.

The course of Volpe's first administration — and a good chunk of Boston's history — were being changed, however, in a block of old South End brick brownstones-turned-rooming-houses, at 362 Massachusetts Avenue, in the back room of Swartz's Key Shop.

In the fall of 1961, the CBS News staff in New York was producing documentaries under the "CBS Reports" format begun by Fred Friendly and Edward R. Murrow. The reports were unique in the industry in that sponsors were not allowed to preview the programs and knew only the general content in advance. They were buying "the prestige, reputations, and integrity of Murrow, Friendly, and CBS."[8]

"CBS Reports" had already made headlines with "Harvest of Shame," documenting the plight of migrant farm workers, and "The Business of Health," an exposé of the American health care system that had infuriated the American Medical Association. In October 1961, the CBS film crew secretly began recording the illegal gambling activities for which Swartz's Key Shop was a front, to use in an episode to be titled "Biography of a Bookie Joint." As all forms of offtrack horse and dog betting, lotteries, and sports gambling were then illegal, bookie joints were not uncommon in Boston. Bookmakers normally operated in bars, news-stands, corner groceries, or through runners who drove delivery trucks and lunch wagons, selling chances for the daily numbers game. At most workplaces, including the State House, it was as easy to place a bet as to send out for coffee. What made Swartz's Key Shop unique was that many of its patrons were Boston police officers — in uniform, driving cruisers, and on duty.

The CBS newsmen were not the only ones to notice the cruisers double-parked along Massachusetts Avenue. About six months before the documentary was produced, the head of the state police, Colonel Carl Larson, requested a private meeting with Volpe and told him about the key shop situation. Normally state police did not get involved with Boston law enforcement but only assisted police in small towns when they were specifically called in to do so. Now there had been complaints about the increasingly blatant activities at Swartz's. What did the governor advise them to do?

Volpe and Larson were in a difficult position. Neither of them wanted to start a feud with the Boston police, and certainly busting one bookie was not going to make a dent in illegal gambling in Boston. But the situation could not be condoned indefinitely, and — Volpe believed — it should not be. Volpe was not morally opposed to gambling. He had grown up in an Italian-American culture in which betting added a little pleasure

103

to a hard existence, like a glass of wine with dinner. The "number" or "policy" (as well as the concept of life insurance) had its roots in the world's first lotteries in the sixteenth-century republic of Genoa. But in Massachusetts, the numbers game was against the law, and Volpe had taken an oath to uphold the laws of the Commonwealth.

"If we didn't know about it, that would be one thing," Volpe told Larson. "But now that we do know, we have to deal with it." He ordered Larson to collect more evidence. But two weeks before the state police were going to announce their case, "CBS Reports" gave its sponsors the title, the general location, and the subject matter of the "biography."

On November 30, "Biography of a Bookie Joint" aired nationally, but producer Fred Friendly had the segment blacked out in Boston because of the state police investigation and possible cases pending against some of the officers shown in the film. Volpe was vacationing in Palm Springs when the show aired, but his vacation did not proceed as planned.

Soon after his election, Volpe had decided to give young Ed Brooke, who, at his request, had run on the Republican ticket for secretary of state, a job in his administration. He had offered Brooke the traditional appointment for a black man, secretary of the Governor's Council. Brooke had refused that but had accepted the position of chairman of FinCom, the watchdog agency set up to deal with corruption in Boston. As soon as the "biography" aired, Brooke took the first plane to Palm Springs and drove, with reporters in tow, to the private resort where Volpe was staying. The club was segregated, and Brooke was forced to wait outside until Volpe was called off the golf course to escort him in. Volpe asked Brooke why he could not simply have phoned, but he knew the answer after seeing the press outside. The two men discussed the situation while they sat beside the pool, and Brooke returned to Boston.

When Volpe returned, Fred Friendly invited him and his legal staff to a private screening. The film was worse than any of them had anticipated. All the police shown were in uniform, and in one scene, an officer stood and joked with the bookie as he burned the previous day's betting slips in a metal trash barrel on the sidewalk. "Now I *know* we have a major problem," Volpe told his staff as he left, and he ordered the lawyers to check on the authenticity of the film. A few days after the showing, Volpe happened to meet Boston police commissioner Leo Sullivan at a forum at the MIT Faculty Club. Volpe angrily collared Sullivan and demanded that he clean up his department.

The next day, after Volpe had calmed down, he asked Sullivan into his office and laid out the evidence the state police had gathered. Sullivan had not run a clean department. Volpe gave him the opportunity to resign "for personal reasons." Sullivan protested; he was innocent! Volpe told him to go home, think it over, and give his answer tomorrow. But the next day, Sullivan still refused, leaving Volpe no alternative but to begin a removal hearing.

Cardinal Cushing jumped into the controversy to defend the police, charging CBS News with "betraying" Boston. Volpe refused to tangle with him, commenting carefully, "I do not believe that my objectives and those of the Cardinal are far apart. He wants to eliminate crime, and so do I."[9] When Sullivan still refused to resign, Volpe began the process of preparing for the hearing, at which he would have to preside as judge. Since he had no legal training, he relied on Frank Lappin, his legislative liaison, to give technical assistance. After searching for a prosecuting attorney, he settled on James St. Clair, a skilled trial lawyer who had served as special counsel to the Army during the 1954 Army-McCarthy hearings.

The trial was bound to be a painful event, and Volpe realized that there was little he could say or do immediately afterward that would help either Sullivan, the police department, or his own crime commission bill. St. Clair estimated the proceedings would take at most three days, and Volpe decided to book a short cruise to Nassau, where he would be unavailable following the trial. He would tackle the crime commission bill on his return.

In the hearing, Sullivan was bitter and took the stand for several long speeches. The proceedings dragged on past the three days, into five. On the day the cruise ship was scheduled to depart from New York at 4 P.M., Volpe concluded the hearing at 1:30. He dashed to the limousine where Jennie was waiting and made the flight at Logan Airport only because a snowstorm had delayed it.

When he returned, Volpe submitted the request for dismissal of Commissioner Sullivan to the Governor's Council. The council held up approval of Sullivan's dismissal for another two weeks. Finally, Volpe approached the senior councilor, Patrick V. ("Sonny") McDonough. McDonough was a Boston power broker of the old school, but he was willing to hear the Republican governor out. Volpe explained that Sullivan *had* been convicted of misconduct in office. If he had to, Volpe would go to the press, which was sympathetic to his crime commission bill. The council approved the dismissal, and Volpe submitted the name of Michael Cullinane, Captain of the State Police Detectives, to become Boston police commissioner. In April, he signed legislation allowing the mayor of Boston to appoint his own commissioner. The tragedy of Swartz's Key

Shop wound down to its final act. Sullivan, bitter and disillusioned, died within a year of his dismissal. Volpe sent the family a Mass card, but Sullivan's widow returned it, unopened.

Neither Kennedy's exhortations in his "City on a Hill" speech nor Volpe's lobbying had produced any legislative action on substantive anti-corruption measures. Now the public mood, triggered by the key shop scandal, was in favor of reform, and Volpe enjoyed the media's full support on the issue. In early January 1962, Volpe began his campaign for public support for his proposed citizens' crime commission. There had been other crime commissions on Beacon Hill. In 1903, then Boston lawyer Louis Brandeis had investigated "misgovernment" in Boston. In the middle 1950s, U.S. Attorney Elliot Richardson had investigated Callahan and the Turnpike Authority. But it was rumored that each time past commissions had gotten close to uncovering something, the parties involved were tipped off. Most commissions simply filed reports, which made headlines for a few days and then were forgotten.

Volpe proposed a crime commission with *no* legislators or other elected officials on it and with the power to subpoena private citizens, public officials, and confidential records. The commission would consist of six members, a general counsel, lawyers, and twenty-five special investigators. On February 1, Volpe called a joint session of the Massachusetts House and Senate to make his personal plea, then he began to campaign in schools, at trade association meetings, and before civic groups.

The campaign hit a small snag when "Duke" Thompson produced his own anticorruption measure calling on newspaper publishers to stop printing racetrack pari-mutuel totals and the day's U.S. Treasury receipt figures (the last three or four digits were the "numbers" at that time). Volpe was then one of six owners of two small newspapers, the *Medford Mercury* and *Malden News,* but had left the papers' operation to editor Dave Brickman, who had served as his press secretary during the 1960 campaign. At a news conference on February 2, a reporter showed the governor that his own papers published the numbers, but the charges had little impact. Volpe, whose own gambling experience was limited to two trips to Suffolk Downs in his younger days, had not been aware of the number in his, or anyone else's, paper. Nevertheless, he sold his share of the papers, which were just beginning to turn a profit.

The crime commission bill received extra impetus in March, when rumors of an investigation into the Boston Common Garage contracts by the Internal Revenue Service began to make the rounds on Beacon Hill. The stories all centered on George Brady, an editorial writer for the

Boston Record American, whom Furcolo had named to the Massachusetts Parking Authority in 1958. Brady was an eccentric who worked at his newspaper office wearing denim coveralls, cowboy boots, frock coats, white cotton gloves, and wigs of varied colors — before the word "counterculture" had been invented. Although Brady had no qualifications for public service other than his newspaper work, Furcolo placed him on the authority after his editorials supported the unpopular project. A year later, William Callahan resigned from the authority and Furcolo named Brady to replace him as chairman. In his speech to the city council in 1959, during an attempt to get title of part of Boston Common, Brady promised: "As chairman of this authority, there is going to be no politics here, and the man who tries to bring politics into it is certainly going to be pushed down by me. I want the garage to be a monument to the city council and the legislature."

His words were prophetic. The garage did become a monument — to the worst corruption scandal the legislature had yet seen. In February 1962, Brady himself triggered the investigation by nervously asking State Public Safety Commissioner Frank Giles to reinspect the garage, which had opened for business in November. Giles set state police captain Michael Cullinane to the task. Cullinane's office found no safety problems but began to check into the qualifications of the previous inspectors. In June, a Suffolk County grand jury indicted Brady and five others for stealing more than $800,000 from the $9.6 million project. Some of the recipients of Brady's largess included a lawyer and a judge in New York who received more than $100,000 for imaginary legal work and an engineer who got $344,000 for visiting the site thirteen times, usually with his taxi waiting. Shortly before the trial, two psychiatrists declared Brady organically brain damaged. The former chairman then disappeared with the Parking Authority's petty cash and seventeen wigs. Despite an extensive manhunt, the FBI did not find him until 1969, when *The Boston Globe* located him in Atlantic City, with only $5,000 left.

By the spring of 1962, Thompson and a majority of both houses were supporting the crime commission bill, and the negotiations on the final appropriations began. Volpe asked for a million dollars for the first year. Thompson offered $250,000. After several weeks of bargaining, the bill passed with a $750,000 appropriation. Volpe believed his biggest break was convincing Alfred Gardner, senior partner of Palmer, Dodge, Gardner, and Bradford, to serve as commission chairman. Volpe knew Gardner at that time only by reputation, but that reputation was formidable. A former president of the Boston Bar Association, Gardner had served as chairman of the Citizens' Advisory Committee on Corrections in 1958. After Volpe approached him, Gardner volunteered to work without pay.

The crime commission eventually included a writer for the *New Bedford Standard Times,* a bank president, a former dean of Harvard, a Boston College law professor, a consultant to the State Department, and one of the commissioners of the Department of Natural Resources. By September 1962, the commission was in place and operating, although the results would not begin to be made public for another two to three years. Before its work was over, the commission would bring charges against a former governor, two speakers of the House, a judge, two members of the Governor's Council, a former head of the state police, and two of Volpe's own men, Charles Gibbons and Frank Giles.

Volpe's first term also marked the beginning of his interest in public education, especially at the state college level. In 1960, Massachusetts boasted some of the best private colleges in the country, but the state university and community college systems were severely hampered by a lack of funding. The state was spending one of the lowest per capita amounts on public education in the United States. Yet for students from poor and working-class families, public education was the only shot at college and an increasingly degree-oriented job market in Massachusetts as the state lost more and more blue-collar industries and gained more jobs for bankers, electronics engineers, and accountants.

Within the first two months of his administration, Volpe had increased the funding for community colleges and the University of Massachusetts' Boston campus. In July 1961, he began to campaign for the creation of a commission to draw up plans for overhauling the entire state educational system. Under the sponsorship of State Senator Kevin Harrington, this proposal became the Willis-Harrington Commission. Benjamin Willis was the author of the commission's report, written while he was still working as superintendent of schools in Chicago.

The summer of 1962 was campaign season again. At the June Republican convention in Worcester, Volpe was renominated without opposition. Also nominated was FinCom Chairman Ed Brooke, for attorney general. Brooke had received good press, and his election seemed likely. Volpe set up a reelection campaign structure but was still spending most of his time setting up the crime commission and drawing up his next batch of legislative reforms as well as tending to the day-to-day operation of the governor's office.

The 1962 Democratic convention, in contrast to the brutal infighting of 1960, was a "model of decorum"[10] in the Springfield Auditorium. The national press corps was present in force to watch the contest between Massachusetts House Speaker John McCormack's nephew, Eddie, and President Kennedy's younger brother, Ted, for the U.S. Senate nomination. Edward F. McLaughlin, Volpe's lieutenant governor, had been the likely frontrunner for the gubernatorial nomination. Many Democrats believed Volpe's reelection was certain.

One of the doubters was Endicott "Chub" Peabody. In 1960, when Ward won the convention endorsement, Peabody had announced late and had fielded a hastily organized effort in the primary. Still, he had made a good showing in the suburbs. In 1962, Peabody announced his candidacy well in advance and pitched it to the same suburban, white-collar audience. Peabody was well suited to appeal to the new suburban bloc. A Yankee by birth, the son of an Episcopal bishop and grandson of the founder of Groton, Peabody started out on the path to glory as an all-American football player at Harvard. A liberal lawyer and admirer of Adlai Stevenson, Peabody was first elected to the Governor's Council in the early 1950s from Cambridge and Back Bay–Beacon Hill. He was tall, handsome, and still athletic. His wife, Toni, was a photogenic blonde, and they had three attractive children. "Chub" seemed to be everything the machine Democrats were not (and perhaps wished they were). He had been labeled a maverick and a loser in the fifties, but times had changed. He won the convention's endorsement and the primary without difficulty, and then he began the uphill battle against Volpe.

On the issues, Peabody took standard liberal postures. He supported a graduated state income tax, which Volpe opposed. He advocated state constitutional reform. And he ran hard. Volpe's campaign centered on his achievements — the code of ethics and the crime commission — and hammered away at Peabody's lack of managerial experience. "Let's not change horses in midstream," Volpe told his audiences. He needed more time to implement the reforms he had begun.

Volpe did not run as hard as he had in 1960, simply because he did not have to. In August, his own poll showed him sixteen points ahead, and the top staffers knew it (after 1962, Volpe never showed his staff polling results). As late as October 19, *Boston Globe* political writer Robert Healy reported that both Volpe's and Peabody's polls showed Volpe clearly in the lead. Volpe refused to debate, reasoning that this would only give his opponent free exposure.

One of Volpe's favorite issues was the graduated income tax. Peabody supported it, yet the voters had rejected it twice in referendums. Volpe decided to produce a television commercial on the issue and run it in the last ten days before the election for maximum impact. Somehow, however, as he busied himself with the crime commission, the staff put the project on the back burner. By the time the show was ready, the television stations had no airtime, and the commercial never ran. There were other small snafus. In October, Volpe, as commander of the honorary Ancient and Honorable Artillery Company (one of the oldest military units in the world) went on a three-day fall "encampment" to Scandinavia and an audience with the king of Denmark. Peabody and some of the press seized on the trip as frivolous.

Also working against Volpe was a force more powerful than any of the issues. Although President Kennedy never tried to harm him, Volpe found himself running against Camelot. In the early fall, Congressman "Tip" O'Neill of Cambridge, Peabody's campaign manager, and Frank Bellotti, the Democratic candidate for lieutenant governor, went to Washington with the suggestion that Ted Kennedy and Peabody have joint billboards. Already, the Kennedys were becoming the target of criticism that they had abandoned the Massachusetts Democratic party when John F. Kennedy became president. Although the president did not campaign for Peabody beyond mentioning his name at a rally, he did approve the billboards.

The fall of 1962, climaxing in the Cuban Missile Crisis, was a time when Massachusetts voters — urban, suburban, rich, or blue-collar — idolized the young president. No three-decker in Dorchester was complete without its Bachrach color portrait of JFK next to the Sacred Heart. Kennedy seemed to have elevated not only the Irish but all Catholics from immigrant backgrounds to hope that their own sons could reach the White House. Peabody's staff "geared the entire campaign around support for the president and giving the president a vote of confidence by electing a Democratic governor in Massachusetts," O'Neill recalled after the election. "Volpe never came back at us that Chub was for the graduated income tax. He never exploited it to the full."[11]

Election night, November 6, 1962, was long, and neither Volpe nor his staff slept. As the Boston returns came in, Peabody led by fifty-three thousand votes, a margin not very different from Ward's, but as the suburbs and then the rural polling places reported in, Volpe did not lead by as much as he had in 1960. Still, the numbers were agonizingly close. At 3:15 A.M., Peabody claimed victory, but Volpe did not concede defeat. When all the polling places had reported by Wednesday night, Peabody led by a scant five thousand votes, the narrowest margin in a gubernatorial election in Massachusetts history. More than two million votes had been cast. Volpe demanded a recount and dispatched state police to eleven cities and towns to guard tally sheets and ballots until they could be recounted. An error of only one or two votes in each of the state's 2,011 precincts could change the outcome of the election, and many ballots had been counted after 4 A.M.

On November 16, the Governor's Council, presided over by Volpe, went over the official tabulation of the vote by thirty-one state bank examiners. Peabody waited near the council chambers. Four hours later, the counting was over. His lead had shrunk to 3,091, but he was still the winner. Volpe still hung on, petitioning for a full recount.

By early December, Volpe had assembled a group of five hundred volunteer lawyers to go around the state challenging ballots. Heading up the lawyers' group was Elliot Richardson, the Massachusetts attorney general who had headed the legislature's crime commission of the 1950s. Volpe's hopes hinged on Springfield, then Massachusetts' second largest city, which he had carried by twenty-two thousand in 1960 but lost by two hundred votes in 1962.

The recount dragged on through the darkening days of early December. Peabody's transition team started work at the State House. At Summer Street, the store windows were dressed for Christmas, and on the Common the Parks Department put out the faded plaster crèche figures, the reindeer, and the strings of colored lights. Boston was the last city to report its official results, showing that Peabody had won by 5,416 votes. Volpe sent his concession telegram to Peabody on December 20 while the new governor was in New Hampshire on a skiing vacation.

In the last days of his administration, Volpe thought back to what he could have done to change that count. Should he have made more of an issue of the graduated income tax? Not gone to Scandinavia? Not shown the staff the favorable polls? The world seemed to have closed in on him. He had worked hard, been honest, fought the good fight. And in return, the people had turned him out.

As he came out of Mass one Sunday morning, the pastor of St. Mary's in Winchester stopped him on the steps. "What happened to that beautiful smile of yours, John?" the priest asked, gently.

"Well, Father," Volpe answered, "I guess I don't have much to smile about."

"Maybe the Lord has something better in store for you," the priest replied. Volpe nodded, but he could see nothing better on the horizon. I'll go back to my business, he thought. I'll start really making money. They don't want me anymore.

On January 3, 1963, the artillery on the Common boomed the twenty-one gun salute for Endicott Peabody. Cardinal Cushing met Volpe as he left his office and put his arm around the ex-governor while the latter genuflected and kissed the Episcopal ring. Sonny McDonough stage-whispered, "Governor, remember the words of General MacArthur at Bataan — 'I shall return.' "

Pale and slightly shaky from a stomach upset that had struck him at a late council meeting the night before, Volpe walked between the lines of State House staff, shaking hands, saying his good-byes. He paused in Doric Hall to look around at the portraits of other Massachusetts governors, then stepped into the sunshine. He had expected perhaps a hundred people, but instead a crowd of more than two thousand lined the huge granite stairway, overflowing onto the lawn and into Beacon Street, waving and cheering. "Good luck, John!" they shouted. "You'll be back, John!" "A good job well done!"

He could no longer hold back the tears and wept openly as he walked alone down the steps. At Beacon Street, the whole family was waiting. Jennie and Filomena embraced him, and they got into a car to drive to a reception at the Hotel Kenmore. It was a black limousine, but on the plates there was no S-1.

NOTES

1. *The Boston Globe,* 22 September 1985.

2. Elizabeth Hardwick, "Boston: The Lost Ideal," *Harper's,* December 1959, p. 65.

3. *The Boston Globe,* 22 September 1985.

4. Robert Lowell, "For the Union Dead," *For the Union Dead* (New York: Farrar, Straus & Giroux, 1960), p. 8.

5. *The Boston Globe,* 10 January 1961.

6. John F. Kennedy, "City on a Hill" speech, Speech File, John F. Kennedy Library, Dorchester, Massachusetts.

7. *The Boston Traveler,* 11 February 1961.

8. Alexander Kendrick, *Prime Time, The Life of Edward R. Murrow* (Boston: Little, Brown and Company, 1969), p. 436.

9. *The Boston Traveler,* 28 February 1962.

10. *The Boston Traveler,* 20 December 1962.

11. *The Boston Globe,* 11 November 1960.

Bottom: The Italian hilltop village of Pescosansonesco, birthplace of Volpe's parents. Volpe, as governor of Massachusetts, returned here to a hero's welcome in 1966. *Right:* Volpe in 1932 with Jennie Benedetto, whom he married in 1934. *Below:* Volpe flanked by brothers Patrick (to Volpe's right) and Peter during World War II. All three served in the navy, as did another of Volpe's brothers, Richard, and his father, Vito.

Top: Volpe with his family in the 1950s. From left, son Jack, daughter Jean, Volpe, and his wife Jennie. *Center:* First headquarters for the Volpe Construction Company, on Eastern Avenue in Malden. The building was originally the Volpe family home, but Volpe's business gradually spread from its location in the front room to occupy the entire building. *Bottom:* Volpe and family at Boston's Old North Church in 1962. Volpe, his wife Jennie, and his mother Filomena (far right) are in the foreground. Behind Volpe are his daughter, Jean, and his son, Jack (center).

Top: "Poppa" and Mrs. Volpe in 1965 with their grandchildren, (l. to r.) John, Roddy, and Joy. *Right:* Granddaughter Joy unveiling the governor's official portrait at the Massachusetts state house in 1964. *Below left:* Governor and Mrs. Volpe during a celebrated return visit to Pescosansonesco in 1966. *Below right:* Ambassador Volpe playing bocce with granddaughter Joy during her family's 1974 visit to the ambassador's villa in Italy. An Italian reporter interviewing Volpe during the visit dubbed the ambassador *"Il Nonno d'America"* (The Grandfather of America).

Top: Volpe (front, third from left) during a 1953 spiritual retreat with board members for the Don Orione Home. During the retreat, Volpe made a lifelong commitment to begin each day by attending Mass. *Center:* Volpe at the groundbreaking for the Don Orione Home in East Boston. Archbishop Cushing is shown holding the shovel. *Bottom:* Volpe meeting Pope John Paul II in 1985, at Archbishop Law's installation as a cardinal.

Left: Volpe in the 1950s with his friend and early political mentor, Governor Christian Herter (center). Volpe's late brother Richard is at right. *Below:* Volpe with Senator Henry Cabot Lodge, on whose 1952 U.S. Senate campaign Volpe worked.

Right: Volpe with President Eisenhower, who advised him in 1957: "You build highways, so you know where the center line is. You can go up to thirty-five percent to the right or to the left of that center line, and you'll be all right. More than that, and you'll land in the gutter."

Right: Explaining the proposed Massachusetts highway system in 1953, while commissioner of the Massachusetts Department of Public Works. Volpe was an early champion of the federal interstate highway system.

Left: Volpe, in January 1961, at the inauguration of his first term as governor of Massachusetts. With him is the late Leverett Saltonstall, former U.S. senator (center), and Lieutenant Governor Elliot Richardson. *Below:* Volpe with some of his top staff members in 1961. Seated, from left, Chief Secretary James Gaffney; Volpe; Commissioner of Administration and Finance, the late Charles Gibbons. Standing, from left, Appointments Secretary Philip Allen; Press Secretary Les Ainley; Legal Counsel G. Joseph Tauro; Positions Secretary "Al" Cole; Legislative Counsel Frank Lappin.

Right: Volpe portrait by Fabian Bachrach. *Below:* Volpe at work on state budget with Charles Shepard while vacationing on Cape Cod in 1965.

Left: Prominent "ethnic" Massachusetts Republicans, Volpe and state Attorney General Edward Brooke, at the 1964 Massachusetts Republican convention. The two would later serve simultaneously in Washington, Brooke as a U.S. senator and Volpe as transportation secretary. *Below:* Volpe with Richard Nixon at the 1968 Republican National Convention in Miami. Also pictured are Nixon's two chief opponents in the Republican presidential primary, Nelson Rockfeller (far left) and George Romney (center).

Above: Volpe, as secretary of transportation, attending the opening of a Transportation Department project in New York City. Audience members include New York City Mayor John Lindsay (second from left) and New York Governor Nelson Rockefeller (second from right). *Right:* Ambassador Volpe visiting the editorial office of an Italian newspaper during his campaign to counter anti-American sentiment, especially among young people, in Italy.

Left: Volpe visiting a Boys Town in Italy. After his retirement from politics, Volpe remained an avid supporter of homes for the aged and for boys through his work as chairman of the Italian Disaster Earthquake Association.

CHAPTER VIII

Bring Back Volpe

VOLPE RETURNED to his office on Eastern Avenue, and to the presidency of his company, in January 1963. Helen Ross came back with him as his confidential secretary. He traveled to Houston, where the Florida branch had obtained two jobs, and considered the idea of opening another branch office in Texas. In the late spring, the State Department asked him to lead a delegation of American construction executives on an exchange program to visit ten cities in the Soviet Union for four weeks. He accepted the offer eagerly. In July, he attended the coronation of Pope Paul VI and was granted a private audience with the new pontiff, who recalled his visit three years before to the Don Orione Home and the Madonna Shrine. From Rome, Volpe flew to Amsterdam to join the rest of the American delegation for the flight to Moscow.

Before they left the States, the delegation had attended the customary State Department briefings for private citizens going on official tours. Although the cold war had thawed somewhat after the Cuban Missile Crisis, the tone of the briefings was cautionary. The delegates were warned that their Soviet hosts might try to test them, that they respected only firmness and tough talk, not conciliation. The State Department also was able to answer Volpe's questions about the extent to which he could practice his religion in an officially atheist country; there was at least one Roman Catholic church in the city of Moscow.

The delegation arrived on a Sunday afternoon. On the drive from the airport to Moscow, Volpe's host almost immediately announced that two of the planned visits to the eighteen construction projects had, unfortunately, been canceled. Volpe had brought his own translator, a Russian-born employee of the Library of Congress, so that he could communicate without an *Intourist* guide. Remembering the briefing, he asked the translator to tell his host that, for every project canceled on this trip, two would be canceled from the Russian delegation's tour of the United States the following year. Their host assured them he would see what could be done. The delegation visited all eighteen projects.

On their arrival at the hotel, Volpe countered with a test of his own. As a guest in their country, he said, he expected to practice his religion. Explaining that he was a daily communicant, he told his interpreter to get the address of the one Roman Catholic church in Moscow. The moment he said "church," the officials escorting the tour seemed insulted but agreed to look it up. After dinner, Volpe questioned them again, but the host still had not been able to find the address. Volpe warned them that if he did not have the address of the church in five minutes, he would book passage the next morning for the entire delegation back to the United States. The address was found in two minutes.

It was still light in the summer evening, and Volpe and his translator set out to walk to the church, to make sure he had been given the correct address. They soon became lost in the maze of identical gray concrete apartment houses. After two or three futile efforts to get directions, the translator asked a couple of men talking in a doorway if they knew where the Catholic church in the neighborhood was. They replied that they were not sure.

When the translator told them that Volpe was the governor of Massachusetts, their attitude changed. One of the two men, who was the custodian of the apartment building, led them toward the church. As they walked along, he began to tell Volpe loudly how the government had tried to take away his faith and how he had resisted. On the other side of the street, coming from the opposite direction, two men in uniform sauntered along. Fearing that the man would get into trouble, Volpe tried to quiet him, but without success. Their new friend took them straight to the small church where a sign said that Mass would be said at nine o'clock the next morning. When Volpe arrived the next day, he found the church open and empty. Two elderly women near the entrance told him that the pastor was away, visiting his bishop. Volpe blessed himself, said a few prayers, and left.

In spite of the poor quality of the hotels and the food, Volpe thoroughly enjoyed the trip. With his translator in tow, he asked questions of everyone he met, roamed around the construction sites and the cities, and even visited private homes, accumulating notes for a series of articles for *The Boston Traveler* and slides for lectures. He found the major projects, such as hydroelectric dams and factories, as well designed and built as any in the United States. But the apartment complexes (the government did not build single-family homes) were of poor quality and comprised boring blocks built with uniform slabs of precast concrete.

Throughout his career, Volpe's only women employees had been secretaries and bookkeepers, and in the Soviet Union, he was surprised to find that more than half the construction workers, as well as many of the managers and engineers, were female. Women did heavy stonework on railroad projects, and the project engineer of the largest hydroelectric plant was a woman. While the delegation was inspecting a cancer research center under construction, Volpe noticed three women stuccoing the outside wall. On impulse, he asked if he could work with them, explaining that this was his old trade. The women laughed and joked with him, and they worked side by side for a while, he in his suit and the women in overalls, while he explained to the foreman that they were using bricklayers' trowels. The work would go much faster if they had plasterers' trowels.

In all, the delegation visited ten cities and the largest hydroelectric plant in the world, which was under construction in Siberia. On his return to Moscow, Volpe finally did attend a Mass, after three cabbies had refused to take him to such a dangerous destination. At the church, he found himself the only man in the congregation. Most of the women were elderly, and at Communion time, three came out of the pews and prostrated themselves in the aisle during the whole Communion period, an act of faith he had never seen before. He had heard that sometimes arrests were made at services, yet none of the women seemed apprehensive. On his return, when he gave talks to church groups, Volpe always mentioned these women. Wasn't it strange that they would take such a chance? Here in America, he would remind his listeners, there were churches open on almost every corner, yet few people ever stopped in even to say a prayer.

In September, Volpe returned to Rome with the Ancient and Honorable Artillery Company for their annual encampment. He happened to notice that Richard Nixon was in Rome at the same time and decided to give him a call. Like Volpe, Nixon had been defeated in the 1962 elections when he ran for governor of California against incumbent Pat Brown. But Nixon had gone one step further — effectively removing himself from the political scene with a caustic denunciation of the press (he would never give them another opportunity to "kick Nixon around") — and now was concentrating on making his fortune with a New York law firm. Despite these losses, Nixon's interest in Republican politics was unabated. Inviting Volpe to his hotel, Nixon asked him what his plans were for the following year. His business, Volpe replied, and to spend more time with the family. No, Nixon told him, you have to run again in 1964. The GOP needs you. Volpe was flattered but still wary. The defeat had hurt, and Jennie was against a comeback. Jack was a senior at Boston College and would be entering the business after his service with the Marines. The business and the family needed his guidance.

Yet events on Beacon Hill seemed to present an opening to the corner office. Governor Peabody was having difficulties his first year. He had made a bitter enemy of Sonny McDonough by declaring his support for a referendum sponsored by the League of Women Voters (the "League of Women Vultures," as McDonough styled them) to strip the Governor's Council of its veto power over executive appointments and dismissals. Peabody's support for the referendum made sense in the abstract. By the early 1960s, the council had grown so powerful that, instead of accepting or rejecting nominations, council members would draw up their own lists of names to start the bargaining process. Reform was needed, but McDonough stood squarely in the way.

An insurance man who had started his career in South Boston with a beer distributorship with John McCormack's uncle "Knocko," McDonough maintained a rock-solid seat on the council through his Irish blue-collar constituency. He wintered in Florida and summered on the "Irish Riviera" in Scituate with a yacht called the *Galway Bay,* but he maintained a voting address in Dorchester. Volpe had worked around him with some success, though he had made a few less than outstanding appointments in the last two months of his administration to gain McDonough's cooperation on other appointments. At the last Governor's Council meeting over which Volpe presided, McDonough reached under his desk and brought forth a bright red football helmet with the $4.99 sticker still attached. "This is for Peabody," he declared. "He's going to need it." It was McDonough who originated the remark that Peabody had played football too often without his helmet, and probably also the joke that the governor-elect was the first man to have two towns named after him: Peabody and Marblehead. While the Bible and the keys were ceremonially transferred from Volpe to Peabody in the council chambers on Inauguration Day, the red helmet reappeared, handed silently from one counci-

116

lor to another, until McDonough, smiling, placed it on the rostrum: a palpable declaration of hostilities.

Although he had projected a handsome, Kennedy-style image during the campaign, once he was in office Peabody performed poorly in the spontaneous give-and-take of the State House press conferences. The harsh light of the television news cameras often caught him off guard, and he quickly developed the reputation of a lightweight, a fumbler. His image problems were compounded by his Bermuda-born wife, Toni. Toni Peabody was attractive, blonde, and outgoing, but her upper-class British accent put her at a disadvantage when dealing with the still Irish-dominated State House regulars. Jackie Kennedy was busy redecorating the White House, so Toni Peabody, lacking a governor's mansion, decided to spruce up the historic State House.

In January, Toni Peabody took her first inspection tour and happened to remark to reporters that the place needed cleaning. The new superintendent of buildings promptly stepped up the pressure on his staff of fifty cleaning women, telling them to submit daily progress reports. But the cleaning staff were not defenseless, menial workers; they were salaried civil servants from the Irish wards of Boston, many of them relatives and friends of the legislators. They were not about to let a lady with a British accent tell them their business. They protested, and the legislators gallantly rose to their defense. Anonymous phone calls flooded radio talk shows, and hate mail arrived at the governor's office for weeks. Mrs. Peabody finally made peace with the cleaning staff after getting them a new locker room, to which they invited her for tea and biscuits.

Toni Peabody became an activist first lady who did a great deal for the cause of handicapped and mentally retarded children, even taking retarded children from state institutions into her home for weekends. She was tireless in promoting the state's cultural events and spent so much time on public business that her friends joked about running her for lieutenant governor. But the damage of the cleaning women's feud was not easily undone.

By his second year in office, Peabody seemed to have regained his footing, although his difficulties did not disappear entirely. He was still at odds with the Governor's Council and had become embroiled in a controversy over the death penalty when he announced that he would not sign any execution warrants, and then he compounded the political damage by nodding in answer to a reporter's question on whether his refusal included the "Boston Strangler," who was then still on the loose. His refusal did indeed include the Strangler, he later explained, although no death warrant related to those murders ever reached his desk.

Despite these problems, by the end of his term, more than half of his legislation had passed, including a reform that had eluded Volpe — the restructuring of the DPW. Under Peabody, the DPW became a five-member commission, with two Republican and three Democratic appointees. He was unable, however, to get a Deomcrat to introduce his tax bill. Peabody's greatest threat in seeking reelection seemed to come not from the Republicans but from within his own party. Peabody's lieutenant governor, Francis Bellotti, was an Italian-American who, like Volpe, had pulled himself from poverty to relative affluence with enormous dedication and intelligence. Born in then Irish Roxbury, Bellotti had worked his way through Tufts University and Boston College Law School selling religious magazine subscriptions door to door, among other jobs. By 1958, he was a successful criminal lawyer, living in Quincy with his wife Maggie and their ten children. That year, he ran for Norfolk County district attorney against Republican incumbent Myron N. Lane, carrying Quincy but losing the election. He was well regarded in Democratic circles but unwilling to wait his turn.

At the 1962 convention in Springfield, during the heat of the Kennedy-McCormack battle, Bellotti had made his move. He began to campaign for lieutenant governor. The regulars asked him to withdraw so that the convention could nominate Lieutenant Governor Edward F. McLaughlin, who was willing to remain in second place and leave Peabody uncontested. Bellotti refused and lost the convention endorsement, but he defeated McLaughlin in the primary. *Boston Globe* writer David Farrell described him then as one of the "strong, aggressive, killer-type power politicians who were not interested in the money they could make in politics."

The office of lieutenant governor was largely ceremonial, but Bellotti persuaded the legislature to allocate him ten full-time staff members, a driver, and a radio-equipped limousine.[1] He became the first Massachusetts lieutenant governor in modern times to file bills. He filed fourteen pieces of legislation (none passed) but spent most of his time traveling around the state, trying to nail down delegates. He was a rough, unpolished speaker but also was charismatic and warm, in contrast to Peabody's aloof, patrician personality. Bellotti became a popular figure, pressing the flesh at Knights of Columbus banquets, Sons of Italy dances, bingo nights, and barbecues all over the state, while Peabody struggled with the legislature and Sonny McDonough. Although Bellotti's activities were no secret, party regulars doubted he would run against Peabody for the gubernatorial nomination. To run against the party nominee was a normal, if not admirable, Democratic party custom. To challenge an incumbent governor from one's own party would amount to treason. Bellotti, the regulars reasoned, must be accumulating support for a power play at the convention in order to demand something else.

When Volpe returned to Winchester from his trip to Moscow and Rome, he thought more and more about what Nixon had said. He had enjoyed public service and felt a great satisfaction in having touched in some way the lives of six million people. And there were nagging thoughts of so much unfinished business in his efforts to rebuild Massachusetts as a competitive industrial state: the unresolved fiscal crisis, plans for revamping the state higher education system, reforms in mental health, the completion of the Inner Belt. Yet he faced formidable obstacles in another campaign. Within his own party he was widely blamed for not having campaigned hard enough, for letting a potential victory slip away through overconfidence. Even getting his own party's nomination would be difficult.

The history of political comebacks in Massachusetts was not an encouraging one. No governor since the Civil War who had been defeated had ever been elected to the same office again. The last man who had tried to make such a comeback was the redoubtable James Michael Curley (best known for his years as mayor of Boston), who had been elected governor in 1934, lost a Senate contest in 1936, and taken the Democratic nomination from Governor Hurley in 1938. But Curley had been beaten by Leverett Saltonstall in the general election. Of the eight governors who preceded Volpe, only one, Saltonstall, had won a statewide election after leaving the governorship.

Throughout the fall of 1963, Volpe pondered his decision. In October, he escorted former King Umberto of Italy around Boston. In November, a poll of the delegates from the 1962 Republican convention showed Volpe still the most popular choice for governor, followed by Ed Brooke (who was not running) and Senate Minority Leader Philip Graham of Hamilton, who had already declared himself in the race.

A few days after Christmas, Volpe called Elmer Nelson, the former Republican State Committee chairman who had run Volpe's 1960 campaign and Herter's two campaigns. Nelson had returned to his prosperous Buick dealership in Milford. At sixty-three and a grandfather, he had left politics behind and was considering retiring from the dealership as well. To his astonishment, Volpe announced that he was running for governor and asked Nelson to run his campaign. Nelson had helped him get a state organization underway during the 1962 recount but lost touch with him after that. Nelson told Volpe bluntly that he had taken the last campaign too easy and let the party down. After such strong words, he did not expect to hear from Volpe again. But he was wrong.

Volpe drove out to Milford a few days later, and the two men went over the possibilities. Nelson told him candidly that if he did not run hard, he might as well stay home. He outlined what he thought a successful campaign would need: a good running mate with a broad political base of his own, issues that could attract public attention, good media work, money, and Volpe's shoe leather. They could expect little money from the Republican State Committee after the 1962 defeat, and the $100 a plate Republican dinner was reserved as the state committee's prerogative. Volpe would have to raise funds from smaller donors.

Volpe called a meeting of his family and closest friends in early January 1964 and told them he was planning to run again. They tried to dissuade him, knowing how much the loss to Peabody had hurt. But in the end, they followed Jennie's lead. If he *did* run, they would give him their full support.

For almost six months, Volpe and Nelson made the rounds to get delegate commitments, trying to convince disenchanted Republicans that Volpe had learned his lesson and would campaign hard this time around. At the same time, Graham and State Representative Francis W. Perry of Duxbury, who had been a candidate for lieutenant governor in 1962, were in the running. Perry did not have much support, but Graham, who had served his time and waited his turn in the Massachusetts Senate, did not intend to let a defeated one-term nonprofessional take this opportunity from him. Graham and Volpe participated in a grueling series of twenty-five debates in the spring of 1964, and by May Ed Brooke was considering entering the race.

By June, the team of Volpe and Nelson had gathered endorsements from 953 of the 1,655 delegates. Still, Nelson was convinced that a strong candidate for lieutenant governor was a necessity. With Peabody the likely opponent in November, a Yankee on the ticket could help to neutralize his ethnic appeal.

As Volpe searched the field, the best possible candidate seemed to be Elliot Richardson. Although he was then only forty-five years old (Volpe was fifty-six), Richardson had already served as an assistant secretary of Health, Education, and Welfare under Eisenhower. A member of a prominent family long associated with Harvard and Massachusetts General Hospital, he had managed Saltonstall's Senate office and then served as U.S. attorney for Massachusetts from 1959 to 1962. In 1962, he ran for the Republican nomination for attorney general on his record of rooting out political corruption with the grim slogan, "Finish the job!" He lost the convention endorsement by one vote to Brooke, possibly as a result of a whispering campaign about an alleged drunk-driving violation that plagued his early political career. He challenged Brooke again in the primary but lost. In 1963, he led a well-publicized United Fund drive for Massachusetts and was receptive when Volpe approached him.

Richardson's only concern was that he might be wasting his time as a ribbon-cutter in the lieutenant governorship. Volpe assured him that there would be plenty of work to do in the fields of education, health, and welfare reform. Richardson agreed and put his full effort behind the campaign. Tight-lipped and reserved, he proved to be a tireless worker who projected an image of integrity and added an intellectual dimension to the campaign.

At the convention in the old Boston Arena, Brooke declared again for attorney general but held an organization in readiness with telephones set up on the convention floor in case of a three-way deadlock. Volpe won on the first ballot. The crowd was not as wild as it had been the first time Volpe was nominated. His supporters had known defeat, and they were uncertain of which Democrat they would face in November. (In May, Bellotti had made the biggest gamble of his career and declared against Peabody, who was certain to be the convention nominee but not guaranteed to win his party's primary.) Despite their worries, Volpe's supporters savored the convention victory, a vindication of the criticisms the party regulars had made after 1962. By mid-June, Volpe's most difficult political campaign was underway.

At best, a political campaign on the street level was draining, hard, physical work. In Massachusetts, home of the "alienated voter," the public often walked quickly by, as if the candidate were trying to sell something they did not want. Old men lounged in tavern doorways, remarking loudly that "they're all crooks and thieves." But the worst political insult was not to brand someone as dishonest or immoral — the most terrible label was "loser."

From June through October, Volpe took to the road on an eighteen-hour-a-day schedule. Many of his staff worked the same hours. Although Elmer Nelson was campaign manager, he was often in the field, and Joe Tauro usually ran day-to-day operations at the campaign headquarters. Every night, Tauro performed the same ritual. About midnight, he telephoned Bellotti's headquarters. If someone answered, Tauro kept on working. When there was no answer, Tauro and his key staff went home.

By the 1964 campaign, Volpe had discovered that in order to keep up the pace, he had to become something of a health nut. With the help of his doctor from the Lahey Clinic, he had devised a regimen that would sustain him. Every night (or in some cases, morning) before going to bed, he left a half glass of orange juice on the windowsill to keep it cool. The alarm clock turned on a hot-water pot, and when he got up, he added the hot water to the orange juice along with a dollop of honey for energy. Then off to Mass he went. Back home, he ate a breakfast of oatmeal with raisins. Jennie always prepared a thermos of tea or cocoa for the campaign station wagon. No coffee. No alcohol. And during campaign season, only plain food without spices or sauce. On several occasions, Jennie entertained the press in her kitchen, feeding them bran muffins and passing out mimeographed recipes from a book by the governor's doctor, *Good Food for Bad Stomachs.*

The health system worked well. Volpe, two aides, and a driver stumped the state in a blue Chevy station wagon with a mattress in the rear for naps. As they drove, the candidate familiarized himself with each town they visited by reading a two-page profile of the community listing the industries in the area; the public officials by name, title, and party affiliation; the numbers of Democratic, Republican, and Independent voters; and the figures for the last gubernatorial election. By the time they arrived at their destination, Volpe was familiar with most of the information and ready to use it.

At each campaign stop, a photographer followed Volpe, taking Polaroid pictures of the candidate with local officials, clerks at town halls, and even people on the street who expressed an interest in the campaign. He would autograph the picture and give it as a memento. College-age girls, "Volpettes," dressed in uniforms, handed out literature. Often an extra aide would follow a few steps behind the candidate to listen to people's comments after he had passed. Meeting hundreds of people at factories, MTA stops, cafeterias, clubs, and coffee parties day after day, Volpe often could gauge public sentiment more accurately than his campaign staff at headquarters.

As he campaigned, Volpe heard that national issues, as well as the problems of Massachusetts, were more and more on their minds. Nineteen sixty-four was a presidential election year, and nationally, Volpe's party was in disarray. Within the political spectrum of the Massachusetts Republican party, Volpe, Saltonstall, and Lodge were emerging as moderates, with Ed Brooke and Elliot Richardson on the left. Volpe was above all a pragmatist and had never been much concerned about ideology. He believed in the Republican ideal of limited government, yet if a human need such as education or care for the mentally ill should be filled, he was not averse to urging government to fill the gap. He had never felt any attraction to the extreme right or to the John Birch Society, whose national headquarters were then in Belmont, not far from where he lived.

In the spring of 1964, the three most important Republican primaries had not given the national leaders a clear mandate. Lodge had won one, Rockefeller another, and Barry Goldwater the largest primary, in California. For two years prior to the 1964 New Hampshire primary, the Goldwater forces had been collecting delegates, and by June the national party leaders woke up to the realization that his movement was headed for victory at the convention in July.

Although a few Massachusetts Republican party regulars expressed sympathy for Goldwater, Volpe and most of the delegation that flew to San Francisco were solidly behind the "Stop Goldwater" movement to nominate Pennsylvania Governor William Scranton. Their experience at the Cow Palace was disheartening. Politics seemed suddenly to be splitting into fanatically opposed factions dominated by a furious emotional intensity they had never seen before. The convention hall was besieged by civil rights demonstrators, anti-Vietnam demonstrators, pacifists who had taken seriously Goldwater's early remarks about "lobbing one into the men's room at the Kremlin," and splinter groups of all persuasions. The hatred of many of Goldwater's followers for the Northeast's liberal delegates was palpable; during the victory celebration on the convention floor, one of his delegates seized the Massachusetts delegation's sign and carried it off into the conga line like an enemy trophy.[2]

When he returned to Logan Airport, Volpe was surrounded by reporters who had only one question to ask: Was he supporting Goldwater? Volpe tried to put as much distance between himself and the party nominee as possible without betraying his own party affiliation. "Goldwater may not have been my first choice," he replied, "or even my second or third choice," he told reporters, who began to laugh. "But I am a Republican and the titular leader of my party in this state, and I personally shall vote for him." None of his campaign literature mentioned the nominee, and Goldwater's picture was conspicuous by its absence from the Volpe headquarters at Court Street. Because there seemed so little support for Goldwater in the eastern industrial states, Volpe and his staff hoped that he would not campaign there at all. But Barry Goldwater's well-oiled, well-financed machine was to carry him all over the United States, including Massachusetts.

After Volpe returned from the convention, his office began to receive individually written letters on the general theme "we voted for you before but not now unless you renounce Goldwater." Soon the trickle of letters became a flood, reaching five thousand. Volpe's office put together a carefully worded reply asking the voters to judge him and his opponent on their respective records and not on his support of other candidates. He reiterated that he himself planned to vote for Goldwater as standard bearer but was not asking anyone else to do so. The campaign leased robotypers and sent off this reply to any letter about Goldwater.

In August, Lyndon B. Johnson was nominated for president at a convention dominated by the memory of the president who had been assassinated nine months before. Robert Kennedy introduced the first showing of the film *Year of Lightning, Day of Drums,* and Adlai Stevenson gave a moving eulogy of Eleanor Roosevelt. And the Johnson team swung into action. Blessed with an unusually large war chest for a Democrat, the campaign committee hired Doyle, Dane, and Bernbach Inc. to develop original television ads playing on the themes of nuclear war and Goldwater's promise to cut federal programs. The most devastating ad ran only once, on "NBC Monday Night at the Movies." The spot featured a little girl in a field of flowers, pulling the petals off a daisy, counting down from ten. At zero, the screen showed only her eyes, mirroring the mushroom cloud.

On the day the call came through from Washington that Goldwater would be staging a rally at Fenway Park in Boston, Volpe called in from the field and ordered his staff to meet and make recommendations. Nelson called his top men together and hashed out the issue. Volpe, as nominee, was titular head of the Massachusetts party. No matter how much he disliked what Goldwater stood for, he had an obligation to the party. The staff recommended that Volpe meet Goldwater at the airport, drive with him to the rally, and say a few words, then continue with his own schedule for the evening. A press release on the matter went out in mid-afternoon.

At 2 A.M., Joe Tauro was awakened by a telephone call from an angry Volpe. "The most important decision of the campaign, and I'm not even told about it!" Volpe fumed. "I have to hear it on the radio that I'm meeting Barry Goldwater!" Tauro tried to reassure him. "I lost before, and I don't *ever* intend to lose again!" Volpe told him, and hung up.

Thinking it over, Volpe realized that Tauro was right. To shun Goldwater would be to take the easy way out, like the liberal governors of other states who were avoiding appearances with the standard bearer. Volpe was the party leader and was obligated at least to acknowledge the leader of the national ticket.

On the night of the rally, Volpe took the limousine to Logan Airport to meet the campaign plane. The Goldwater Girls were already there, dressed up in cowgirl outfits trimmed with gold braid, but the plane was five minutes early, and few reporters had arrived. Volpe had met Goldwater only once and had not yet formed an opinion of him personally. As the two men got into the car, a *Boston Globe* photographer knocked on the window. "Senator, could I take your picture with the Goldwater Girls?" he asked. "I'll get it on the front page of the *Globe* tomorrow."

Goldwater looked at him coldly. "Shut that window," he told the driver. "I'm not getting out for *anybody.*" First impressions are the lasting ones, Volpe thought, as they drove through the tunnel beneath Boston Harbor. That evening at Fenway Park, a crowd of between twenty-five thousand and thirty thousand people had gathered. Volpe was the only Republican candidate from the statewide ticket to appear. He spoke briefly, to enthusiastic applause. The audience knew he was going out on a limb to appear for their candidate during a comeback campaign. Then he proceeded on to the two fund-raisers he had scheduled for that night.

September 11 was primary day. Although the polls had shown him running somewhat behind, Frank Bellotti topped Peabody by only a thousand votes in Boston and then went on to carry almost all the other urban areas, defeating Peabody by a little more than thirty thousand votes. Now Volpe knew who his opponent was. The biggest issue that separated them did not emerge until a month later, however, when Massachusetts held its first televised gubernatorial election debate.

In early October, Father Seavey Joyce, dean of the Boston College School of Business Administration, called the candidates' offices and asked whether they would like to debate what to do about Massachusetts' financial difficulties. Volpe called a staff meeting at his house. The entire staff was opposed to his participation in the debate. Bellotti was a skilled trial lawyer who had been on a debating team in college, they argued. Volpe countered that he knew much more about the subject, which was state finance, after two years in office. Bellotti had spent his time in office seeking delegate support and probably knew little about the nuts and bolts of state government. And Volpe felt the old competitive instinct, the drive to show that he could compete with any man on his own ground. They think I'm just a dumb contractor, he thought, but we'll see.

If he chose to debate, what solution would he propose to bail the cities and towns out of their dependence on the regressive property tax?

Volpe outlined three options: streamline government, revamp the tax structure completely, or begin a limited sales tax. He did not, after two years of trying to trim state government, believe that enough fat could be cut from the state budget to lower taxes and still finance crucial programs in housing, education, and welfare. Changing the entire tax system would be impossible without overwhelming support in the legislature — which neither Volpe nor Bellotti was likely to get. That left the sales tax. Massachusetts was then one of only eight industrial states that did not have some form of sales tax.

The history of the proposals for a sales tax was not comforting. The issue had been deadly to Furcolo. The liberal Democrats used the standard arguments against it: It was a regressive form of taxation because it fell more heavily on the poor, who had to spend a greater proportion of their income than the rich. Further, the sales tax had become a bone of contention between two Democratic party rivals, former Senate President John E. Powers and Boston Mayor John Collins. Boston financed all its municipal services with one of the highest property tax rates in the nation. Almost one-third of all Boston property was tax-exempt, including hospitals, schools, gove..iment buildings, and dormitories. By law, businesses were assessed at full market value (private homes were not), and as a result, the city was steadily losing its small industries.

Collins was a strong supporter of the sales tax as a way to bail Boston out of the cycle of increased taxes, businesses leaving, and taxes increased again because of a shrinking base. After Collins upset Powers in the 1958 Boston mayoral election, the sales tax became mired in the internal party quarrel between the two men. When Maurice Donahue took over as Senate majority leader, he continued Powers's opposition. Many observers felt that it was Collins himself who had suggested the debate idea to the Jesuits at Boston College.

Volpe's staff adamantly opposed supporting a new tax just before an election. What politician would promise that, if elected, he would raise taxes? Volpe reminded them that this was not just raising taxes but replacing an inequitable tax with a fairer substitute. The staff was unconvinced and voted unanimously against the sales tax. Volpe cast his one vote for the debate *and* the tax. Since he was the candidate, he won. "The point of the matter is that the team doesn't run for office," John F. Kennedy had proclaimed in his acceptance speech in August 1960. "One man runs."

A week before the debate, Bellotti's press office announced that he was sick and might not be able to go on. But on October 20, both candidates stood on the stage at Faneuil Hall in the glare of the television

126

lights. Both men were tense. Volpe, nervous himself, thought that he could see Bellotti's knees shaking. Boston Mayor John Collins sat in a front row seat, and the press watched his reactions as carefully as they observed the debaters.

In the course of the debate, the two men seemed to be running neck and neck until the sales tax issue came up. As his solution, Bellotti proposed increasing tourism, stimulating economic growth, and getting more federal aid. As a Democrat, he hinted broadly, he would be better able to get help from a Democratic president. Volpe pounced on this. He had not known that the federal government allocated funds on the basis of party affiliation instead of merit, he countered. By the summation, Volpe was rattling off budget figures, while Bellotti was forced to speak in more general terms. Collins, when asked his opinion, did not endorse the Democratic nominee.

The real verdict would come from the voters. The next morning, Volpe toured the Watertown Arsenal. Upstairs, the managers and engineers greeted him warmly, assuring him of their support. That meant little, however, as they probably would vote Republican anyway. With some trepidation, he ventured downstairs to the shop floor to shake hands with the men behind the lathes. Volpe had two young campaign workers with him, one to "front" him — introduce him and move him along to keep on schedule — the other to stay a few steps behind and take notes on what the men were saying after the candidate was out of earshot. Of every ten workers on the shop floor, about three said that they were Democrats and planned to vote the straight ticket. Of the other seven, three or four said they liked the idea of the sales tax to help reduce the property tax and would vote for Volpe. The others said that they did not agree with the sales tax plan, but that any candidate who had the courage to come out and tell the electorate he would raise taxes must be an honest man and would get their vote.

The sales tax issue suggested a new theme: credibility. Although it meant sending the underfinanced campaign deeper in debt, the campaign committee changed all the billboards, with only a few weeks to go, from "Bring Back Volpe" to "You Can Trust Volpe." At the same time, the flip side of the honesty issue began to appear. Unauthorized signs such as "Peabody Trusted Bellotti. Can You?" appeared on store windows, and allegations about Bellotti's receipt of "Rhode Island money" (a code word for the Mafia, whose New England headquarters were believed to be in Providence) surfaced in the last weeks of the campaign.

None of the "dirty money" innuendos against Bellotti were ever proven, or even brought into the open, and in the context of Massachusetts politics they probably did minimal damage. But the Peabody "betrayal" did. After the primary, hundreds of former Peabody workers volunteered for the Volpe campaign, and the wounds were slow to heal. At about the same time, the issue of taking power from the Governor's Council probably hurt Bellotti more than Volpe. Unwilling to antagonize McDonough and his supporters unless it was absolutely necessary, Volpe and Richardson held off on the issue until October 20, when the polls were showing a clear victory for the constitutional reform, and then they announced their support for the plan. Bellotti could not support the referendum without seeming to "betray" his own running mate, John W. Costello of Boston, who was then a member of the council.

The turnout was heavy on election day, and in most of New England, the trend was heavily Democratic. John F. Kennedy had pulled only 56 percent of the total New England vote in 1960, but Johnson's total was 71.1 percent. In Massachusetts, the final count at the top of the ticket was 76.2 percent Johnson, 23.4 percent Goldwater.

As the night wore on, the outcome of the gubernatorial election was unclear. Ed Brooke was racking up a landslide victory against State Senator James W. Hennigan for attorney general, but Volpe and Bellotti were now running neck and neck. Some Volpe staffers turned in after midnight, believing they had lost. But as dawn broke, the small towns and the rural areas began reporting after the long count of their paper ballots, and Volpe took the lead.

By mid-morning, his ultimate plurality was predicted to be about forty-five thousand votes. Bellotti conceded just before noon. Jubilant, Volpe announced that after two or three hours of sleep, he would depart by helicopter for a swing through Pittsfield, Springfield, Worcester, Fall River, and New Bedford to thank the voters.

On November 7, five days after the election, the final figures showed that Volpe's margin was much closer than he thought — a plurality of only twenty-four thousand votes. But in order for a recount to take place, there had to be less than a 12,500-vote difference. He was safe. The Volpes left for a vacation in Miami, then a Thanksgiving trip to Jean's house in Schenectady, where the family was living while her husband did graduate work at Cornell. The inauguration was scheduled, and preparations for the transition began. This time Volpe ordered a different portrait to be hung behind the desk — Marcus Morton, the last governor who had returned to the corner office after defeat, in 1840.

The election also had changed profoundly the operation of the executive branch Volpe was to lead. The League of Women Voters referendum had abolished all the powers of the Governor's Council over executive appointments or dismissals, though the council did retain the veto over judicial and regulatory agency appointments and pardons. The terms of major departments and commissions were still not synchronized to the gubernatorial term, yet now Volpe was free to make his own appointments when openings did come up, without being asked the council's question: "What have you done for me today?" The voters also had amended the constitution to extend the governor's term of office to four years, beginning with the 1966 election.

The three top constitutional offices were now Republican, for Brooke had finished with an impressive 725,000 votes. The legislature, however, was more solidly Democratic than in 1960: 170 to 69 in the House (with one Independent), and 28 to 12 in the Senate. John E. Powers had been succeeded by Maurice Donahue of Holyoke. "Duke" Thompson, who had died less than a year after having been indicted by the crime commission, had been replaced by John F.X. Davoren. Both Donahue and Davoren were traditional Irish-American moderates. In the Senate, Philip Graham still led the Republicans; in the House, Minority Leader Sidney Curtiss ("The Squire of Sheffield") was being challenged by Alfred Shrigley of Hingham.

Volpe was determined to improve his relations with both the legislature and the media. After his 1962 defeat, three charges had especially bothered him: that he had not campaigned hard enough, that he had been a "do nothing" governor because so little of his legislative package had passed, and that he had failed to get his ideas across to the public through the media. In the campaign, Volpe felt vindicated on the first count. To make sure his programs got through the legislature this time, Volpe would need more conciliation, more diplomacy, and more cooperation. Hard work and intelligence alone would not always win votes in the legislature, and his honesty ruled out traditional horse trading.

For his new team, Volpe assembled a group of men who were much younger than the staff that had worked for him in 1960. Volpe had appointed his closest advisor of the 1960 campaign, G. Joseph Tauro, as associate justice of the superior court after he had worked as legal counsel to the governor's office for a little less than a year. Tauro's son, Joseph L. Tauro, had then replaced his father as unpaid legal counsel. "Young Joe" at the age of thirty-three had served not only as the Volpe Company's legal counsel during the time Volpe was out of office but also as close friend and advisor during the second campaign for the governorship. While "Old

Joe" had been formal and somewhat distant, Young Joe was flamboyant and hard-driving. A Cornell graduate, Young Joe became the staff's chief speech writer. He also functioned as protector, forming a buffer between the governor and the other staffers' demands. He was so close to the Volpe family that Jennie would jokingly refer to him as her other son; she had been the nurse who assisted at his birth. After a long briefing, it was invariably Young Joe who would call a halt, tell the staff that the governor needed a break, and warn him that he was working too hard. On any major policy decision, Young Joe was consulted.

Tony DeFalco, then thirty-nine, was appointed chief secretary. Volpe had met DeFalco in 1960 while campaigning in DeFalco's hometown of Dedham. DeFalco was then president of Contolomat, a data processing firm with offices in Boston, Detroit, and San Francisco. In 1961, he was hired as a special assistant to the commissioner of administration and finance to develop computer systems for various state offices, starting with the Registry of Motor Vehicles.

Leslie Ainley, who had been press secretary in Volpe's first administration, moved up to special assistant. The elder statesman of the staff, Ainley was a courtly, white-haired newspaperman who did much of Volpe's speech writing and prepared him for his encounters with the press. Volpe's new press secretary was a young public relations man named Barry Locke. Born in the working-class Jewish neighborhood of Mattapan, Locke had worked in the newspaper business until he became press secretary to the governor of Vermont, then public information officer for the IRS in New England.

None of Volpe's staffers were ideologues. They were practical, sometimes cynical, political workers — well liked on Beacon Hill. Joe Silvano, Volpe's patronage chief, was the gregarious proprietor of a barbershop in Brookline who had been elected a state senator. None of the staff had political aspirations of their own, so interoffice rivalries were few. From Volpe's side, the relationship was slightly distant and avuncular. "One or two days after the inauguration in 1965, he called us all into his office," Christopher Armstrong, then serving on Young Joe's legal staff, remembered. "He gave us a fatherly pep talk. Actually, it was very good advice. He warned us that now that we were working for the governor, people would want to be our friends — but stick to your old friends. We were to have no dealings with the legislature or the press unless it was cleared through Tauro. All letters were to be answered within forty-eight hours, even if you could only send an acknowledgment. And there was to be no drinking in the State House — he was very strict about things like that."

Although none of his staffers attempted to follow Volpe's puritanical lifestyle, they idealized their boss and were fiercely loyal to him. They complained about his innocence and yet loved him for it. More than once at conferences or conventions, Volpe met some of his staff returning from a night of partying when he himself was leaving for early Mass. Once, during a convention, he met DeFalco in the hotel elevator at 5:30 A.M. Volpe, smiling and rested, asked if DeFalco would like to attend Mass with him. DeFalco was too tired to refuse, and off they went to church.

Another incident that became part of the Volpe myth happened at a Republican conference in Colorado Springs. Barry Locke, DeFalco, and several reporters were drinking at the hotel bar about 11 P.M., when a call came through from Volpe's suite. The governor was getting ready for bed and discovered that he had lost the tiny screw from his eyeglass frame. "Where do you think you lost it, Governor?" DeFalco asked. Volpe thought it must have been in the conference room where his committee had met that afternoon. The staffers located the conference room, turned on all the lights, and began crawling around on the floor. Under the table, they found the tiny screw. They went upstairs and knocked on the governor's door. His room was dark. "We found it!" they shouted, but Volpe was unimpressed. "Put it on the bureau," he told them without getting up. "Good night."

From the beginning of his second term, Volpe made an all-out effort to improve his dealings with the press. During his first administration, he had not been an easy governor to cover. In the pre–tape recorder era, the reporters at the State House scribbled helplessly trying to keep up with his drumfire recitals of facts and figures. At social gatherings, he could give a pleasant, anecdotal talk, but when the speech covered substantive issues, he often would rush through a twenty-minute presentation in fifteen, then wait impatiently for technical questions. But the press, unlike businessmen, were not interested in long lists of percentages and detailed explanations. He did not provide good copy. While out of office he did not, as some believed, take speech lessons. But he did try to slow down his delivery, and he did practice.

After taking office for the second time, Volpe held a mock press conference before every real one. The staff would brief him; this was the easy part, for he soaked up facts like a sponge. Then, in the corner office, the staff would role-play, asking any questions that might possibly come up, the harder the better. The briefing sessions frequently turned out to be rougher than the actual press conferences. For the staff, the most difficult part of the briefing was to get Volpe to agree to a "no comment." In the briefing, the staff would all agree that some issues, where Volpe's personal religious beliefs differed from what he thought was legally justified, should not be discussed. Birth control and the death penalty were two such issues. But Volpe seemed incapable of sustaining his "no comment." The press soon discovered this, and would simply rephrase the question. He would dodge the first time, but eventually, while his aides squirmed in their chairs at the back of the room, his opinion would come out.

By February, editorial writers were talking about the "new John Volpe," a better speaker, more patient, easier to deal with. He also had begun to master television, the medium that had been so hard on Peabody. He learned to flash the camera his "million-dollar smile" and pace his delivery. On screen, he looked confident and occasionally cocky, but likable.

Volpe also had limited his objectives to what he could reasonably accomplish while in office. In his first term, he had rushed in to reform the DPW, the MDC, and the MTA all in one term, and he had failed. Now he chose to build on what he had already started: to restructure the DPW, get construction on the rest of the Inner Belt started, and carry through his programs in mental health and the rebuilding of the state college system. The crime commission that had been his primary goal in the first administration had done its work and was scheduled to end in 1965.

During the campaign, Volpe had taken on a new objective. Before he took office again, he embarked on what would become yet another crusade for something he believed to be not only correct policy but also the will of the voters — fiscal reform through the sales tax.

NOTES

1. *The Boston Traveler,* 8 December 1963.
2. Theodore H. White, *The Making of the President, 1964* (New York: Atheneum, 1965), p. 231.

132

CHAPTER IX

Managing the Issues

T HE GREAT TAX DEBATE that had begun on the stage of Faneuil
Hall reached the legislature in February 1965, when Volpe filed
the first of his sales tax bills. The prospects were not good. Senate
President Maurice Donahue of Holyoke opposed the entire concept,
favoring instead an increase in the income tax. House Speaker John F.X.
Davoren also rejected the initial legislation, though he was willing to look
at compromise exemptions. A normal course of action for a minority
governor who was so strongly opposed in both houses would be to file two
or three times and then quietly drop the issue. Volpe was disinclined to
pursue this course for two reasons. He believed that the legislation would
go far toward reducing the property taxes that were strangling urban areas
as well as small towns. And he thought he had the mandate of the electorate, if not their elected representatives, behind him. The polls showed that
a majority of voters favored a sales tax, albeit a limited one. Volpe's visit
to the Watertown Arsenal had marked a personal turning point. His stand
on the sales tax, he felt, was one of the issues that had led to his election in
a Democratic landslide year. He would be breaking faith with those voters
if he let the issue go.

By March, a statewide organization was in place under the chairmanship of Elliot Richardson, ready to promote the sales tax in a series of
public hearings of the House Committee on State Administration in six

cities across the state. The League of Cities and Towns, the League of Women Voters, and the Republican city and town committees held public forums on the issue. Just as he had campaigned for the crime commission, Volpe went to the media, campus forums, and civic groups, appealing to the public directly. And changes were made in the sales tax bill each time it was filed.

From the beginning, the 3 percent sales tax was limited, with the goal of affecting the very poor as little as possible. Food was exempt, as were medicine and clothing under $200 per item. The House debated for hours over items such as soap and toothpaste. Each time, the margins were narrower, but in 1965, the bill was defeated five times. It had passed twice in the House, only to be defeated in the Senate. At press conferences, reporters would ask what was the matter, couldn't the governor sweeten the deal with a few more summer jobs?

Volpe always involved himself in the creation of legislation that came from his office, reading every word of any document he signed, but with the sales tax his concern became obsessive. Staff members involved in drafting the bills would receive phone calls, often at night, asking for explanations of technical terms, even checking on spelling or typing errors. As the S-1 limousine pulled out of the State House parking lot, the reading light would be on in back while Volpe went over his paperwork on the drive home to Winchester.

By the spring of 1965, the sales tax was still stalled, but Volpe's popularity with the public was high. Freed from the restrictions imposed by the Governor's Council, he had gone outside the Massachusetts political system to the business community to fill vacancies in top state jobs. John J. McCarthy, a former General Electric executive, was appointed commissioner of administration and finance and given the task of getting more production from state employees. The new state commissioner of commerce and development, Theodore Schulenberg, was the ultimate State House outsider, having been hired on the strength of his record as director of the Indiana Department of Commerce.

With the help of three full-time staffers, Elliot Richardson ran a separate office that drafted legislation and coordinated the Departments of Public Health, Mental Health, Education, and Welfare; the Youth Service Board; and the Commonwealth Service Corps with the activities of related federal agencies. As lieutenant governor, Richardson had run slightly ahead of Volpe on the ticket with a margin of twenty-seven thousand votes but showed no inclination to challenge Volpe; his ambition at that time was to serve in the U.S. Senate. Richardson considered himself a member of Volpe's staff or cabinet.

The first big issue that Richardson tackled in 1965 was the reform of the mental health system. The first goal of the Volpe-Richardson mental health reform was simply to get adequate funding to improve the facilities the state already operated and to hire more doctors and nurses. In 1964, the state was paying $7.69 per patient per day in a mental hospital, while rates at a general hospital were $56 per day. Even the most conservative experts believed the figure should be doubled. On March 16, at Volpe's request, Dr. William Menninger of the Menninger Clinic in Topeka, Kansas, addressed a special joint session of the legislature and a legislative dinner meeting of the Massachusetts Association for Mental Health to urge allocation of more funds and implementation of a report calling for the founding of community mental health clinics to replace the warehouse hospitals.

Volpe's second administration marked the beginning of the deinstitutionalization movement in Massachusetts that would lead to the closing of the regional hospitals, the large, prisonlike facilities that had seen previous use as tuberculosis sanitaria. Richardson's office advocated a two-tiered approach. Instead of living in hospital wards, acute mental patients would live in twelve- to twenty-bed "cottages" located across the state. Some cottages would be built on institution grounds or on other extra land already owned by the state; others could be built close to the neighborhoods from which the patients came. Medical care could be provided in neighborhood clinics for patients able to live at home. The first of these clinics was built to serve the Lowell-Lawrence area. These reforms were made possible by the development of drug therapy that enabled mentally ill patients to function, with medical support, in a community setting. Increased federal funding also was available at that time as the "Great Society" social programs began to come on-line, so the whole burden of reform did not fall on the Massachusetts tax base.

As Richardson's office planned the reform of social services in Massachusetts, new issues were coming to the forefront. Among them was the question of civil rights for the black community. Black people had lived in Massachusetts since colonial times, and the city of Boston had been a center of abolitionism before the Civil War. Yet until the end of World War II, the size and influence of the black community was minimal. Blacks were simply one of many small ethnic groups scattered throughout the urban areas of the state, with the greatest concentration in Boston's polyglot South End and Roxbury.

The "racial" conflicts of Volpe's youth had been played out by the Irish, Italians, and Jews. But in the early 1950s, the migration from the

West Indies and the rural South that had swelled the ghettos of New York, Detroit, Chicago, and Washington, D.C., had reached Boston. Black families had moved into all of Roxbury as the Irish migrated to the South Shore. Between 1950 and 1960, Boston lost about a hundred thousand whites and gained twenty-five thousand blacks.[1] The Boston Jewish community of Mattapan-Dorchester also dispersed to the suburbs, abandoning the commercial centers of the urban ethnic neighborhoods.

Many black families moved north to Boston not for better jobs — industry was then leaving the city — but to get an education for their children. They knew about Harvard, MIT, and the Boston Latin schools. Surely Boston, the "hub of the universe," must have a school system better than the segregated classrooms of the rural South.

But Boston, and the Boston schools, did not absorb black people in the same way that they had assimilated the Irish, the Italians, the Jews, and other newcomers. In the late 1920s, when author Theodore White was growing up in the Jewish ghetto of Mattapan, each neighborhood had elementary and intermediate schools within a child's walking distance. Segregation was by gender only. As the neighborhoods changed ethnically, so did the schools. In White's time, positions on the Boston School Committee, an unpaid citywide elective office, were held by Yankees, but the schoolteachers and administrators were almost uniformly Irish. "Whatever the general theory of the Boston School Committee was, in the state in which Horace Mann had first preached the idea of free public education, its practice, when I was going to school, was excellent," White wrote.[2] But as the white Catholic population prospered, more and more of their children entered the parochial school system, leaving only the poorest students behind. By the early 1960s, the system as a whole, with the exception of the Boys' and Girls' Latin schools (admission by examination only) had deteriorated, and the schools where black children were in the majority were visibly inferior to those in white neighborhoods.

As the civil rights crusade moved through the segregated South, blacks in Boston began to look at their own position. Massachusetts had never had Jim Crow laws, yet a network of informal, unwritten codes seemed to restrict blacks to certain ghetto neighborhoods and segregated schools. The schools became the focus of initial black demands for equal treatment, and when the Boston School Committee proved unwilling to meet the demands, the state legislature was seen as the most likely vehicle for redress.

The leader of the movement to obtain integration and improvement was Thomas Atkins, the young Harvard-educated executive secretary of the Boston branch of the National Association for the Advancement of Colored People (NAACP). On June 18, 1963, a coalition of church and civil rights groups led by the NAACP held a public school boycott that kept half the system's five thousand high school and junior high school students home for one day. In 1964, they followed with a better organized boycott that put four thousand black students into special Freedom Schools for one class day.[3] In early 1965, Atkins filed suit in federal court against the Boston School Committee on the grounds that the black children were being denied equal protection under the Constitution. On the state level, however, there was no vehicle for change.

In July 1964, an interim report to State Education Commissioner Owen Kiernan on racial segregation was issued by an advisory committee composed of some of the most distinguished men in Boston, among them the president of Brandeis University, the president of Boston University, the Cardinal, and the editor of the *Christian Science Monitor*. The Boston School Committee, under the leadership of the redoubtable Louise Day Hicks of South Boston, had taken the position that black children were being given equal access to all public schools through the policy of "open enrollment." In theory, a child could attend any school in the city. But in practice, the city would not pay transportation costs, and transfers from black to white schools were nearly impossible for black children to get.

The Kiernan Commission report documented a clear pattern of segregation. Of the forty-five schools in Boston with greater than 50 percent minority attendance, twenty-eight were more than 80 percent black and sixteen were more than 96 percent black. And in Boston, separate was not equal. Sixth grade children in many of the segregated schools were as much as three years behind the reading levels of children in white schools, and they fell further behind each year. In-class expenditures for Boston as a whole averaged $275 per pupil per year. In the black schools, the figure was $213.[4]

Volpe read these figures carefully and thought back to his days at Camp Peary and the segregated system he had fought. He did not want these injustices established in his own home state at the same time that they were being eliminated in the South. As governor, Volpe could not intervene directly in the policies of the Boston School Committee. Like black community leaders and liberals who had tackled the issue before him, Volpe found that the unpaid school committee was normally regarded in Boston politics as simply one rung on the political ladder. Most of its members were Irish-American lawyers whose own children attended the parochial schools, and the committee members often seemed less inter-

137

ested in the findings of study commissions than in the political capital they could make from championing the cause of "neighborbood schools" against the imagined terrors of integration by busing.

Yet the state did have potential leverage over school districts. In the past, state aid had been withheld when districts did not fulfill educational requirements set by the Department of Education. Federal laws were being enacted that would allow Washington to deny federal aid to school districts with de facto as well as de jure segregation. Richardson and several black leaders proposed that Massachusetts enact similar legislation to force a school district to desegregate or lose state funding. Volpe directed Richardson to begin drafting a bill in early April, though he still hoped that the Boston School Committee would have a change of heart once its members saw that the state was not going to back off. Neither Volpe nor any of his advisors could foresee that the school committee members could not back down; their electorate would not let them.

From the beginning of the discussions on drafting the racial imbalance bill, a new and emotionally laden word entered the political vocabulary: busing. In the early 1960s, black students were already being transported by bus from racially changing areas to black schools. But if the racial imbalance bill were enacted, some busing of white students would be unavoidable. Volpe and Richardson envisioned ending segregation in Boston by building new schools with federal and state aid in border areas to attract both white and minority students. Some busing would be necessary while the new schools were being built, but they estimated that in three to five years, the system would have not only an equitable distribution of resources but better facilities as well (there had been no new schools built in Boston since the 1930s).

Both Volpe and Richardson underestimated the emotional impact of sending white children by bus to ghetto neighborhoods, even temporarily. The reaction from the Italian-American neighborhoods of the North End and East Boston was vehement and uncompromising. East Boston, cut off from the rest of the city by the harbor and accessible only by tunnel, considered itself a city apart; parents would no more consider sending their children by bus to Roxbury than to an alien country. In his public speeches, Volpe downplayed busing: "I regard busing as a last resort and only then a temporary expedient, if the cities and towns exhaust all powers of human persuasion," he told a reporter in May 1965.[5] Yet if the racial imbalance bill passed, some busing would come to Boston.

In following the civil rights movement on the national level, Volpe was particularly drawn to Martin Luther King, Jr.'s, nonviolent, Christian way of conducting a social revolution. Like everyone else in politics, Volpe heard rumors that King and his movement were communist inspired. He could find no basis for these rumors, so he took the man for what he said he was. Two months after his inauguration, Volpe appointed James Bishop, the Boston chairman of the Congress of Racial Equality, to the newly created job of secretary of intergroup relations, to work specifically on racial issues. Richardson also spent considerable time with black leaders in Boston and Springfield.

In early April, demonstrations against segregation in the Boston and Springfield schools were planned, and Martin Luther King, Jr., was scheduled to arrive in Boston to participate. But it was the governor who made the headlines the day before King's arrival. After a dinner speaking engagement in Northampton, Volpe and his state police aide George Luciano boarded a helicopter at the closest airport for the return trip to Boston. When they were fifty to seventy feet off the ground, the helicopter stopped dead and began to fall. The pilot tried to cut the speed of the descent by pitching from side to side, and the helicopter hit the ground just beyond the concrete landing pad. It had rained the night before, and the earth was soft, so none of the occupants was injured. Relieved, Volpe told Luciano to drive him back immediately, but the policeman, more experienced in life and death situations than his boss, recommended that they stay the night in Northampton instead. A few hours later, Volpe found that Luciano was right; the brush with death had shaken him.

The incident had an even greater effect on Helen Ross. Hearing the news over the police radio at the State House, Ross began to consider how closely her career was bound up with Volpe's. For seventeen years, she had changed jobs whenever he had, never accumulating a pension or retirement fund. Without telling any of the staff, she resolved to ask Volpe for the next suitable state job that came across his desk. In May, a vacancy occurred on the Public Utilities Commission, and Ross was appointed to become a full-time commissioner. In 1967, she would become the commission's first chairwoman.

On April 22, 1965, King and other members of the Southern Christian Leadership Conference led a peaceful march from Roxbury to Boston Common. At the State House, they met briefly with Volpe and Richardson and held a photo session. A week later, the state Department of Education filed its first racial imbalance bill. The proposed legislation would empower the commissioner to withhold state funds if he found "resentment or resistance" to desegregation and suggested that the best remedy was not busing but construction of larger, regional schools. Kiernan's filing was the beginning of a protracted struggle. Working with Richardson and Brookline Representative Beryl Cohen, a Jesuit priest from Boston College named Robert Drinan fielded a team of six civil rights lawyers to lobby the legislators. Black picketers kept a vigil outside school committee offices on Court Street for 114 days, rain or shine.

Although a core of liberal legislators already favored the bill, suspicion and fear of the civil rights movement deepened with every demonstration and racial incident. These fears crystallized in a last-minute amendment to the legislation barring from the Racial Imbalance Advisory Committee any person who was a member of an organization "listed in any federal or state document as a communist front."[6] The final version included both incentives to integrate through extra funds for balanced schools and penalties in the form of withdrawal of funds from imbalanced districts. Suburban and rural legislators could take comfort from the fact that the legislation was drawn strictly on municipal lines. Under the bill's definition, only Boston was imbalanced. No matter how many buses rolled, trouble would end at the city limits.

By the summer of 1965, race riots had broken out in the black ghettos of Los Angeles, but Boston was quiet. Then, abruptly, demonstrations began in Springfield in the wake of charges of police brutality after a series of arrests at a black nightclub in July. The demonstrations quickly turned violent. After six hours of meetings, Volpe, Richardson, and Secretary of Intergroup Relations James Bishop persuaded community leaders to call off further demonstrations, but the situation simmered all summer. Volpe found the negotiation process among black leaders, police officials, and the mayor's office much like the bitter labor-management talks of the 1960 MTA strike. Here he was, again the mediator, trying to soothe and reach agreement.

Tensions were at the breaking point in late August. On August 18, Volpe formally signed the racial imbalance bill into law in a ceremony in the Hall of Flags, with King and other black leaders watching. The vigils at Court Street and the State House ended, but more demonstrations were planned for the weekend of August 19 in Springfield.

On Saturday afternoon, Volpe's mother Filomena suffered a heart attack and died. She was eighty-four.

Filomena Volpe had been well and active up until the time of her death. Often she had attended state functions with her son and daughter-in-law. Her favorite public event had been Perry Como's appearance in Boston. On March 4 of that year, a month after the War Memorial Auditorium (now Hynes Auditorium) opened, Perry Como had been

140

scheduled to broadcast his show live from the new stage, and Volpe was to present the singer with the customary Revere bowl. Remembering his mother was a Como fan, Volpe telephoned Como's agent and asked if he could bring her along. Como's family had come from the Abruzzi too, and he had welcomed Filomena in Italian, embraced her onstage, and sang her an Italian folk song. After that day, no event had been too important for her to miss "The Perry Como Show."

Now she was gone. But the tension in Springfield was unabated. On Sunday morning, as the plans were being made for her funeral, Volpe was on duty at the State House to monitor the course of the demonstrations. Fortunately, there was no violence in Springfield that weekend, and Volpe was able to spend the rest of Sunday with his family.

On August 24, Filomena Volpe's funeral was held in Malden; the church in Wakefield was too small to hold all the mourners. Even the Immaculate Conception Church was crowded, as more than thirteen hundred people attended and more than a thousand lined the streets to see the procession. Cardinal Cushing presided at the Mass, and virtually every Catholic church and state dignitary in Massachusetts came to pay respects.

The summer of 1965 marked a turning point in another issue that would surface soon. During Peabody's administration, the DPW had been restructured into a five-member commission. Peabody had then appointed the customary two Republicans and three Democrats; the Republicans were State Representative Donald Dwight of Holyoke and Francis Sargent III of Cape Cod. Sargent, a second cousin of Elliot Richardson, was an affable, low-key Yankee. He had gone to MIT to study architecture, but after a World War II stint with ski troops, he had decided he preferred the outdoor life and opened a sporting goods store and a modest charter boat business on Cape Cod. When gill netters began wiping out the striped bass off the Cape, Sargent led the sportsmen's protests so effectively that Governor Bradford appointed him director of the Department of Marine Fisheries. Eisenhower later appointed him to the Northeast Atlantic Fisheries Commission, and finally Peabody made him one of the five DPW commissioners in charge of the Division of Waterways. In early 1965, Volpe demoted the Democratic DPW chairman, replacing him with Sargent.

Within a few weeks of his elevation to the chairmanship, Sargent publicly opposed Volpe's plan for further reorganization of the DPW. Attempts at reorganization, Sargent argued, would be too risky at a time when he needed all the support of his department to get the Inner Belt and Southwest Expressway completed on schedule. Despite Volpe's years of effort to change things, the DPW still functioned with senior staff whose service had begun in the Depression under Callahan, and hiring policies were still governed by a combination of the state's civil service mandate of absolute veterans' preference and interference from the legislature. Unlike the modern highway departments of California and Texas, the Massachusetts DPW still lacked enough highly skilled personnel to do its own design work and relied heavily on expensive consultants. Faced with a choice between concentrating on the visionary goal of revamping the department and the very real possibility of completing the Inner Belt, however, Volpe chose to push on with highway construction.

Sargent shepherded an amendment abolishing the local veto over federal highway programs through both the House and the Senate in July. Suddenly, the way seemed clear, and none too soon. According to federal funding requirements, construction on the Inner Belt and Southwest Expressway would have to begin in 1968 and end in 1971 or 1972 to receive the 90 percent federal reimbursement. "I don't see how, realistically, the New Boston and several communities can afford not to have these two roads," Sargent commented at the time the local veto provision was killed. "Without the Southwest Expressway, in four, five, or even ten years time it will be unbelievable — jammed with traffic that will take hours to straighten out. The city will be strangled."[7]

The Inner Belt route plan was still what it had been in 1948, an eight-lane circle around the core city through Roxbury, the Fenway, Brookline, Cambridge, Somerville, and Charlestown. The Central Artery portion would then form one-third of the total circle. The Southwest Expressway was to be the route Interstate 95 would take on its way from Florida to Maine. Using I-95, interstate travelers could bypass the core city on a path that would take them through Milton, Hyde Park, Roslindale, and Jamaica Plain. The Inner Belt and I-95 would then meet in a massive five-level interchange in lower Roxbury, the heart of the black community. The Inner Belt alone would cost more than $300 million.

When Volpe had first pushed for the Inner Belt as DPW commissioner, chamber of commerce president, and finally governor, the obstacles in its way were the legislative patronage system, political pressure from local elected officials whose districts were threatened by land-taking, and simple bureaucratic inertia. No one questioned the basic assumptions that General Lucius Clay articulated in his 1955 report to President Eisenhower — that the private automobile represented progress and that urban workers should shop and work downtown, then commute by tax-supported highways home to bedroom communities, bypassing the old city neighborhoods that had grown up around the streetcar and bus systems. "We have been able to disperse our factories, our stores, our people, in short to create a revolution in living habits. Our cities have spread into suburbs dependent on the automobile for their existence. The automobile has restored a way of life in which the individual may live in a friendly neighborhood, it has brought city and country closer together, and it has made us one country and united people," the Clay Report authors wrote in 1955.[8]

But times had changed since Boston's initial involvement with the Inner Belt. In the mid-1960s, new political players were coming onto the highway scene — from colleges, from ghetto housing projects, from old Victorian mansions and triple-deckers in the old streetcar neighborhoods. Before the contest over the Inner Belt and Southwest Expressway was over, the debate would not be about whose homes would be taken and who would get the paving contracts but about the underpinnings of the whole national transportation plan.

From the beginning of the Inner Belt debate, the sticking point had been Cambridge. The Elm Street–Brookline route went through Congressman Thomas P. ("Tip") O'Neill's crowded district, and O'Neill had consistently opposed it. In May 1960, when Furcolo was still governor, more than twenty-five hundred Cambridge residents, including priests and local politicians, had held a rally to oppose the route. In 1963, one of the future key figures in the Inner Belt battle, an MIT graduate engineer named Fred Salvucci, had joined the Boston Redevelopment Authority and studied the Inner Belt plans, concluding that the DPW studies were "loaded" and inaccurate. After Salvucci had spent a year studying transportation systems in Italy, he had returned to work full-time on the issue in 1965. Shortly after Salvucci had returned from Italy, Jim Morey, a high-tech systems analyst turned community organizer, had started his own study, concluding that "something was needed to counteract the DPW, the BPR [Bureau of Public Roads], the Governor, the highway interests, and the highly paid consultants."[9]

Morey and other young organizers fresh off the college campus began to rally support in Jamaica Plain along the proposed I-95 route, eventually linking up with the Cambridge activists to form a "Save Our Cities" committee. Under Sargent, the DPW went ahead with its plans. Neither he nor Volpe imagined at this time that more than a few route changes would be necessary, perhaps changing some elevated routes into depressed sections. But in the old neighborhoods, the forces that would lead to a greater confrontation were already at work.

January 1966 began another election year. With this election, the next governor would begin the first ever four-year term. At the turn of the year, a political rift within the Republican party developed suddenly. All through the fall of 1965, Senator Leverett Saltonstall's wife had been in poor health, but few people outside the family knew about the senator's personal life. In the past, Elliot Richardson had expressed an interest in running for the senator's seat if Saltonstall ever chose to retire, but Brooke had been the big Republican vote-getter in the 1964 election. On December 29, 1965, Saltonstall invited the press to his office in the federal courthouse and formally announced that he would not be a candidate in 1966.

Sometime in early December, Brooke, Volpe, and Joe Tauro met to discuss the question of who should run for Saltonstall's seat, hoping to make an agreement that would avoid a primary fight. No notes or recordings were kept, and as is often the case, all three men remembered the conversation differently. Brooke's version, in his authorized *Ed Brooke: Biography of a Senator,* has Brooke telephoning Volpe the night before the Saltonstall announcement to warn him of a "premonition" he had that the senator would retire. After the announcement, he phoned Volpe again, asking him what his intentions were. Volpe asked for a month to think it over, but Brooke would not give him "a month, a week, or even a day."[10] After the telephone conversation, Brooke rounded up his key staff and spent the next seven hours on the phone calling Republican leaders to a meeting at the Sheraton Plaza. By the end of the day, the staff had contacted nearly five hundred Republicans.

In Tauro's version, Brooke asked to meet with Volpe about three weeks before the Saltonstall announcement. The three met in Volpe's office in the State House, and Brooke opened with an explanation that he was certain Saltonstall was going to retire, that the secret could not be kept long. Brooke then came straight to the point: One of them should run for governor and the other for the Senate. "Which one do you want?" he asked Volpe. Volpe hesitated, explaining that he would need some time — a month perhaps. Brooke agreed. Two weeks later, Volpe called Tauro into his office. "I have to make a decision now," he told Tauro. "Put down on a piece of paper the pluses and minuses of each one." Tauro did so, and the analysis favored the governorship. As Republican governor of a large industrial state, Volpe was likely to become more of a national figure. As a senator, he would be just one of a hundred legislators — and junior senator to Ted Kennedy. On the personal side of the equation, Jennie would not want to move to Washington. But before Volpe had communi-

144

cated his decision to Brooke, the attorney general announced that he was entering the race.

Volpe remembers a meeting between himself and Brooke, without Tauro, in the corner office. Volpe had assumed that, as titular head of the party, he would be the first to know when Saltonstall made a decision. When Brooke informed him that he had been told first, Volpe was surprised but assumed the news had come indirectly through a leak. Brooke then told Volpe that he was going to enter the race. Volpe had at that time no desire to serve in the Senate; his training had been in management, not law. He was already planning for his reelection campaign and knew Jennie would not want to move. But his sense of propriety was offended. Brooke, he felt, should first have asked his blessing, which he would have been happy to give.

For Volpe, the great unfinished business of the new year was the sales tax. In 1965, after five rejections, the staff was unanimous in advising him to give it up. But, as often happened, Volpe disregarded the counsel of the "no" men. On the third and fourth tries, the votes had been tantalizingly close in the House, but the Senate still firmly supported Democrat George V. ("Gee-gee") Kenneally's increased income tax bills. On the fifth submission, Tauro suggested to Senate Minority Leader Philip Graham that he call the Democrats' bluff — have the Republican senators move to support Kenneally's bill. If the bill passed, the Democrats would have to take the blame for increasing income taxes. From the Senate visitor's gallery, Tauro watched as Donahue understood their tactic and voted the Democrats' bill down.

On the sixth submission, Volpe tangled with Donahue over one of the state's perennial no-win issues: the "beano bill." As a fund-raising mechanism for parochial schools, bingo (with its variants "beano" and "blitz") was then both illegal and immensely popular. Donahue's mother was reputedly an avid beano player and favored legalization. Most of the legislators and the lobbyists on Beacon Hill assumed that Volpe, as a prominent Catholic layman, would support the beano bill, but they were wrong. Although he had been careful not to go on record on the issue, he did not want to legalize the games. Several studies linked organized crime to the professionals who actually operated the games in other states. This, combined with the fact that the operators often took as much as 70 to 80 percent of the profits, had convinced Volpe that he should not sign a bill legalizing the game. But neither did he want to go on record as having vetoed it in an election year. At the last minute, Volpe made an exception to his usual methods, called in some debts in the Senate, and defeated beano. Donahue retaliated by killing the sales tax for the sixth time.

For the seventh submission, Volpe himself came up with the idea of a new presentation. From the first discussions, the most telling argument against the sales tax had been that it fell most heavily on the poor, who had to spend a greater proportion of their income than the rich. The bill now exempted food, clothing, rent, and medicine. Volpe decided to help low-income families further with a rebate. For any family with an income under $5,000 a year, the family would receive a $7 rebate for each parent, with an $8 rebate for each child. Using charts showing a typical poor family's budget for rent, food, and clothing, Volpe explained at press conferences that a low-income family would get back almost all the money it paid on the sales tax if the family had three children. With four children, the tax would cost them nothing at all.

Volpe signed the sales tax bill into law on March 2, 1966, in Gardner Auditorium beneath the State House in front of three hundred guests, press, and television. "Volpe has a lot of courage," a lobbyist remarked. "If I were governor, I'd sign any tax bill in a closet."[11] Senator Kenneally wore a black suit to the ceremony, explaining to the press that he was going to a "funeral" because "the people are going to be saddled with an unfair, inequitable, and inefficient tax bill."[12] It did not take a very astute observer to read the subtext of Kenneally's comment: The political funeral he was attending was the governor's.

In January, Volpe had started working out implementation plans for the new tax with the commissioner of corporations and taxation. Normally, after the signing of such a bill, setting the mechanism in place to collect revenue would take from three to four months, but the state was actually collecting the new sales tax by April 1. By starting the process early, Volpe guaranteed that the cities and towns would be receiving extra revenue in September, well before the election. As soon as the sales tax was enacted, a labor coalition began the process of getting signatures for a referendum to defeat it at the polls. Again, Volpe had asked Richardson to take charge of a speakers bureau to campaign for the tax. In November, the referendum was defeated by more than two to one.

When Volpe formally announced his candidacy for reelection in April, he seemed unstoppable. The sales tax had become a plus, contrary to all normal political logic. Highway opponents were still scattered and lacking real political clout. Volpe also had managed to neutralize the death penalty issue, which had damaged Peabody, by declaring a month after his second inauguration that he would sign death warrants if the facts in each case were indisputable. From a moral standpoint, Volpe saw nothing inconsistent with his Church's teaching in his position. But neither was he convinced, as the hard-liners were, that capital punishment was a deterrent. He hoped that ultimately the issue would be resolved directly by the electorate.

Yet the electorate was divided. There had not been an execution in Massachusetts since 1947, and since then, five governors had declined to send any convicted prisoners to the electric chair. Polls generally showed a slight majority in favor, but the figures changed dramatically in relation to public fear of crime.

Tauro's strategy to disarm the death penalty had been to delay and postpone, hoping that eventually the problem would be handled by court action, referendum, or legislative reform. When appeals were exhausted, the condemned man was granted a ninety-day "respite" and his case restudied. Tauro's legal assistant James O'Leary negotiated delays and reprieves with the Governor's Council. This was a difficult juggling act; often it seemed that no sooner had one respite been granted than another case came up. By early 1966, there were eight men on death row, but in the end, Volpe was able to finish his fourth campaign for the governorship without having had to wield the state's ultimate power.

At its inception, Volpe's campaign strategy seemed unbeatable. His personal popularity was high, not only within Massachusetts but nationally within the Republican party. His route to power on the national level was the same one that had taken him to leadership in the state organization. He had done the work, served on the necessary committees, raised money, and asked nothing in return until he was certain he would make his move. Just before the 1962 election, he had been advised by the top Republican leadership to win big, for there might be a place for him on the national ticket in 1964. Now that dream, once dead, seemed alive again. Volpe did not envision himself competing with men like Nelson Rockefeller, Richard Nixon, George Romney, or Charles Percy for the presidential nomination, but possibly getting the nod for vice president if he picked the right candidate to support early on.

In the series of Lincoln Day speeches he made in February 1966, Volpe laid out his prescription for victory for the party and his own credentials as well. "Over the years," Volpe told the Summit County Republicans in Ohio, "we excluded the minority groups who were, in fact, the very life blood of our party." Now things had changed. "As the son of Italian immigrants, a one-time card-carrying plasterer, I have been honored by the Republican party in many instances, state and national, and I know that my counterpart exists within our party in many states throughout the nation."[13]

Of Volpe's possible opponents in the 1966 election, only two appeared to be serious contenders: Edward J. McCormack and Kenneth O'Donnell. Maurice Donahue had toyed with the idea of running for governor but chose to stay in his secure power base within the Senate. O'Donnell in early 1966 was almost an unknown but had a strong background as one of John F. Kennedy's closest aides. Like the rest of the Kennedy team, he had already proven himself a capable speaker and organizer. Eddie McCormack, a former attorney general, was the nephew of U.S. House Speaker John W. McCormack.

In the earliest days of the 1966 race, the Republican party's biggest problem was the office of attorney general, left vacant by Brooke in his quest for the Senate. In Republican hands, this office had become a powerful weapon against the Democratic establishment. Under Brooke's direction, the most devastating indictments based on material unearthed by the crime commission had become public just before the 1964 election. The job had enjoyed high visibility during the Boston Strangler panic, and Brooke also had taken an active role in prosecuting organized crime figures. One by one, the Republican leaders interested in running for attorney general bowed out. Blocked from the Senate by Brooke and Kennedy, Richardson had been aiming for the governorship. If Volpe were to win the vice presidential nomination in 1968 or were appointed to the cabinet, Richardson, as lieutenant governor, could step into his place without running. To move down to attorney general would mean a considerable sacrifice. Yet Richardson chose to put party ambitions above his own and in January agreed to step down and enter the race for attorney general.

Waiting in the wings was DPW Chairman Frank Sargent. Although he was not close to the Volpe inner circle, Sargent's position was strong. Sargent had a solid reputation as an environmentalist, to help balance Volpe's image as a friend of the construction industry. Sargent had not come up through the legislature and presumably owed few favors to the established system. And, like Leverett Saltonstall before him, he seemed both impeccably Brahmin and charmingly folksy at the same time.

By April, the Republican ticket was set, and it looked like a sure winner. At the top, in the middle of the civil rights movement, Brooke was hoping to be the first black man elected to the Senate since Reconstruction. An Italian-American and a Yankee rounded out the ticket nicely. But less than a month later, an accidental discovery in a hearing room at the State House set up the first charges of corruption that Volpe had ever faced in one of his own administrations.

Almost since the beginning of Volpe's second administration, his administration commissioner, John J. McCarthy, had shown a talent for making headlines in the newspapers and enemies in the State House. McCarthy had never held elective office, and he set out to increase the productivity of civil servants as if they could be hired or fired at will. Through the eyes of the media, he appeared — especially in comparison with most state administrators — to be a flamboyant, shoot-from-the-hip operator as he pursued one state agency after another in his quest for efficiency. His demands that state employees work as productively as those of the private sector did not endear him to the Beacon Hill regulars. In May, the Senate established a special committee to investigate McCarthy's setting of hospital rates. While aiming for the broad target of Commissioner McCarthy, the Senate investigators stumbled on the potentially more interesting fact that Peter Volpe had apparently been advising McCarthy's office about the qualifications of architects seeking state work.

Peter Volpe was then president of the Volpe Company, but the governor was still a director and the major shareholder. At that time, state construction contracts were awarded by public, competitive bidding, but architects' work was not. The obscure Senate hearings quickly blew up into a media circus. On May 21, in the glare of television lights, the investigators called a surprise witness, an architect who testified that he had gone to the Volpe Company's Malden office, talked with Peter about contracts in the budget, and given him a $1,000 check for a testimonial dinner for the governor — a dinner that had already taken place. Peter Volpe, in the same afternoon, had testified that he had, on an informal basis, passed on some advice about the competence of architects being considered to design the new state medical school but that he had never taken any contributions from an architect in the Malden office. Patrick Volpe was the treasurer for the testimonial dinner and collected the funds, not Peter. As soon as the day's hearings were over, the governor went on the attack with the press, condemning the hearings as politically motivated and comparing his advisory relationship with Peter to that of John and Robert Kennedy and Dwight and Milton Eisenhower.

Since his first race for the governorship, Volpe had worried about the possibility of hurting his family. His brothers had helped him in politics out of love and loyalty but often found his driving ambition hard to comprehend. From childhood, Peter and John had had markedly different temperaments. Peter was genial, somewhat reserved, soft-spoken, and deliberate. His own ambitions centered on his home and family, his

149

business, and the Associated General Contractors. While the governor built his mansion in Winchester, Peter was content to stay in a modest garrison colonial house, where he spent his spare time in a basement workshop or tinkering with his collection of antique cars. While John was making speeches, Peter was minding the store. Now Peter was forced into the limelight, and there was little his older brother could do to keep him out of the headlines.

For the average Massachusetts politician, the architect's contribution scandal would have been a minor event, worth one day's headlines and then forgotten. But Volpe had made his name campaigning against corruption. His strategy had been to belabor the legislature and "business as usual on Beacon Hill" in his campaigns, trying nonetheless not to overstep the line beyond which the legislature might later retaliate by killing his bills. A June 1966 poll by Opinion Research Corporation showed a sudden decline of ten points in Volpe's favorability rating, while his unfavorability rating rose twelve points. Fifteen percent of the poll's respondents mentioned hearing rumors about Volpe, and all of these related to the state Senate investigation. "Largely, the Governor's image problem is one of a diminishing of favorable characteristics rather than an accumulation of unfavorable ones," the authors concluded.[14]

The June poll showed that Volpe was much better known than either of his two possible Democratic opponents. But in trial heats, he and McCormack were running neck and neck, and McCormack was more likely than O'Donnell to benefit from the exposure guaranteed by the Democratic primary contest. Although the news media portrayed Volpe as a sure winner, the poll data showed that, at the start of the campaign season, victory was far from certain. Volpe and Tauro studied the poll results carefully. Once before the media had declared him a sure winner, and the voters had decided otherwise. He planned to run again as hard as before, no matter what the numbers told him.

The 1966 campaign turned up no compelling issues, no more scandals, and little drama. The architect's contribution issue disappeared as quickly as it had come. In late summer, the Democrats in the legislature made political capital of the state's participation in the new federal Medicaid program. When the program began, states could opt to exclude the "working poor" from the system. Richardson's office studied the issue and concluded that the state did not have the funds or the systems in place to handle the more inclusive Medicaid plan. Richardson recommended entering the program in stages — first covering welfare recipients, then other low-income families. This appeared to be a fiscally sound decision but did not prove to be politically palatable.

150

The legislative leadership seized on the fact that about 161,000 children of low-income families in Boston, Springfield, and Worcester would be excluded during the first year. A millionaire Republican governor was standing between needy children and federal aid! In late August, Volpe agreed to the more inclusive plan. As Richardson had predicted, however, by 1968 the state ran into massive funding problems trying to meet the sudden demand for medical care with the few doctors who were willing to take Medicaid patients in core city neighborhoods. The crisis did not begin to subside until new neighborhood health centers could be built in the early 1970s.

At the end of the 1966 legislative session, Volpe aimed a counterstroke at the legislature when Donahue held up proposals to reorganize the Department of Mental Health and establish twenty-seven clinics across the state. In the press, Volpe belabored the Democrats for failing to help thousands of mental patients and threatened to bring the legislature into special emergency session after the election — whether he won or not — until the bill passed. True to his word, Volpe did reconvene the legislature between sessions and succeeded in getting the funding for his community clinics.

Kenneth O'Donnell ran a hard campaign but had virtually no political base within Massachusetts. In the September primary, McCormack defeated him easily. Frank Bellotti received the nomination for attorney general. Both Hubert Humphrey and Robert Kennedy campaigned for McCormack. Volpe's organization passed the word back to Republican party officials that a proffered visit from Nixon would not be helpful. On October 17, Volpe debated McCormack in a synagogue in Worcester, but no new issues came to the fore.

Although his 1966 campaign was better financed than the 1964 race, Volpe took no chances, continuing with his shoe-leather effort, touring manufacturing plants, shops, and streets with his Polaroid. Now he traveled in a camper equipped with a stove, refrigerator, telephone, and conference table that made into a bed. At the end of the day, the candidate could put on his pajamas and catch an extra hour or two of sleep on the way home from the last stop.

By mid-October, Volpe was running ahead again in the polls, but the size of the November victory surprised even his own supporters. As the results came in from the more prosperous wards of South Dorchester, Jamaica Plain, West Roxbury, and Hyde Park, Volpe became the first Republican to carry the city of Boston in more than forty years — despite the fact that his opponent was a city resident.

The final figures gave Volpe a record-breaking plurality of 524,683 votes, enough to put him well into the forefront of the Republican party. In a state that had nearly twice as many Democrats as Republicans, he had received more than 63 percent of the vote, a better showing than George Romney of Michigan (62 percent), Nelson Rockefeller of New York (45 percent), or Ronald Reagan of California (58 percent). On the morning of November 9, he took off again for his postelection helicopter tour. The time for dreaming, for talking with his closest supporters about the "what ifs," and for speculating was gone. Volpe was fifty-eight years old. He now had a convincing electoral victory and a mandate to bring about reform within his state. If he chose to go for the long shot at the vice presidency or even the presidency, this was the time to begin.

NOTES

1. Alan Lupo, *Liberty's Chosen Home* (Boston: Houghton Mifflin, 1978), p. 143.

2. Theodore H. White, *In Search of History* (New York: Warner Books, 1979), p. 30.

3. Lupo, *Liberty's Chosen Home,* p. 151.

4. Massachusetts State Board of Education, *Interim Report of the Advisory Committee on Racial Imbalance and Education,* 1 July 1964.

5. *The Boston Globe,* 5 May 1965.

6. *The Boston Globe,* 12 August 1965.

7. *The Boston Globe,* 25 July 1965.

8. U.S. Congress, House, *Needs of the National Highway Systems 1955–1984,* 84th Cong., 1955, H. Doc. 120.

9. Alan Lupo, Frank Colcord, and Edmund P. Fowler, *Rites of Way* (Boston: Little, Brown and Company, 1971), p. 16.

10. John Henry Cutler, *Ed Brooke: Biography of a Senator* (Indianapolis: Bobbs-Merrill Co., 1972), p. 156.

11. *The Boston Globe,* 3 March 1966.

12. *The Boston Traveler,* 3 March 1966.

13. *The Boston Globe,* 22 February 1966.

14. Opinion Research Corporation Survey, June 1966, unpublished.

CHAPTER X

Favorite Son

I N THE DAYS FOLLOWING the 1966 election, as Volpe, Barry Locke, and Joe Tauro looked at the national scene, the long shot seemed a better and better possibility. The Republican party had rebounded somewhat from the Goldwater disaster, picking up forty-seven seats in the House of Representatives and three in the Senate. The extreme conservatives who would never support Volpe had been discredited, but the leadership of the moderate and liberal wings was in dispute. Volpe decided to wait until the picture became clearer.

Two weeks after the election, the Volpes were on a hastily organized trip to Italy on a rescue mission. Heavy rains had swollen the Arno River, sending floodwaters sweeping through the center of Florence just as winter was setting in. Bringing donations collected throughout New England, the Volpes toured the stricken city and the surrounding countryside for five days and sent back a series of articles for the *Boston Globe.*

Joe Tauro and his wife accompanied the Volpes through the flooded city. The first morning of the trip, Tauro was awakened early by their guide. The governor had asked if he would go to a private Mass. Tauro usually did not attend services with his boss, but this time he agreed. In the gray dawn, Tauro found himself in a tiny, medieval chapel, kneeling on the cold stone floor beside Volpe while an elderly priest said the Mass in Italian. The three men were alone in the silence of the stricken city. Tauro later recalled the stillness of the moment. The pressure and details of the last campaign seemed to drain away, and he felt only a strong bond to the man beside him. They seemed, for that moment, brothers. Tauro knew he would follow this man wherever the journey took them.

But Tauro had come to Italy for more mundane reasons as well. In the suitcase-size briefcases Volpe carried on business trips were the management survey team reports on the operation of all state agencies, Tauro's rough drafts of Volpe's next inauguration speech, and outlines of legislation he intended to file in 1967. If Volpe were to have the freedom to pursue national ambitions as well as get his legislative package passed, there must be peace at home. The tone of the inaugural speech would be conciliatory.

Volpe's relations with the legislature had been changed considerably by the outcome of a referendum granting the governor new powers of executive reorganization. Under the new powers, a governor could propose reorganization of any executive department in the legislature. Either branch could then veto proposals but not amend them. If the legislature took no action in sixty days, the plan automatically became law.

Although Republicans were still heavily outnumbered in both Massachusetts houses (170 to 69 in the House and 26 to 14 in the Senate), a slight Republican increase in the Senate now enabled Republicans to sustain the gubernatorial veto. There also was a new face in the Democratic legislative leadership, House Majority Leader Robert Quinn, a low-key team player and moderate Democrat from the conservative blue-collar Savin Hill section of Dorchester. Quinn would replace Davoren, ending the strained Davoren-Donahue relationship that had often split the Democratic majority.

Just before Christmas, 1966, Volpe suffered a pinched nerve and was forced to go about his official business in an orthopedic collar. By inauguration day, January 4, he was well enough to offer his olive branch to the legislature. The inaugural address was peppered with references to "our joint responsibility," "cooperative spirit," and "working together." Volpe's speech did not even mention new proposals to cut the size of the House, and gone were references to the state sales tax and mental health reorganization battles of the recent past. Even the new reorganization plans were downplayed. He would, he told the legislators, seek support from both parties before submitting reorganization proposals. Now that he had the power to push through his long-awaited reorganization plans, there was no need to be heavy-handed.

The conciliatory strategy was, by and large, successful. On February

10, Volpe signed a bill raising the base pay of the 280 legislators from $5,200 to $10,000 per year.[1] In 1965, he had vetoed a similar raise and had the veto overridden. Five days after the pay raise signing, Volpe was able to abandon the orthopedic collar and set off on a speaking tour of New Jersey, New York, and northern Ohio, all areas with heavy concentrations of Italian-American voters. He praised front-runners Richard Nixon and George Romney of Michigan, telling reporters that he was considering going to the Republican National Convention as a "favorite son" and telling audiences that he had won big as a Republican in "Kennedy land" and could do it again on a national scale.

But Volpe did not abandon the corner office. In early March, he plunged into a controversy over auto insurance rates. In the late 1960s, Massachusetts car owners were paying the highest insurance premiums in the country, almost twice as high as those in New York. Rates were set by the state, according to the number of accidents and thefts in each district. In Boston's low-income neighborhoods of Roxbury, Mattapan, Dorchester, and the South End, drivers were paying first-year premiums of nearly half the value of a new car.

Volpe approached the auto insurance problem by proposing changes in the system of compulsory insurance sold by private companies at the rates set by the insurance commission. Although the car-owning public was demanding change, the insurance industry lobby was well entrenched in the legislature, where lawmakers often either sold insurance themselves or made part of their income as lawyers from auto insurance cases. Volpe's plan proposed the repeal of the compulsory system and the substitution of a claims fund to which each uninsured driver would contribute $50 annually, as well as the creation of a well-funded fraudulent claims bureau to track down and prosecute drivers filing phony damage claims. The most controversial part of the Volpe proposal was free competition in rates. Legislation was filed, and hearings were held, but resistance within the legislature was massive, and momentum on the plan was lost. Leadership on the auto insurance issue fell to a young Brookline liberal Democratic representative named Michael Dukakis.

An issue much harder to let go was the death penalty. During his second term, adroit legal maneuvering had enabled Volpe to avoid having a death warrant on his desk. But eventually, all appeals would be exhausted for one of the men on death row in Walpole; it was only a question of time. The electorate seemed to have no clear consensus except in times of panic such as the Boston Strangler era. And the statistics gave Volpe no clear verdict on whether capital punishment really deterred crime. Rhode

Island, which had abolished capital punishment in 1852, had homicide rates almost identical to those in Massachusetts for the 114 years during which one state punished by execution and the other did not.

In April 1967, Volpe threw the question back to the legislature, asking for a special study commission to determine whether the death penalty was a deterrent. The study commission bill was killed in the House by nine votes, as the alleged Boston Strangler had picked that week to escape from the state's hospital for the criminally insane at Bridgewater. The proposal was refiled with some changes, among them a one-year moratorium on the use of the electric chair, only to be rejected by seventy-eight votes.[2] By August, Volpe drove his staff to use every weapon in the executive arsenal and finally secured passage. A referendum on the issue was planned for 1969, and Volpe hoped that this time the electorate would give a clear verdict.

As Volpe and Tauro looked at the national Republican scene in early 1967, the picture that emerged was confusing, the candidates tentative. With Goldwater discredited, party chiefs looked to the moderate/liberal wing. The 1964 debacle had cut through the lower ranks of the Republican party as well as the national ticket, and in 1965 Congress had its greatest Democratic majority since 1936. Of the fifty states, only seventeen had elected Republican governors in 1964. New York City's young mayor John V. Lindsay had shone as a possible national leader of the liberal wing, but his advance into state or national office had been blocked by three other New York liberals: Jacob Javits and Robert Kennedy in the Senate and Governor Nelson Rockefeller in Albany. The 1966 elections had given the Republicans a comeback and brought another potential national leader to prominence when Charles Percy won an upset victory for a Senate seat in Illinois. But like Lindsay, Percy found his way blocked within his state by more senior political figures, among them senior senator Everett Dirksen. California Governor Ronald Reagan also entertained presidential hopes in 1966 and early 1967, but Goldwater's defeat had temporarily demoralized the right wing of the party where Reagan's greatest political strength lay.

In the months that followed Volpe's third gubernatorial victory, the national front-runner seemed to be Governor George Romney of Michigan. Handsome, deeply religious, sincere, and somewhat humorless, Romney had gained considerable support at the 1966 December National Governors' Conference, held at the Greenbriar resort in West Virginia, when he unofficially announced his candidacy at a private breakfast meeting. Governors Love of Colorado, Chafee of Rhode Island, Rockefeller of New York, and (initially) Bellmon of Oklahoma were among Romney's earliest supporters.

At the Greenbriar conference, Volpe too expressed admiration for Romney but still felt closer to the possible candidacies of Nixon and Rockefeller, men he knew better on a personal level. Although a "dark horse" theory of his own candidacy was being spread around, Volpe was under no illusions that he could successfully compete with either Nixon or Rockefeller for the presidential nomination. He lacked their national standing and their experience in foreign policy, an area that was becoming increasingly important as the Vietnam War escalated. Instead, Volpe saw the vice presidency as a possible final accolade to his career, honoring the Italian-American community in the same way that John F. Kennedy's election had honored the Irish. He also saw the race as an opportunity to prove his loyalty to the party leadership and provide unity at a time of increasing dissension — giving the next Republican president a loyal second in command instead of a potential rival.

Volpe was not the only Republican governor interested in a possible vice presidential role. At the National Republican Governors' Conference in Colorado Springs the week before the Greenbriar conference, both John Chafee of Rhode Island and John Love of Colorado had gone all out to win the largely symbolic chairmanship. Love had won the job, some headlines, and talk about his vice presidential chances. Volpe had stuck to the unglamorous job of working within the organization in Massachusetts and building alliances. Although Joe Tauro and Barry Locke were actively promoting the race for the national ticket, Volpe himself was still concentrating on the goals he had set himself to achieve as governor. The vice presidency seemed like a very long shot, almost a fantasy, while the briefcases he took home every night were real, the business of running the state pressing on his attention every day.

The presidential race was barely a year away, but Lyndon Johnson was still in office, and the increased federal government spending on the War on Poverty necessitated more and more contact between federal and state administrations. Although the two men were opposed in their philosophies of government, Johnson and Volpe developed a mutual respect and a warm personal relationship, and Volpe found himself more often a guest at White House social functions during the Johnson years than he had been in the Eisenhower administration. After one state dinner, Johnson and the Volpes met at the door as the party was breaking up. Johnson bent down to have a word with Jennie: "Mrs. Volpe, I want you to know that John never knocks my block off just because I'm a Democrat. He may be criticizing me sometime next year, at election time, but he won't be antagonistic. I hope we could all act like that," he added, thoughtfully. "I would hope that for three years out of four, we could act like Americans, rather than Republicans or Democrats."

Johnson also appreciated Volpe's restraint on the issue of Vietnam. Antiwar sentiment was strong in Massachusetts, and the state was producing leaders of the still-amorphous "movement" from within the universities, private schools, and liberal religious denominations such as the Quakers and Unitarians. Volpe declined to take the State Department–sponsored tour of South Vietnam that was becoming de rigeur for politicians with national aspirations. He doubted he would really learn anything from an official trip through a country about whose language, culture, and history he knew nothing, a journey in which he would see only what his guides wanted him to see. But Volpe did make many unpublicized visits to men in local hospitals who had been wounded in Vietnam. He was disturbed to see that the men were so young, almost children. When he had served in the Navy, he had been an established businessman with a family of his own. The average age of the men serving in Vietnam was nineteen. The war seemed a terrible thing. Yet to Volpe it seemed more terrible still to undermine the president, to create dissension within the country when the nation was at war.

By April 1967, Volpe's personal relationship with Johnson had grown to the point that the president, breaking party precedent, invited him to serve on the Advisory Commission on Intergovernmental Relations, a committee created to level the bureaucratic roadblocks that impeded the flow of federal funds into state programs. The commission dealt with one of Volpe's greatest concerns: his fears that state machinery could not handle the influx of federal dollars and the enormous demands those dollars created in terms of reporting and accountability at the local level.

With the War on Poverty in full swing, the state was shifting gears into providing intangibles never even envisioned ten years before: legal aid, storefront and street corner social work, rent subsidies. Creating systems to ensure honest contracting for macadam and bricks during his DPW days had been difficult but not beyond Volpe's personal experience. Creating fiscal accountability in the human services was a new challenge, not only to Volpe but to government as a whole. Volpe accepted Johnson's invitation to serve in the unpaid commission position and then discovered that a state constitutional amendment provided that a governor who accepted a federal appointment automatically was forced to resign. Federal law, however, provided him with an out. Federal appointments do not become legal until accepted in writing, and Volpe had accepted only orally.

Volpe's run of bad luck was not quite over. In March, Barry Locke's office produced a short biographical pamphlet for Volpe, which the legislative leaders pounced on as a government-sponsored campaign document. And then came the hair color joke. During one of their briefing sessions before a press conference, Les Ainley mentioned to Volpe that a reporter might bring up the color of his hair, now that he was competing for national office against younger men. Although he was fifty-eight years old, Volpe's hair was still thick and, instead of graying, had darkened with age. "Someone might ask you if you color your hair," Ainley mentioned. Volpe bristled; it was none of their business! Then, searching for a possible comeback, he remembered what Italian men of his father's generation had used to slick back their hair. Not long after Ainley's warning, a reporter asked why, over the years, as the reporter's hair had turned white, the governor's had darkened.

"You don't use olive oil," Volpe retorted. Pencils froze, and a hush fell over the pressroom. The reporters began to laugh. How much oil? Taken internally? "Oh, about a teaspoonful," Volpe guessed.

In the corner office, the staff laughed about olive oil, thinking the joke would wear thin in a few days. But people remembered. Years later, when he was in retirement, a guest approached him after a Sons of Italy fund-raiser and asked whether he still used olive oil. "No," he replied, touching his now gray hair. "You know how the price has gone up."

Throughout 1967, Volpe turned his attention to the auto insurance program, civil service reform, plans for overhauling the state's welfare system, and the simmering Inner Belt–Southwest Corridor controversy. After Sargent left the chairmanship of the DPW to become lieutenant governor, Volpe had appointed Colonel Edward Ribbs to replace him. Ribbs, a veteran of the Army Corps of Engineers, was a man of unquestioned integrity, had great technical skill, and was an administrator of the "can do" school. But he was politically inexperienced, and the highway issue was rapidly becoming dominated by political concerns. In dealing with labor problems, technical difficulties, hard terrain, and weather, Ribbs was outstanding. But angry picketers lying in front of bulldozers were beyond his expertise. His problems were compounded by open opposition from Boston Mayor Kevin White and the Boston Redevelopment Authority. Ribbs was building a highway through a city whose officials seemed dedicated to throwing every possible obstacle in his way.

Volpe involved himself more and more in the legislative process as the confrontations continued. Gradually, opponents came to a consensus that *no* highway should be built — not simply that plans should be altered. The possibility of compromise vanished. Volpe persisted, however, directing Ribbs to go ahead with land-takings. The DPW cut a swathe through the housing stock of Jamaica Plain and the black community of Roxbury. The activists mobilized, demonstrated, and complained, but they could not stop the wrecking crews. Black frustration expressed itself in other ways. In June, a sit-in by welfare mothers demanding increased benefits triggered violent protests in the Grove Hall section of Roxbury. But the black community's anger focused primarily on the mayor and, increasingly, the school committee, not the state.

At the National Republican Governors' Conference in late June, Volpe's campaign began to be taken more seriously by the national leadership. At the conference, Nixon sent law partner John Sears and another top advisor to sound out Volpe. Sears hinted, at a meeting with Volpe and Tauro, that Volpe was seriously being considered for the vice presidential nomination. Sears asked only that Volpe hold off on making a commitment. Tauro wanted to plunge ahead and endorse Nixon, arguing that they had nothing to lose. Still, Volpe was not certain; he admired Nelson Rockefeller and thought he would make a good candidate. On a terrace after breakfast, with the national political reporters present, Volpe gave a short talk about not ruling out Nixon, despite his defeat in California, and giving Nixon his warm encouragement, if not his open support.

By July, Romney seemed to be in front. Chafee of Rhode Island, the only other Republican governor in New England, was openly supporting Romney, and Volpe was considering entering the New Hampshire primary himself. His work on the national political circuit was beginning to pay off. "Republican governors respect him for his ability to win in a predominantly Democratic state, the home of John Kennedy," Robert Healy, the *Boston Globe's* political editor, wrote in mid-July.[3]

The next test of Volpe's political strength came in October 1967 aboard the USS *Independence*. The fall National Governors' Conference took place aboard the last of the American luxury liners en route to the Virgin Islands. The chairmanship of the conference alternated between Republicans and Democrats, and this was a Republican year. As soon as the announcement of the conference's location was made, Volpe received a call from Boston businessman Max Wasserman, who owned a hotel on Sapphire Bay in the Virgin Islands. Wasserman offered to give a luncheon at the hotel so that the conferees could enjoy a swim and a break from the routine aboard ship.

As the ship sailed from New York on October 16, John Love, who had been vice chairman the previous year and was still chairman of the

Republican Governors' Association, let it be known that he wanted the conference chairmanship and was seriously interested in the vice presidential race. Daniel Evans of Washington also expressed an interest in the chairmanship.

At the start of the voyage, Volpe was more concerned about whom he should support for the presidency than with a possible battle over the chairmanship. He was still leaning toward supporting Nixon, but he wanted to make certain that Rockefeller really was not going to run. As Volpe jogged around the promenade deck on the voyage down (Rockefeller's stateroom was on the more desirable upper deck facing outside), the two men would meet and talk. Volpe pressed him. Are you sure you won't run? But Rockefeller's pride had been hurt by the jeers of the Goldwater delegates in 1964 and by the brutal publicity surrounding his divorce and remarriage in 1962. He would sit this one out.

Usually the election of a conference chair was a routine formality, but as the ship headed for St. Thomas, the proceedings began to turn into a political test of strength. While Volpe attended committee meetings, Tauro and Locke had picked up a ground swell of support to challenge Love and were contacting the other governors' aides. At the first Republican caucus, the governors split evenly, eleven to eleven, between Volpe and Love. Governor Raymond Shafer of Pennsylvania was absent but had sent a proxy vote for Volpe. Love let it be known that he might challenge the proxy. Undeterred, Tauro and Locke looked for support among the Democratic governors and found some help from, among others, John Bailey, chairman of the Democratic National Committee and father of Tauro's wife's Trinity College classmate, Congresswoman Barbara Bailey. The Sapphire Bay luncheon party, planned long before the start of the voyage, suddenly assumed a political significance, though Volpe himself did not talk about the upcoming vote at all. About twenty governors attended the luncheon, while their staffs worked aboard ship.

The next day, Love decided not to object to the proxy, and Volpe was elected chairman of the conference by acclamation. At the press conference following the vote, Volpe declared himself "quite likely" a favorite son candidate in the Massachusetts presidential primary in April. He still had not made up his mind, either publicly or privately, about New Hampshire. In the unsettled atmosphere of the 1968 campaign, favorite sons could wield more power than was usually the case. Rockefeller was still thought to be interested, and the moderate wing of the party was splitting between Nixon and Romney. Favorite sons Volpe, James Rhodes of Ohio, Spiro Agnew of Maryland, Raymond Shafer of Pennsylvania, and Claude

Kirk of Florida could play a decisive role in a deadlock situation. The possibilities for these governors looked promising, yet at the same time other, disturbing forces showed themselves. The Democratic governors voted to take a position supporting President Johnson's efforts in Vietnam; the Republicans held back. In addition to the usual sessions on revenue sharing and fiscal responsibility, the governors discussed mobilization tactics, response time, and riot training for the National Guard. The war was beginning to come home.

In the months following the Virgin Islands conference, Romney faded from his place as front-runner. Although he was a personable and efficient administrator, his relations with the national press were poor from the start. One reporter following him on the campaign trail confessed later that he liked the man but that he had come away with an empty steno pad. In public, Romney had given the same speech, word for word, every day, and in the private give-and-take in hotel rooms and cars, he was pleasant but said nothing remotely interesting. Romney's Mormon convictions seemed to the press sincere yet baffling. A billboard for the New Hampshire primary read: "The way to stop crime is to stop moral decay." What did that mean?

Romney's worst blunder came as a result of his sincerity. On national television, he confessed that "when I came back from Vietnam, I just had the greatest brainwashing that anybody can get when you go over there." Years later, when the weakness of the South Vietnamese democracy and the extent of the American cover-up lay exposed, his words rang true. At the time, however, they seemed a confession of his own weakness. His standing in the polls slipped from the fall of 1967 on, and Nixon's percentage grew.

Early in January 1968, Volpe received a call from former Oklahoma Governor Henry Bellmon, then Nixon's campaign manager. Bellmon came to the point quickly, asking for Volpe's endorsement. Volpe would promise nothing but indicated that he was favorably inclined. A month later, Nixon visited Volpe in the corner office, and the two men talked for nearly an hour while the press outside waited. After the meeting, Nixon told the reporters that Volpe was one of the four or five men being considered as his possible running mate.

Two weeks later, Volpe met with Nixon at his New York apartment and offered his endorsement. Again Nixon brought up the vice presidency. Volpe mentioned that he himself would be sixty years old one month after the 1968 election. If Nixon served two terms, Volpe as vice president would then be considered too old to run for president. Nixon would not have to worry that his second in command was pursuing ambitions of his own during his terms. Nixon nodded, conceding that was a point he had not thought of before. Then he introduced Volpe to the campaign manager who had succeeded Bellmon: John Mitchell.

At the start of 1968, the Nixon campaign was gaining the most prized political quality: momentum. His two key themes, law and order at home and peace with honor in Vietnam, struck a responsive chord as he hammered away at Johnson's troubles in the inner cities of America and the villages of Southeast Asia. But within the Republican party, support for Rockefeller was still strong. In February, Rockefeller was supporting Romney, but the Michigan governor slipped inexorably in the polls. Seeing that victory in New Hampshire was impossible, Romney dropped out at the end of February. Yet Rockefeller did not throw his support behind another candidate. Although still publicly out of the race, Rockefeller hinted in private that he might be moved to reconsider. He held long discussions with friends and supporters in his apartment in New York, asking them whether this race was his duty and whether it was appropriate that a millionaire should be president. While Nixon pushed on with his well-financed and well-organized campaign, Rockefeller seemed to be asking himself the kinds of questions that might have been appropriate two years before.

Among those who believed that Rockefeller would reenter the race was Ed Brooke. In January, Brooke and Volpe disagreed on the composition of the thirty-four-member delegate slate to be elected in the April 30 Massachusetts primary. Technically, any Republican with five hundred signatures could run as a district delegate to the national convention; in reality, both district and at-large delegates were picked by the party leadership. Brooke fought to get delegates who might break away from loyalty to the state's favorite son and be prepared to vote for Rockefeller, if the opportunity came. Although publicly Brooke was supporting Volpe's candidacy, he also was contacting liberal Republicans across the state on a possible "Draft Rockefeller" campaign.

In early February, Volpe was still considering the possibility of entering the New Hampshire presidential primary, then decided against it. But the New Hampshire popularity polls were both surprising and encouraging. Forty-three percent of the New Hampshire voters polled agreed that Volpe would make an excellent vice presidential candidate, with only 29 percent disagreeing.[4]

Just before the New Hampshire primary in March, Rockefeller issued another withdrawal statement, this time so suddenly that many of his supporters were taken unawares. Governor Spiro Agnew of Maryland, the chairman of his state's "Draft Rockefeller" committee, was one of those who got the news first from the media. Agnew promptly gave his allegiance to Nixon. While Rockefeller's supporters had waited and wondered, Nixon's workers had been methodically implementing a well-thought-out strategy town by town, precinct by precinct. His victory in New Hampshire placed Nixon far ahead. Now it was the Democratic picture that became unclear.

Throughout the early jockeying for position within the Republican party, the opponent was always presumed to be Johnson. But the antiwar movement had fielded its own candidate, Senator Eugene McCarthy of Minnesota. In addition to the usual block leaders and neighborhood association officers, suddenly thousands of college student volunteers — exhorted to cut off their beards and flowing hair to "come clean for Gene" — were tramping through the snow, ringing doorbells in old mill towns, handing out literature in front of discount stores, showing slides in church basements. Although McCarthy did not win the New Hampshire primary, his vote was impressive in a conservative state. McCarthy was a single-issue candidate, and a profound change had taken place since late January, when American television viewers had watched U.S. Army regulars fighting the Vietcong on the grounds of the U.S. embassy during the Tet Offensive.

On March 31, President Lyndon Johnson appeared on national television to announce that he would not seek reelection. Democratic party regulars were stunned, and the race was now suddenly, bewilderingly open. In Massachusetts, the antiwar movement picked up more and more support. On April 4, more than ten thousand people marched from Faneuil Hall, Cambridge Common, Boston University, and the University of Massachusetts in Boston to Boston Common. Two hundred young men turned in their draft cards.

On the following day, an even more devastating shock struck the political process and anyone old enough to understand its significance. The black leader who had come to symbolize peaceful revolution, Martin Luther King, Jr., was assassinated in Memphis, Tennessee.

On the day that King died, Volpe was in Japan with Barry Locke on a government-sponsored exchange visit. Every other year, eight or ten American governors would visit Japan, and the next year the same number of governors of Japanese prefectures would visit the United States. When the Japanese governors had visited Massachusetts, they had been to the Volpe home in Winchester for a reception and dinner, and Volpe had gotten to know some of them fairly well. Volpe was visiting Hiroshima at the time of King's death.

Joseph Bosco was a young assistant legal counsel in Volpe's office when the news came that King had died. On the Common outside the State House, crowds began to gather, grieving, talking, many weeping openly. Bosco felt as they did, but he also was fearful. "There was already fear of rioting," he remembered later. "What would happen in Boston?" The governor's staff met with Acting Governor Sargent, discussing what to do about Volpe in Japan. Bosco argued that Volpe should come back, but his was the minority position. Sargent got through to the governor on the phone, assured him that everything was under control, and advised him not to cut short the trip.

Although Boston did not explode into rioting on the scale of the disturbances in Chicago, Detroit, or Washington, D.C., the city was far from peaceful. On Blue Hill Avenue, the center of Mattapan's black business district, and in Grove Hall in Roxbury, bands of youths roamed the streets through the night, smashing windows, stoning cars, and starting fires in abandoned buildings. In the city of Boston, the National Guard was put on alert. Twenty people were injured and fifteen arrested. With help from city officials, youth workers, black leaders, and often ordinary volunteers who came forward spontaneously from within the black community, Roxbury and Mattapan gradually came together. Volpe was criticized in the press for not having returned early to deal with the crisis. Nationally, thirty-nine people died, fifty thousand federal and National Guard troops were called out, and twenty thousand people were arrested in more than a hundred cities.

Massachusetts was lucky: There were no deaths. But confrontations, violent as well as nonviolent, between the black community and the city lasted throughout April. Three weeks after King's assassination, hundreds of protestors pitched makeshift tents in a South End parking lot bordering the site of the Southwest Expressway. Some of the demonstrators had once lived in the block of brownstones that had stood on the muddy ground before the street was cleared for redevelopment on one side and Route 95 on the other. Other protestors were local residents demanding more affordable housing for the poor. All were angry. They blocked cars from entering the lot, called in the news media, and proclaimed the area "Tent City." Although the demonstrators occupied the lot for only a few days, for the next eighteen years, the Tent City lot was to remain empty, a symbol of the failure to replace the neighborhoods being destroyed both by city redevelopment and by the state highway projects.

165

In 1968, the Massachusetts primary, the only presidential contest Volpe was to enter, took place on May 1. Deferring to Volpe's favorite son candidacy, no other Republican presidential candidate had entered his name, although a scattering of write-ins was expected. The *Boston Globe* predicted he would receive 80 percent of the vote. But on the night before the election, Rockefeller scheduled a press conference for the following day, and rumors began to circulate. Was Rockefeller really in or out? Volpe had received a call from the New York governor on the night before he publicly endorsed Nixon. Rockefeller had asked him to wait. Volpe replied that on the basis of Rockefeller's word, he had believed he was not going to run; Volpe could not go back on his pledge to Nixon. There were no calls from Rockefeller on the night before the Massachusetts primary.

With his name the only one printed on the ballot, Volpe had seen no reason to campaign in Massachusetts. But at 11 A.M., three hours after the polls opened, Rockefeller appeared on national television and announced that he *was* a candidate. Unknown to Volpe, Rockefeller supporters, probably led by Brooke, had organized a write-in campaign. When the returns were in, Rockefeller was the clear winner, with nearly 29,000 votes. Volpe was second with 27,000, and the Nixon write-ins totaled 24,000. Eugene McCarthy topped the Democratic ticket with 103,000, nearly double the total of his closest rival, write-in candidate Robert Kennedy.

Twelve hours after the polls closed, Volpe held his weekly press conference on schedule and opened with a brief statement of the results. He smiled ruefully and shrugged. "That's politics," he said. A reporter mentioned that the chairman of the Democratic State Committee had labeled Volpe a "dead duck" as a vice presidential hopeful. At that, Volpe smiled. Republicans did not rely so heavily on standings in the polls, which changed daily, he reminded them.

In both parties, primaries were not the way to the vice presidency. A more reliable strategy was to pick the eventual winner and stick with him, building an organization. In Nixon, Volpe seemed to have chosen wisely. It was Nixon who had encouraged Volpe's entry into the Massachusetts primary, and shortly after the votes were in, Nixon met with him again. He had narrowed the list to three, Nixon confided. Volpe was still on it.

Nationally, Nixon's southern strategy was evolving. Heading off the only serious opposition from the right when he defeated the Reagan forces in the Oregon primary on May 28, Nixon brought his delegate total from primaries to an impressive 112. On June 1, Nixon met with Senators John Tower (Texas) and Strom Thurmond (South Carolina), along with several other southern Republican leaders, in Atlanta to discuss civil rights and other issues of concern to the South. The meeting was closed to outsiders, but whatever Nixon told them apparently pleased the party chairmen, for they reached a cordial understanding. With Reagan's effort blunted, there was little room for Rockefeller to open up the process by August.

The political clock stopped again on June 5. The antiwar movement's new challenger, New York Senator Robert Kennedy, was assassinated on election night in Los Angeles, as he won the California primary and seemed ready to go on to capture the nomination. Now the lead fell to Johnson's vice president, Hubert Humphrey. The Democratic party, seemingly assured of victory just three months before, scrambled to regroup in the face of Nixon's forces to the right, independent George Wallace to the extreme right, and the antiwar movement on the left.

After the Atlanta accord, Nixon turned over preparations for the convention to the capable, if somewhat unimaginative, Richard Kleindienst. Miami Beach was the location for the 1968 convention. The tropical heat made the site somewhat less than ideal in August, but the location adjacent to — but not in the middle of — the city of Miami helped to isolate the conventioneers from possible disruptions. This was a wise choice. On the night of the first ballot, rioting broke out in Miami's largest black neighborhood, Liberty City. Four people were killed, but the convention delegates knew nothing more about it than what they heard on the radio.

By the first week of August, Rockefeller led in delegate counts in only one region, New England, largely due to his victory in Volpe's home state. Yet even in New England, Nixon had some pledged delegates. Still the Rockefeller forces persisted, trying to whittle away individual delegates here and there and cut a possible deal with Reagan — any strategy to force Nixon's first ballot total below six hundred and throw open the next ballot. From their headquarters in the Americana, the northernmost of the big hotels, the Rockefeller forces went out on their mission, but the results of the first ballot had already been determined when the delegates arrived. The question that interested the convention was who would take second place.

Nixon had already outlined some of the criteria he intended to use in choosing his vice presidential candidate. The candidate should have some knowledge of the cities. He should be a governor, to encourage the other twenty-five Republican governors to campaign hard for the ticket. And he might possibly be an "ethnic." Although Howard Baker of Tennessee was considered a strong favorite because of the southern strategy, only two men seemed to fill the three designated categories: Spiro Agnew of Maryland and Volpe. Agnew's experience was much more limited: he had been governor for only eighteen months and before his election, had been involved only in county-level politics. Volpe seemed much the stronger candidate and had known Nixon for sixteen years.

On August 8, at 1 A.M., the convention completed the first ballot. Nixon had 692 delegates and needed only 667 to win. Rockefeller trailed with 277; Reagan gained a respectable 182; the rest belonged to a scattering of favorite sons. As the celebrations went on in the convention hall, the bars, and the hotel suites, Nixon met with seven of his key people and reduced the list of choices for vice president to two: Agnew and Volpe. One of the seven men present telephoned Volpe that night in confidence to tell him the results. Agnew had known Nixon for only four months, the Nixon aide reasoned. Volpe seemed to him the logical choice.

The Massachusetts delegation had been assigned the Algiers, a less-than-luxurious hotel far from the action in the grand hotels. Joe Tauro was there to see that all went well with the Massachusetts delegates. He had heard the rumors about Volpe's being chosen, and all night and into the morning, the calls kept up. No one slept. By mid-morning, the television network reporters were calling to tell him that Volpe had it sewed up. Nixon had scheduled a press conference for noon.

The Volpe family was staying at a suite in the Fountainbleu, and Barry Locke, as press secretary, was taking the phone calls. At about 11 A.M., the Nixon aide who had phoned after the initial meeting of seven advisors called again. "You're it," he said simply. "Congratulations."

Volpe thanked him but still could not fully accept the news. I'll believe it when he calls me himself, he thought. In the construction business, he had sometimes been tipped off in advance that he would get a job, but he had learned not to lease equipment until he saw the names on the contract. Tired from the long night but too keyed up to sleep, he sat on one of the beds and watched the press coverage on television. About thirty minutes after the call came an announcement: The naming of the vice presidential candidate had been postponed for a half-hour. Something went wrong, Volpe thought. It's not so certain after all.

As Locke manned the phones, the New England press corps began to gather in the outer room of the suite. Robert Healey from the *Boston Globe* came in to offer his congratulations. As more reporters were knocking on the outer door, ready to congratulate him, a phone call came from Nixon's office. "You better put John on," the caller told him. Silently, Locke passed the receiver to the governor. Volpe nodded, the disappointment showing on his face.

"Well, tell Dick I appreciate very much his having considered me," Volpe said, and passed back the phone. "I can't believe it," he told Locke. The press was still at the door, ready to start the victory celebration. Locke walked out of the bedroom to tell them the news.

At the Algiers Hotel, several delegates were gathered informally in Tauro's room to watch the press conference. Tauro was certain now, though he had not yet told the others. As Nixon built up the suspense, Tauro hung on every word. "A deeply religious man," Nixon described the nominee. Yes, that was true. "A governor." The long wait was over. Tauro felt his heart pounding as if it would come out of his chest. "Spiro T. Agnew!"

Tauro stood up, looking around to see if the others had heard the same thing. They had. Slowly, he left the crowded room and walked outside to the pool. He ordered a glass of orange juice. Although it was early in the day, he changed the order — "Put something stronger in it," he told the waiter — and then wandered down to the beach. Every morning, when they traveled together, he and Volpe went jogging, and they had been running together on this packed white sand only a day before. Now the race was suddenly over. It had been so close. But in the end, the prize had vanished. Tauro plunged into the soupy-warm water and began to swim.

When they returned to Massachusetts from Miami, the Volpes rented a large house on Cape Cod, with a verandah overlooking the sea. As they sat together one evening after dinner, Jennie said gently, "You know, the dear Lord was good to you in Miami."

"What do you mean, good to me?" Volpe asked.

"Can you name one person who has been happy in the vice presidency?" she asked.

"Well, I haven't taken a survey of all the men who have been vice president, but I've never heard anyone say they were very happy with it."

"Then what makes you think *you* would have been?" she asked. "Maybe the dear Lord has something else planned for us."

NOTES

1. *The Boston Herald,* 10 February 1967.

2. *The Boston Herald,* 8 August 1967.

3. *The Boston Globe,* 10 July 1967.

4. *The Boston Herald,* 12 February 1968.

CHAPTER XI

Mr. Secretary

I N THE DAYS FOLLOWING the 1968 convention, several theories surfaced to account for Nixon's apparent switch from Volpe to Agnew. Political columnists noted the fact that Volpe came from a liberal state. Yet Volpe himself was not known as a liberal in national Republican circles. At state delegates' meetings in Florida and Louisiana before the convention, Volpe had been warmly received and assured of support. He had gotten along well with southern politicians at the National Governors' Conferences as well. He was known as a moderate, a pragmatist who could work a compromise, not an ideologue of the right or left.

A more persistent theory held that South Carolina Senator Strom Thurmond, at the Atlanta meeting that cemented Nixon's southern strategy in June, had demanded that the vice presidential candidate be a southerner or a man from a border state. For a time, Volpe himself gave credence to this theory. On the night that Nixon made his acceptance speech at the Miami convention, Thurmond happened to be Volpe's partner in the procession of ten dignitaries who escorted the nominee to the podium. As they waited for the line to form, Thurmond told Volpe that there was no truth to the rumor he had blocked his nomination — he would have accepted him gladly. Volpe turned the conversation to other topics, but Thurmond brought the subject up again. And again a third time. By the third time, Volpe had begun to wonder whether the senator was protesting too much. Just after the convention, yet another rumor circulated among Massachusetts Republicans that Tom Pappas, who had raised money for Nixon, preferred Agnew because of his Greek ancestry. Many of those close to Nixon doubted both theories, knowing that Nixon at that stage owed little to any single power broker; he was secure in the nomination and very much his own man. The choice could easily have been his own, for his own reasons.

One week after Nixon's nomination, at his request Volpe flew to Mission Bay near Los Angeles to discuss his role in the campaign. The issue of the vice presidency was never mentioned. Together, the two men reviewed the campaign strategy. Volpe's time would be limited, for he was still governor of Massachusetts, but he agreed to chair the "nationalities" committee and to campaign in ten states with high concentrations of Italian-American and other ethnic voters. The targeted groups would normally vote Democratic, but in the turmoil of 1968, Nixon's message of loyalty to traditional values could be immensely appealing. As Volpe was about to leave, he asked the nominee one last question: If there were one state where Volpe should spend more time than the others, which would it be? Without hesitation, Nixon answered, "New Jersey."

Throughout the rest of the summer, Volpe campaigned in New Jersey seven times, a day or two each time. He found the campaign well organized and smoothly run. Scheduling and advance functions were well coordinated, and transportation was first class and on time. For the duration of the campaign, the committee had leased three trijet Boeing 727s (christened *Tricia, Julie,* and *David* for the occasion) to be on call every day. For the candidate and his family, the pace was geared to television and "photo opportunities" rather than personal contact, with only two or three stops a day. But Volpe's schedulers put him into a frantic round of Italian religious feasts, Polish picnics, and German Oktoberfests. He addressed the Sons of Italy, danced the tarantella with pretty young girls and older women, admired babies, and shook hands with construction workers, police officers, firefighters, factory workers, and housewives. At the blue-collar rallies Volpe addressed, there were no hecklers or protestors. The message he brought was simple and compelling: He was one of them, a former union plasterer and the son of immigrants. Nixon had promised to bring their sons home from Vietnam with honor. Volpe had known Nixon for sixteen years and knew that he would keep his promise. The vote in New Jersey was very close, with Nixon carrying 46.1 percent and Humphrey close behind with 44.0.

On election night, Volpe waited with a number of other Nixon supporters at the campaign headquarters in the Waldorf-Astoria Hotel in New York. It was a long night, and victory was not certain until the Illinois returns came in at 5 A.M. Nixon had swept thirty-two states with a total of 302 electoral votes. Humphrey's electoral votes (191) came from the old industrial states of New York, Pennsylvania, Massachusetts, and Michigan. The old Catholic/Protestant split between Democrats and Republicans had apparently healed since 1960. Much of Nixon's margin of victory came from the "nationalities" Volpe had courted: voters of Italian, Irish, Polish, and Jewish ancestry.[1]

Late in the morning after the election, Nixon came downstairs to the ballroom of the Waldorf-Astoria with a group of his closest associates for his first postelection news conference. After Nixon had thanked his supporters and told them that he would try to "bring us together" — his campaign theme — he invited a group of his closest friends and campaign workers up to his suite for a reception. There, Nixon took Volpe aside and asked him to serve in the new cabinet. "We'll be thinking about the post that we feel would be most appropriate, and that you could do the best job in, but we can discuss it later." Volpe answered that if the job were a challenge for which he was qualified, he would consider it a great honor. He would be the first cabinet member from Massachusetts since Harry Truman had appointed Governor Maurice Tobin as secretary of labor.

Two weeks later, John Mitchell telephoned Volpe in Boston and offered him the job of postmaster general. Since the election, Volpe, his staff, and the press had engaged in considerable speculation as to what cabinet position he probably would be offered. The consensus had been labor; housing and urban development; commerce; transportation; or health, education, and welfare. Postmaster general had traditionally been a patronage appointment, often for a man with years of loyal party service but without an independent income. Volpe did not refuse outright but did not even take up the matter with Jennie; he felt that he was no more qualified than a thousand other people for the post. He called Mitchell back with a polite refusal. A few days later, Mitchell had another offer: secretary of the new Department of Transportation. "You're a manager," Mitchell told him. "That's what the president thinks we need."

Volpe thought back to his twenty years in the construction business, his years in highway construction with the Massachusetts DPW, his short tenure as federal highway administrator under Eisenhower, and his more recent involvement in the railway issue with the extension of the Boston public transit system along the old New Haven Railroad line to the South Shore. This assignment would be challenging. The department was only twenty months old and still being organized. And the federal highway system Volpe had worked on in 1957 was now approaching its most crucial phase, the building of highways through major cities. Both the private long-distance passenger rail systems and the urban public transit systems were in a state of crisis. The massive federal funding being poured into urban renewal would be of little benefit if there were no systems available for urban residents to use to go to work, shop, and do business. After talking it over with Jennie and two or three friends, Volpe called Mitchell back and accepted.

In the last week of November, Volpe met with Nixon again in California, and the two men talked briefly about what they hoped to accomplish. "I hope you realize that I'm not a 'yes' man, that I like to think things out, and if I feel that you or other people on your staff come up with an idea I disagree with, that for your interests and the best interests of the nation, I will tell you so," Volpe told him.

Nixon seemed pleased. "That's one of the reasons that I want you. Because I know you're *not* a 'yes' man, and I'll always get your best advice."

Breaking with tradition, Nixon arranged to have all twelve cabinet nominees introduced at once on national television on December 13. The night before, all the secretaries and their families had stayed in secret at the Sheraton Park. Also breaking precedent, the wives too were briefly introduced before the cameras and gave short speeches. Only Jennie was not able to give her speech, as she had come down with the flu. After the television broadcast, the secretaries and their wives attended a day of lectures on subjects ranging from national security to party protocol, while the cabinet children took guided tours of Washington, shepherded by the presidential daughters and the campaign staff. In his speech to the new appointees, Nixon explained that his new secretaries were to run their departments free from White House interference; White House staffers were there only to coordinate and assist, not to dictate policy. He recommended that the secretaries call him at 4:30 or 5 P.M., when he had scheduled a break in his day, if they needed to contact him.

Shortly after the cabinet announcements came the news that Nixon had appointed Elliot Richardson under secretary of state. As soon as the new administration took office, a major reshuffling would occur at the Massachusetts State House. Lieutenant Governor Sargent would become acting governor; the lieutenant governor's office would be vacant; and House Speaker Robert Quinn of Dorchester would become attorney general. Of the three Massachusetts Republican "strong men" — Volpe,

Brooke, and Richardson — all would be in Washington. This was a loss from which Massachusetts Republicans, already a minority party, would be slow to recover.

There was still unfinished business for Volpe in Massachusetts. While he and Jennie had vacationed in the Virgin Islands after the November elections, a tense confrontation between Mothers for Adequate Welfare and the Welfare Department culminated in a sit-in at Roxbury and Dorchester welfare offices and the corridors of the State House, followed by the arrest of forty-one mothers who were demanding special allowances for winter clothing.

The welfare issue figured largely in the problems Volpe's team sought to address in his sweeping reorganization package proposed in December. Under the modernization plan, virtually all state agencies, authorities, and commissions were to be brought under departments whose directors would report to the governor and whose terms of office would be coterminus with his. The reorganization plan proposed thirteen "groupings": human services, communities and development, education, manpower affairs, consumer affairs, transportation and construction, environmental affairs, public safety, personnel, general services, and finance. Much of this plan was later enacted into law and implemented under Sargent's administrations, and it remains the basic blueprint for the Massachusetts state bureaucracy today.

Under Commissioner of Administration Tony DeFalco's guidance, the outgoing administration also worked up plans for potential trouble spots in the Human Services Department, such as reimbursements for state contracts with private nonprofit social service agencies. To ensure equitable funding for private agencies doing business with the state, DeFalco designed an independent rate-setting commission to negotiate human service contracts on the basis of an agency's actual costs. Before the institution of the commission, contracting procedures had been arbitrary and sometimes influenced by political considerations.

There were preparations to be made in Washington as well. Volpe's taking on the management of the fifth largest federal department meant subjection to close scrutiny by the press and those on Capitol Hill. Between 1960 and 1969, his company had done $13.3 million in work on federal buildings in Washington, and it was working on eight more federal installations when Volpe was named transportation secretary. Two years before the 1968 election, the company had been hired by Boston developer David Nasif to build a ten-story office building in Washington's redeveloped southwest area. Nasif then leased the building to the General

174

Services Administration, which in turn planned to house the Department of Transportation (DOT) there. Signs posted on the huge construction site read, "The John A. Volpe Company."

When Volpe had first run for governor, he had ordered Peter not to bid on state or even city and town jobs so as to preclude the possibility of any conflict of interest. But he had retained a controlling interest in the company and still served as chairman of the board. Before being appointed to the cabinet, Volpe could have placed his shares in a blind trust and stayed within the law. He chose instead to sell all his shares to Peter, paying capital gains taxes of nearly a quarter million dollars in the process, and to sell stocks in any company remotely connected with the transportation industry. He then asked Peter not to bid on any DOT contracts, even though he could no longer benefit personally. The day after the transaction was completed, sign crews painted over the "John A." on the Volpe construction sites in Washington.

For Volpe, the loss was more than a financial one. He had invested much of his adult life in the company, and severing the last legal ties was painful. Before the election, he also had sold the Winchester home that was once Jennie's dream house. They moved into the apartment he maintained at 151 Tremont Street, Boston, and then registered to vote at Boston City Hall before leaving for Washington.

For the Nixon appointees, confirmation hearings in the Senate were expected to be routine, but Volpe's staff anticipated some attacks on the highways issues. The Inner Belt question was still in dispute, and Harvard economist John Kenneth Galbraith charged Volpe with being a "compulsive road builder." "I *am* a compulsive *everything*," Volpe admitted in an interview shortly afterward. "I like to get things done."[2] Despite some opposition from Inner Belt opponents, the ninety minutes of questioning by the Senate Commerce Committee went well for Volpe, and approval was unanimous. Senator Norris Cotton of New Hampshire joked that Volpe was the only nominee who had ever built his own building.

Volpe left the corner office at the State House for the last time on January 17, flew to Washington, and went straight to Walter Reed Army Hospital to see former President Eisenhower. Volpe had planned a visit in November or December, but the former president had had a setback and was unable to see him. This time the nurse allowed Volpe only twenty minutes, but as he began to tell Eisenhower about his plans for DOT, the president sent the nurse away. Volpe found his host thin and wasted, but his mind was unimpaired. Eisenhower told him that when he was president, he had wanted to do something about transportation from cities to airports so that planes could land farther from urban centers, perhaps including a helicopter service or a rapid transit line with baggage capacity. At last, Mamie Eisenhower came in and advised her husband to get some rest. They parted, and Volpe never saw him again.

On January 22, the new cabinet officers were sworn in by Chief Justice Earl Warren at 8 A.M. "In view of the hour," Nixon joked, "we will call it a working Cabinet."[3] And Volpe found that there was plenty of work to do. DOT's first secretary, Alan Boyd, was a young Florida lawyer who had been Civil Aeronautics Board chairman. Boyd had spent an average of eight out of twenty working days out of town making speeches as an "educator and salesman."[4] Education and salesmanship were needed, but Volpe found the department badly in need of organization as well. A conglomerate of more than thirty transportation agencies that had once been scattered throughout the federal government, the department included the Federal Aviation Administration (FAA), which had existed semiautonomously within the Commerce Department; the new Urban Mass Transportation Administration (UMTA) from the Department of Housing and Urban Development (HUD); the Coast Guard, during peacetime a part of the Treasury Department; the formerly independent St. Lawrence Seaway Development Corporation; the Federal Highway Administration that Volpe had directed under Eisenhower; and the newly created Federal Railway Administration, with responsibilities for rail and pipeline safety.

The FAA, the Coast Guard, and the Federal Highway Administration were established agencies, with their own entrenched civil service bureaucrats, special-interest constituencies, and allies in Congress and other departments. Simply placing them together in one building did not ensure their cooperation. Nor could the new organization immediately reverse the dominance of highways and aviation over mass transit. For the first year and a half of the department's existence, the component agencies had simply continued on as they had before they were thrown in together, but this policy could not endure long. Political pressures were building as the federal highway system moved inexorably to close the last gaps through urban, often black, neighborhoods just as black community consciousness and political power were rising.

Volpe began the selection process for his top staff as soon as he himself was nominated. Young Joe Tauro was not able to leave his law practice in Massachusetts, though he did open an office in Washington. For a time, he considered running for elective office but in the end decided against it. Barry Locke was hired as special assistant to the secretary and moved his family to Potomac, Maryland. Joe Bosco, a Democrat, had refused to take part in the Nixon campaign but had sent a series of memos on the civil rights issue to Volpe, and Volpe in turn had passed them along to the Nixon campaign committee. Bosco was surprised to be asked to come to Washington with Volpe, yet here was an opportunity to play a role in civil rights and urban affairs on a national level. Shortly after Volpe's nomination, the *New York Times* and the *Washington Post* had run critical editorials about Volpe's urban and environmental policies, editorials that worried Bosco. "*I* know you're not like that," he told Volpe, "but the public doesn't."

"I guarantee that within a year, they'll be saying different things about me," Volpe assured him. Bosco, like Locke, accepted the position as special assistant to the secretary and soon became a key player in the transformation of the department's urban and civil rights positions. In less than a month after his appointment, Bosco was representing Volpe on Nixon's Urban Affairs Council, a committee chaired by presidential advisor Daniel Patrick Moynihan, to advise the president on city concerns.

The other two departments represented in the Urban Affairs Council were HUD (under George Romney) and HEW (under Robert Finch). A year and a half after taking office, Volpe asked Boston attorney Thomas Trimarco to become assistant general counsel. Volpe was rarely seen at DOT without at least one of the three: Bosco, Trimarco, or Locke. While he was "Mr. Secretary" to the rest of the department, to these three men he was still "the governor."

As assistant secretary for policy and international affairs, Volpe recruited Paul Cherington, a professor of economics at Harvard with a background in airline, water, and railroad transportation. For under secretary, Volpe named NASA Associate Administrator James Beggs. Beggs was at first reluctant to leave his job at NASA. While interviewing him in the secretary's office, Volpe pointed out the window to the Capitol dome nearby. "You see how close it is?" he asked. "It takes more than twenty minutes to get there. I'd like to be able to get a person to the Capitol as easily as you get someone into space." Beggs accepted. Charles D. Baker, a vice president of Harbridge House, a Boston consulting firm, was named deputy under secretary.

White House advisor John Ehrlichman recommended former Seattle Mayor James Braman, an outspoken environmentalist. While he was a lawyer in Seattle, Ehrlichman had represented anti-highway groups and had come to respect Braman's political acumen. When Volpe took office, the department had three assistant secretaries: policy and international affairs, public affairs, and research and technology. In addition to these, Volpe created another, urban systems and environment, for Braman.

During his first few weeks on the job, Volpe found himself working sixteen to eighteen hours a day just to familiarize himself with the com-·plexities of the department and the Washington bureaucracy. The Nasif building was not finished, and Volpe worked in the FAA building on Independence Avenue, not far from the brick towers of the old Smithsonian on the Mall. The city had changed enormously since he had lived there during the Eisenhower administration. The predominantly white, middle-class government employees had moved to the suburbs in Maryland and Virginia, and the city of Washington was now approximately 80 percent black, with much of its old brick row housing deteriorating into ghetto conditions. The old trolley lines had been abandoned; public transportation was provided by a privately owned bus company; and the highways were choked with cars as the government workers commuted each evening to the safety of their split-levels, leaving the downtown with its marble monuments and elegant parks deserted and dangerous. During the riots that followed Martin Luther King, Jr.'s, death, less than a year before Volpe had arrived, mobs had looted and burned much of the business district surrounding 14th and G streets. Between the two gray stone "anchor" department stores, the smaller shops stood boarded up and gutted, as if the war had come home.

The Volpes had thought of moving into a modest three-bedroom apartment in Rosslyn near the airport on the Virginia side of the Potomac, but traffic crossing the bridges was so heavy that Volpe felt too much time would be wasted in the short commute. They bought a penthouse next to prominent Republican hostess Anna Chennault's apartment in the new Watergate complex on the Potomac and furnished it with Jennie's blue and gold French provincial furniture and Italian paintings. With no yard to plant in, Jennie improvised a garden on the roof, created a miniature bower on the mantelpiece surrounding the porcelain figures of saints, and took up Japanese flower arranging. She gave up making hats; styles had changed, and no other Washington wife wore them.

Volpe, too, was making his adjustments to official Washington. In Massachusetts, he had had three state police aides assigned on a twenty-four-hour basis if needed, and at least two usually accompanied him to social events, one to drive and the other to escort him and smooth over potential problems. After three terms as governor, Volpe and his aides had the social functions timed so perfectly that he could attend four dinners in one evening, eating the fruit cup at the first, the main course at the next, and the dessert at the third, then giving his speech at the last event while the other diners had their coffee.

In Washington, the secretary of transportation was assigned an official limousine and driver, but the chauffeur's assignment was to protect the car, not the secretary. For speaking engagements, Volpe was on his own, trying to find the correct room, where to put his coat, and whom to see. A few weeks after his arrival, Volpe was being driven home at dusk with his large briefcases in the back seat. While the car was stopped in traffic, a man appeared from behind, opened the back door, and reached in to grab the briefcases. The driver got out the front door to chase him, and the thief abandoned the attempt and disappeared into the night. After this incident, Volpe talked to the president about the need for better security, and two Coast Guardsmen were assigned to work in shifts and accompany him on his travels.

By the summer of 1969, Volpe had settled into the routine of his new job, "going full speed ahead with caution." His department had moved, floor by floor, from the old FAA offices into the new marble-fronted headquarters in southwest Washington, next to the new HUD building. The DOT and HUD buildings stood in a neighborhood recently cleared for urban renewal and cut apart by railroad tracks and freeways. A few streets of row houses had been cleaned up and fitted with iron bars on the lower windows, but the old maze of warehouses, oyster bars, and shacks that had once lined the waterfront had disappeared, replaced by housing projects and a few expensive restaurants. The neighborhood where people sat on front steps and children played in the streets was gone.

The DOT building itself was more spacious, with wider corridors and larger offices, than the old Roosevelt era government offices around the Mall, and Volpe decorated his own suite, with Jennie's help, on the eighth floor. The suite included a tiny private dining room, lounge, and shower; he could virtually live at the office. At 7 A.M., he would arrive at the DOT gym and go through his regular exercises, finishing off with a whirlpool bath. Then, as he had for sixteen years, he attended Mass, usually the 8 A.M. service at St. Dominic's just behind the DOT offices. After hearing about Volpe's physical fitness routine, Nixon joked at a press conference that Volpe was exercising with the space team and "might be one of our next astronauts." The new DOT building featured a gym with a weight room and a tiny wooden track on the roof. From the windows on the opposite side of the building, DOT employees could watch their boss patiently jogging his laps in the humid heat of a Washington summer or bundled in a sweatsuit in January. Employees began to use the new

179

facility, too, while a few high-ranking officials even copied his hot tea and graham cracker snacks, hoping to get some of the same benefits he seemed to derive from his regimen. At home, the Volpes lived quietly, avoiding the Washington party circuit and accepting few invitations except those from old friends.

Before he had left office, Alan Boyd had given Volpe and his transition team two pieces of advice: Get out of Washington and see what is going on in the rest of the country, and don't get involved in the Washington, D.C., highway controversy. Volpe followed his first piece of advice. During the first few months of his administration, there was no early warning system in place to give notice that a highway project would encounter local opposition from neighborhood activists or environmentalists. Federal Highway Administrator Francis Turner (who had worked for Volpe as chief engineer of the Bureau of Public Roads under Eisenhower) and most of his staff were resolutely pro-highway. Several of the projects they gave Volpe looked good on the map but proved disastrous in the field. During his first two months in office, Volpe approved projects based on the reports he was given. From his first day in office, he continued his practice of reading everything he signed and insisting on forty-eight hours' notice, no matter how tight the deadline. Soon he discovered, however, that the paperwork sometimes ignored or glossed over serious political problems.

Nor was there a mechanism to warn of trouble in the civil rights area. In February 1969, Volpe scrapped the Johnson administration's practice of prequalifying highway contractors on the basis of what they stated they *would* do about hiring and promoting minorities. Clarence Mitchell, director of the Washington NAACP and author of many civil rights bills and federal regulations, promptly blasted Volpe for "spineless capitulation" to the highway lobby. But in March, Volpe incorporated stricter minority hiring provisions than the department had used under Johnson and stepped up the postaward compliance reviews to make sure that contractors actually were following through. By April, Mitchell had been a guest at a DOT luncheon and admitted, "He has impressed me." Mitchell became a frequent guest at DOT conferences, and Volpe began to count on his advice. The two men became friends, drawn to each other by their similar experiences in early life. At a DOT conference, Volpe told the story of his father's teaching him how to balance the hod, check that the ladder was secure, and balance the load on the way up. "But when you are older, you must learn how to climb the ladder for yourself." The man sitting next to Mitchell saw that he had tears in his eyes.

180

As Volpe became more involved in the civil rights issue, he found out just how large a job it would be to implement minority hiring practices even within his own department. There were no women or minority "supergrades" (the upper ranks of the civil service) at DOT. The FAA and Coast Guard were nearly all white, and there were few blacks in state highway programs, particularly in the South.

In his first year in office, Volpe created a departmental Office of Civil Rights, and each office was assigned its own director of civil rights. He began to enforce the minority hiring requirements for private contractors very strictly, sometimes over the objections of southern congressmen. State highway departments receiving federal reimbursements also were forced to comply and to undergo periodic compliance reviews. In November 1970, the *Christian Science Monitor* ran a story naming Volpe as the man in Washington blacks most identified with, as they had looked to Attorney General Herbert Brownell in the Eisenhower administration. In southern states, there were virtually no blacks on federal highway work crews before 1969. By 1970, crews were 20 to 50 percent black in Mississippi, Georgia, and Alabama, and the department itself had more blacks in decision-making jobs than any other federal department.

Throughout his tenure at DOT, civil rights was one of Volpe's top priorities. The subject was brought up at any official meeting. Progress reports were read, and if Volpe did not think real efforts were being made, he pushed. "He would bang his fist on the table — 'I want to see more black faces, more brown faces,' " Bosco recalled his saying. "No one had ever talked to them like that before. And suddenly, you walked down the hall and you did start seeing more black faces and brown faces."

Volpe's civil rights views also were intrinsically tied into the inner-city highway crisis, for many of the neighborhoods through which interstates were routed were predominantly black. The interstates that had been built without trouble through farmland and forests were stalled at at least twelve urban borders, delayed by local opposition. San Francisco Mayor Joseph Alioto not only refused 90 percent federal funding but also began tearing down elevated arteries that had already been built, hoping that the BART (Bay Area Rapid Transit) system then under construction would make them obsolete. Protest groups were organizing against proposed freeways in Philadelphia, St. Louis, Buffalo, and Des Moines.

The urban freeways issue became a theme that ran through Volpe's entire term of office and beyond, and it gave him more publicity than any other. Relations with the media sometimes were confused because his policies did not fall neatly into a prohighway or antihighway position.

When he first took office, he was pegged as prohighway. His first two appointments in the highway field were pegged as prohighway. He named Francis C. Turner, former chief engineer of the Bureau of Public Roads under Eisenhower, as federal highway administrator. Then he appointed Ralph Bartlesmeyer, former chief engineer of the Illinois Highway Department, to head the Bureau of Public Roads. Some critics suggested that he instead appoint an urban expert, but Volpe contended that he was simply being practical; these men knew how to build roads. Braman's office would handle environmental and urban problems.

In March 1969, after only three months in office, he appealed to "so-called conservationists and civic groups" for common sense and compromise, and set about finding ways to speed up highway construction. He opposed a regulation from Alan Boyd's administration that required state highway departments to hold two public hearings before seeking federal aid for highways. On this he was supported by most of the states' governors and highway superintendents but opposed by the U.S. Conference of Mayors, the National League of Cities, and several conservation groups. Despite this opposition, Volpe's one-hearing rule was implemented.

In practice, Volpe often made extraordinary efforts to reroute or even cancel highway projects he believed could hurt inner-city neighborhoods or places of natural beauty. In July 1969, Volpe intervened directly in a local highway dispute for the first time. A six-lane freeway was being built between the waterfront and the historic French Quarter in New Orleans. A 690-foot tunnel had already been dug, and the project was supported by local business groups as a necessity to move traffic to the new Rivergate convention facility. But preservationists warned that the highway would detract from the atmosphere of the historic area of narrow streets, overhanging balconies, bars, and jazz clubs. Volpe had not made up his mind when he left Washington, but when he arrived in New Orleans and saw that the highway would cut the French Quarter off from the sea, he decided to cancel the project, leaving the tunnel uncompleted. Not long after the French Quarter reversal, Volpe also withdrew funding from the proposed Miami Jetport that could have irreparably damaged the ecology of the Florida Everglades.

As Braman's Office of Urban Systems and Environment developed connections throughout the country, Volpe's office began to be alerted sooner to possible trouble spots, making it possible to reroute or redesign controversial projects rather than make the drastic and expensive decision to cancel. But on some projects, compromise was still not possible. In March 1970, Volpe halted construction of Interstate 93 (Boston to Montreal) on a path that would have cut through the White Mountain National Forest, near the Old Man of the Mountain rock formation. In Charleston, West Virginia, an expressway routed through a black neighborhood was halted. After surveying the site from a helicopter, Volpe canceled a federal highway that was to cross a wilderness area in Lake Altoona, Georgia, although both Georgia Highway Commissioner Burt Lance and Georgia Governor Jimmy Carter supported it.

When his successor in Massachusetts, Francis Sargent, proclaimed the moratorium in February 1970 that killed the Southwest Expressway, Volpe was furious. The land had already been taken, people relocated, and homes destroyed, and Volpe felt the highway and rapid transit line that would have used the same right of way were badly needed to ease Boston's traffic problems. But Volpe could do nothing except remember Callahan's prediction that the Inner Belt would never be completed in their lifetimes. Volpe did not speak to Sargent for six months after the moratorium. At last, with Sargent's election campaign imminent, the Massachusetts governor sought Volpe's support. The two men met in Boston and made their peace, but Sargent's reversal on one of Volpe's dearest projects bothered Volpe long after the highway was forgotten.

In the spring of 1972, Volpe intervened in a highway dispute involving one of the oldest Italian-American neighborhoods in the United States, "The Hill" in St. Louis, Missouri. The Hill had been an Italian settlement since the early 1900s, when workers had come from Lombardy to mine clay under The Hill itself. In 1971, Interstate 44 began to cut through The Hill, and housing prices fell. While he was in St. Louis on other business, Volpe was approached by Father Salvatore Polizzi, a community activist who pleaded his case (in Italian) for an overpass to link the now-divided neighborhood — a request the state highway department had denied. Volpe was greatly impressed by the residents' fundraising drive that had resulted in a $50,000 contribution toward the expense of the overpass. He believed that the long-term health of the neighborhood was more important than immediate economic considerations and overruled the state highway department. The overpass was built, the highway was rerouted, and The Hill began the slow process of recovery.

A 1972 U.S. Supreme Court ruling that protection of parkland was to be given "paramount importance" in highway decisions gave Volpe more legal justification to stop highways when he believed this was necessary. In San Antonio, Texas, defining an open field as parkland was grounds enough for stopping an expressway through a crowded Mexican-American neighborhood. After Volpe's last decision to halt an expressway in Memphis, Tennessee, that would have cut through Overton Park, a 342-acre forest of oak and hickory with a zoo at the edge, Jack Kramer, director of the environmentalist Highway Action Coalition, commented: "This shows at last that we need not accept the concrete cloverleaf as the national flower."

Nonetheless, Volpe did not bring all highway construction to a halt. More than a thousand miles were completed by the end of his first year as secretary. The trouble spots constituted only a tiny fraction of the system. By 1970, two-thirds of the system was finished, and work continued on schedule.

The most bitterly contested highway routes were within miles of Volpe's office in Washington, D.C. Activists opposing freeway construction possessed little real political power, although they lived within sight of the Capitol and the White House. The mayor of the District of Columbia was still appointed by Congress, and the District's one congressman had no vote. The home rule movement was gaining momentum, and cars driving downtown sported bumper stickers such as "D.C. — The Last Colony." The congressional committee overseeing the District's administration had for years been considered a political backwater, and its members had little interest in working with ghetto activists who could not vote. Volpe's predecessor Boyd, after tangling with some of the District's more vocal community leaders, simply took all the proposed D.C. expressways off the map. Federal Highway Administrator Francis C. Turner's first move was to put them back on.

Instead of following Boyd's lead and avoiding the issue, Volpe plunged into the D.C. highway morass and began a series of meetings with community groups. The antihighway groups were an uneasy coalition of well-off Georgetown liberals and black activists whose principal weapon was the lawsuit. Often the rhetoric was strong, and the style was confrontational. Within the department, Volpe had little tolerance for unconventional dress and behavior. One employee at the UMTA who was given to wearing embroidered jeans and flowing robes to the office was forced to promise that he would appear before Volpe "properly dressed." The man later appeared before the secretary in white tie and tails.

Volpe stayed calm under fire at D.C. community group meetings as the language grew bitter, and even as one protestor waved a matchbook in his face and threatened to burn down DOT. After prolonged negotiations, Volpe withdrew funding from the North Capitol Freeway, which was to run through a densely populated northeast section. Volpe canceled the three most controversial D.C. highway projects: the Three Sisters Bridge over the Potomac (named for three rocks in the river's main channel),

184

I-66, and a tunnel that would have passed directly under the Lincoln Memorial.

During one of the D.C. highway lawsuits, Volpe encountered the judge who would later preside over the Watergate trials. John Siricca, a Republican appointee, called Volpe as a witness. As was customary, Volpe's office submitted an affidavit instead. Siricca refused to have anything but an oral deposition, and so Volpe appeared in person to testify, learning in the process that Siricca ran his court by the rules, not by Washington custom.

Simply canceling highway projects could only exacerbate Washington's traffic problems. Washington was long overdue for a public transit system, and Volpe intended to build one that would serve as a model for the country as a whole. In 1969, only five American cities had any significant public transportation besides buses: New York, Chicago, Philadelphia, Boston, and Cleveland. For more than thirty years, the idea of building a Washington subway had been studied, considered, and often ridiculed. At the same time, the last of the trolleys had been phased out in the 1960s, and the city made do with the old green buses of the privately owned D.C. Transit.

When the subway idea was first proposed, it did indeed seem impossible. Central Washington is built on marshland, and a conventional tunnel would have filled up with water. But by the early 1970s, the technology of building concrete tubes to carry trains was well developed in Europe. Still, in Congress, funding for the proposed "Metro" system was held hostage to highway funds. The highway lobby insisted on more Washington area highway appropriations — or no subway.

When Volpe began deleting District highways, his chances of getting Metro funded lessened, although regional authorities in Maryland and Virginia had appropriated their respective shares of the cost. Congressman William Natcher, chairman of the D.C. Committee, would not agree to release Metro funds until more highway construction actually began. Volpe had to have environmental impact statements before beginning any new highway work, or his department would be inviting lawsuits. Volpe asked Nixon, who had first been elected to Congress the same year as Natcher, to intervene. The president invited Natcher to the Oval Office for a talk, but the congressman was adamant. Volpe finally was able to break the impasse by persuading other members of Natcher's committee to support release of funding. Through the National Capital Transportation Act of 1971, DOT was able to "guarantee" revenue bonds rather than donating funds directly, and construction began.

The Washington area was Volpe's model for urban transportation, but he realized early on that little could be changed in other cities without massive federal aid both for design and for the early stages of implementation of new systems. After barely three months in office, Volpe began a campaign to redress the highway/public transportation imbalance. "If we had gone along with mass transportation at the same speed and started it at about the same time as we did with the highway setup, we wouldn't be in the mess we are today."[5]

Volpe's office first began submitting legislative proposals in 1969, and in 1970 the Urban Mass Transportation Assistance Act came into law, after strong support from both sides of the House and Senate. Before 1970, the largest annual investment in public transportation had been $175 million. The new legislation increased this to a level of $1 billion a year and guaranteed a continuing program for at least five years by giving transit systems the authority to make long-range project commitments.[6]

Yet Volpe was not content with simply beefing up existing mass transit by putting more subway trains and buses on-line. From his first day at DOT, he was fascinated by new technology. After the lunar landings in 1969 and 1970, NASA was winding down its space exploration program and laying off engineers and research scientists. Volpe envisioned using these people and the technologies they had developed to create more efficient transportation systems on earth. His choice for chief of the UMTA was Carlos C. Villareal, a sales executive and engineer at an aerospace research and development firm. "He's not a transit man," Volpe explained at the time of his appointment, "and that was deliberate. I wanted someone who wasn't wedded to old concepts but who could think fresh and was familiar with technological research."

A few novelties, such as the turbo train, were already in the works at DOT. The turbo train was a high-speed train powered by an aircraft-type engine and built by United Aircraft Corporation. It could take corners in excess of 165 miles per hour, but antiquated roadbeds on the routes where it was tested severely limited its capabilities. When the train finally went into service between Boston and New York in 1970, it cut only twenty minutes off the time conventional trains took to make the run.

Another even more exotic system financed by DOT was the "dashaveyor." Each unit was small (from six to twenty-four passengers) and looked somewhat like the gondola in a cable car. The dashaveyor ran on rails above and below the car, to prevent possible derailment, and could attain a maximum speed of 80 miles per hour.

Shortly after funding the dashaveyor (which was later dropped),

Volpe became intrigued by the "gravitrain," a development financed by a private inventor named Lawrence Edwards. The gravitrain was to be powered by a combination of compressed air and gravity through sloping tunnels a thousand feet underground. Compressed air would push the train downhill, accumulating enough force to push it uphill to the next station twenty miles away.

The gravitrain proved to be unworkable in practice, but there was still the "tracked air cushion vehicle" (TACV). In the summer of 1970, DOT announced plans to build a sixteen-mile TACV line with electric-powered trains riding an air cushion on the median strip of the freeway from downtown San Diego to the airport.[7] The TACV, called the "Aerotrain," was already operational on a test track in France. In Washington, Congressman Joe Broyhill of Virginia referred to it as "Volpe's ventilating vehicle." Although a prototype of the TACV was built at a DOT test facility, it never went into service. Another innovation was the personal rail transport (PRT), a system of small, programmable cars that could be run on air cushions (like the TACV) or rubber tires, or it could be suspended from a monorail. This system was actually put into use for a time on the University of West Virginia campus in Morgantown.

Volpe's most direct effort to channel Space Age technology into earthbound transportation systems came in March 1970, when he was able to convince President Nixon to transfer the entire NASA Electronic Research Center in Cambridge, Massachusetts (including most of the eight hundred employees and $20 million in funding), to DOT. The center's director, James C. Elms, had already given the employees notice of the center's closing, but through James Beggs, Volpe had received advance notice of the layoffs and persuaded the White House to approve the transfer. After he had been told the good news in New York, Elms drove to the airport, only to find it closed on the first day of the air traffic controllers' "sick-out." He rented a car instead. Although Elms had never used a seat belt before, both he and his wife put on belts and shoulder straps for the drive to Boston. On the Connecticut Turnpike, Mrs. Elms lost control of the car and crashed into a guardrail.

Before he checked into the hospital to have his broken ribs taped, Elms managed to introduce Volpe to his cheering employees in the packed auditorium. Instead of working on space exploration, the center switched over to projects involving noise and air pollution abatement, electric guidance systems for highways, and devices to test drivers' reflexes in order to prevent drunken driving.

In the spring of 1970, DOT showed off its new projects at an exhibit call TRANSPO at Dulles Airport near Washington, D.C. Volpe began the program with the idea of staging an American counterpart to the Paris Air Show, but the department quickly broadened it to include the experimental ground transportation systems then under development. Exhibitors came from the major American aircraft and ground transportation companies, as well as from Canada, West Germany, and Great Britain. Volpe had planned to have DOT stage a similar show every four years, but the event was not repeated.

DOT's most expensive and advanced technological project was never built. When Volpe became secretary, the Boeing Corporation in Seattle was nearing completion of the development stage of the American supersonic transport (SST). The SST was, however, encountering opposition from environmentalists who feared that the sonic booms would be too damaging when the plane used airports near urban areas. Volpe discovered that a bewildering variety of factors had to be considered: foreign policy, the national balance of payments, aviation technology, unemployment in the aviation industry, and the budget deficit.

In early June 1969, Volpe took Jennie, Joe Bosco, Barry Locke, and Tom Trimarco in the Coast Guard's executive jet to Paris for the air show. The president also designated Senator Barry Goldwater, who was then a general in the Air Force Reserve, to represent the United States. Both Volpe and Goldwater wanted to look at the Soviet Union's entry in the SST race, the Tupelov-144 (Tu-144), but when Goldwater asked for a tour of the new plane, he was turned down.

Nevertheless, on the appointed morning, at the edge of the airfield, Goldwater showed up. He was not recognized and simply filed in with the other dignitaries. The plane's interior turned out to be narrow and cramped, a far cry from the luxurious Boeing mock-up. After the guide had given his speech, Goldwater raised his hand. "Have you had any objections from environmentalists in your country?" the senator asked. The guide seemed confused by the question. Volpe stood up to explain. "Senator Goldwater was saying . . ." he began, and then stopped. The guide looked at him in horror, then regained his composure. The guide assured the Americans that no patriotic Soviet citizen would object to *their* SST. No one at the Paris Air Show was permitted to see the Tu-144 fly. Volpe did fly on the prototype *Concorde* (built by a British-French consortium) at the air show and found it cramped and a little noisy. He was sure that Boeing had a better plane.

The SST issue simmered on through 1970 and 1971. On Earth Day, April 1, 1970, Bosco was delegated to address a student demonstration at the Mall in Washington, D.C. Although the invasion of Cambodia was in progress, most of the questions he was asked concerned the SST. By early 1971, ten years and $1.1 billion in federal money had been invested in the SST, and test flights were scheduled for 1973. Volpe decided that the project was so near completion that the pros outweighed the cons and gave it his full support. By March 1971, even Nixon seemed to have lost interest, only to be pulled back by Volpe's personal appeal to his patriotism. "How would you like to go out to Dulles Airport and see an SST with the words 'Made in the USSR' on it?" Volpe asked.

The crucial vote on further funding came in March 1971, when the Laos incursion was going on and a grass roots revolt against the president was taking place in Congress. Republicans in the House and Senate defected in record numbers. "They weren't voting against the SST. They were voting against John Ehrlichman and the staff at the White House," Volpe commented at the time. Within a year and a half of scheduled flight tests, the SST was dead. Throughout his tenure at DOT, a model of the SST sat on Volpe's desk as a reminder of unfinished business. The SST that was to land at Dulles Airport, the *Concorde,* made its first commercial flight in 1976. The *Concorde* did turn a profit, after ten years of losses.

Nixon's turnaround on the SST was one of the few occasions when Volpe had a discussion with the president on any substantive issue. Volpe had taken the president at his word that he would be available to his cabinet, but within a few months of the inauguration, it was difficult to get a call put through to the Oval Office. Within a year, for Volpe it had become nearly impossible.

In the years Volpe served in the cabinet, Nixon called him only once at DOT, on a day Volpe happened to be speaking on the West Coast. A wall seemed to be forming around the White House, impenetrable to all but a few insiders. Robert Ellsworth, who had been one of Volpe's contacts in the campaign, left for Brussels to become ambassador to NATO (the North Atlantic Treaty Organization). John Sears returned to his New York law practice. At one of Volpe's first meetings with Nixon after the inauguration, he suggested that the president meet with each cabinet member for a half-hour every six weeks or so; the president was agreeable. As time passed, however, the idea was dropped. Word spread among the upper levels of the administration that the only way to see the president was through two White House staffers: John Ehrlichman, a young Seattle lawyer, and his friend H.R. Haldeman, a California advertising executive.

Still, Volpe persisted in trying to contact the man who had appointed him. Attorney General John Mitchell and his wife, Martha, lived on the

189

seventh floor of the same building where the Volpes had a penthouse, and the couples sometimes met socially. On one such evening, Volpe complained that he could not get through to discuss substantive policy issues on which the president should be informed. Mitchell suggested calling in the evening, as he himself did, but Volpe could not get through in the evening either. He decided to wait until he had good news to report.

After Senate passage of his first major piece of legislation, the 1970 Airport/Airways Improvement Act, Volpe decided to tell the president about it personally and to get a good quote for the press to promote the bill's passage in the House. He reached Ehrlichman about four in the afternoon and was told that the president was in conference and would get back to him in about forty-five minutes. An hour passed, and Volpe called again, only to be told that the president had left for Florida about fifteen minutes earlier. "I'll call him on *Air Force One*," Volpe said.

"I wouldn't do that if I were you," Ehrlichman warned.

"I didn't ask for your advice, and if I want to call him on *Air Force One,* I will," Volpe replied. After allowing for travel time from the White House to Andrews Air Force Base by helicopter, Volpe called the number for the president's plane and got White House staffer Alex Butterfield. "The president is in conference now, Mr. Secretary," Butterfield told him, smoothly. But Volpe was never one to quit easily. "Well, will you please tell him that John Volpe has a very important message for him and would like to talk to him?"

"Oh, I couldn't do that. He's in conference, and I would catch hell for disturbing him."

The two men sparred for a while, and soon the president came on the line.

"The Airport/Airways Development Act passed by a margin of 88 to 4 in the Senate," Volpe told him. Nixon congratulated him, and the two men talked about transportation problems for a few minutes. "John," Nixon concluded, "you know you can talk to me anytime you want." But when he called again a few weeks later, the gates were shut.

Volpe was not the only cabinet appointee experiencing difficulty contacting Nixon. The other two former governors, Walter Hickel at interior and George Romney at HUD, lost Nixon's confidence within a year of their appointments. By the summer of 1970, HUD's budget was being squeezed hard as Nixon gutted Romney's pet project, the Model Cities Program, but Romney did not take the hint. Hickel's disagreements with the White House took a more public turn.

In March 1970, Hickel had come under fire from the media for advocating offshore drilling and the Alaska oil pipeline, issues that voters in his home state of Alaska approved but environmentalists opposed. Then on May 6, 1970, Hickel composed a letter to Nixon telling him that he lacked "appropriate concern" for the young war protestors who were then demonstrating in Washington. Hickel leaked the letter to the press before sending it to the White House and became an instant hero of the antiwar movement. Nixon did not ask for his resignation until November, but Hickel was effectively shut out after the letter was published.

Although some of his staff would have liked him to, Volpe never criticized Nixon's Vietnam policies and often gave speeches sent from the White House to bolster support for the war effort. As secretary of the department that included the Coast Guard, Volpe was directly responsible for a small percentage of that effort. He visited South Vietnam briefly in 1970. Openly criticizing the conduct of the war while part of the government would, he believed, have constituted disloyalty.

Frustrated in his efforts to obtain support and guidance from the White House, Volpe turned his attention to Congress and the passage of his own legislative agenda. Here, his experience in fighting for his bills in the Democratic State House, his years of service with the national Republican party, the contacts he had made as federal highway administrator, and his time as a member of the Labor Relations Committee of the Associated General Contractors came into play. In an administration short on experienced politicians and long on media experts and advertising executives, Volpe was one of the few effective lobbyists the White House had. Volpe's best-known legislative accomplishment was the implementation of a concept that had long been the norm in Europe but was politically unpopular in the United States: a government-subsidized passenger rail system.

Early in the summer of 1969, Assistant Secretary Paul Cherington told Volpe that there would be no more passenger rail service in the United States within two or three years unless the federal government intervened. Beggs and Baker agreed with Cherington's analysis, and Volpe went to the president to propose a federal program. Nixon agreed in principle. With the president's approval, DOT began an in-house study. The study was then sent out to be approved by the Office of the Budget, then on to the White House.

In January 1970, when the passenger rail study was being reviewed at the White House, *The New York Times* printed a story on the "Railpax" proposal. Ehrlichman called Volpe, accusing his office of "leaking" the story. Volpe replied that the story also could have come from the Office of the Budget, the congressional leaders with whom the White House staff had directed Volpe to check, or even within the White House itself. "Why do you think it was leaked here?" Volpe asked. "Well," Ehrlichman replied, "I have a hunch that's where it came from."

By the middle of February, the bill had still not been approved by the White House, and Volpe was called by the Senate Commerce Committee's ranking Republican, Norris Cotton. Cotton told Volpe that the only bill under consideration to save rail passenger service was one sponsored by Vance Hartke of Indiana. Where was Volpe's bill? Volpe went to see Ehrlichman personally and had it out with him, banging his fist on the desk and threatening to pack his bags and go back to Boston the next day unless the president saw him the following morning. This time Ehrlichman relented, although he and other White House staffers opposed Railpax. Volpe met with Nixon, and as he had with the SST, Volpe appealed to Nixon's sense of patriotism. What would America be like without any passenger trains?

Nixon agreed in principle to support Railpax, but now that Hartke's bill had already been reported out of the Senate Commerce Committee and was ready for consideration on the floor, they could not send down Volpe's piece of legislation. "You'll just have to leave that to me, Mr. President," Volpe replied.

Volpe met with Senators Warren Magnussen and Norris Cotton and told them that at last he had White House approval. "Fine," they told him, "but first you'll have to make your peace with Hartke." Hartke agreed to let his staff work with Volpe's to modify the Hartke bill. Then Volpe asked Senate Majority Leader Mike Mansfield to hold the original bill for a month. Mansfield refused. "How about twenty days?" Volpe bargained. Mansfield agreed. The new bill, now 90 percent DOT bill and 10 percent Hartke's original bill, was ready in eighteen days.

The enabling legislation, as it was finally passed, set up a quasi-governmental corporation with a bare minimum of $340 million in capital under the control of a board of directors selected by the White House and the four major railroad corporations that became stockholders. Volpe, as DOT secretary, was the first chairman. By 1971, the National Railroad Passenger Corporation had been renamed "Amtrak," and on May 8, Volpe joined a crowd of dignitaries and reporters aboard the Metroliner from Union Station in Washington to New York. A band on board one of the cars played at each station. Although the train was late for its first run, Volpe was elated. He hoped that within five years, after eliminating marginal lines, the new corporation would turn a profit and no longer rely on government subsidies. This was not to be the case, but Amtrak did save the passenger train and cut down on the need for new highway construction in the Northeast.

Vance Hartke, ironically, was later involved in Volpe's only verbal fight with a congressional committee, at a time when other White House appointees regularly came under attack on Capitol Hill. As many White House officials were doing, Volpe went on the road during the 1970 congressional election season to campaign for Republican candidates. He made one stop on behalf of Hartke's opponent in Indiana. Up until then, the two men had enjoyed a relatively good relationship; Hartke had even invited the Volpes to be his guests at the Indianapolis 500 auto race.

The 1970 election in Indiana was close, and Hartke interpreted Volpe's campaign stop as a betrayal. A week after the election, Hartke berated Volpe during committee hearings for failing to submit written statements seventy-two hours in advance. For two hours, Hartke grilled him so thoroughly that Norris Cotton banned television cameras from the hearing room. Volpe remained outwardly calm, but relations between the two men were strained for some time afterward. The Hartke incident was an exception, for Volpe's relationship with Congress remained close as his relationship with the White House staff grew more and more distant.

Although the focus of his administration was to redress the imbalance between the automobile and public transportation (Volpe came to prefer this term to "mass transportation" because better service also was needed in rural areas), he did not neglect highway or airline problems. When Volpe took office in 1969, congestion at major airports was reaching a critical point, and airline hijackings had begun again after seven years of quiet. Volpe worked on two fronts: improving airport security and negotiating an informal agreement with Cuba, where most of the hijackers had landed. If the Cuban government imprisoned or returned hijackers, he reasoned, air piracy should cease.

But on September 6, 1970, a member of the Palestine Liberation Organization (PLO) commandeered an American jet in Israel, landed it in Cairo, and blew it up. After working around the clock with the FBI, the Treasury Department, and the State Department, less than a week later, DOT put a "sky marshal" force of plainclothesmen on board U.S. planes and began requiring airlines to hire security personnel and to install metal detectors at boarding gates.

When Volpe met with the president to brief him on the hijacking situation, Nixon stressed the importance of having a top administrator run the program. Air Force General Benjamin O. Davis, Jr., one of the first black aviators in World War II, had just resigned as Cleveland, Ohio, commissioner of public safety. Volpe called him, and Davis accepted the assignment at once, without even asking the salary. Gradually, the number of hijackings leveled off, until November 1971, when a passenger listed as D.B. Cooper introduced a new twist to air piracy. On a flight from Portland (Oregon) to Seattle, Cooper demanded four parachutes and $200,000 in cash. He bailed out in darkness high above the Cascade Mountains and was never found. Twelve similar efforts followed in two weeks, but none was successful. The numbers continued downward. By 1972, Volpe's last year at DOT, only twenty hijack attempts were made, and none was successful.

At the same time that hijackers were making headlines, Volpe was dealing with a more mundane, but equally intractable, problem: airport congestion. Between 1960 and 1969, the number of aircraft using FAA control towers had doubled, but few new facilities had been built to accommodate them. Congestion was especially severe in the "golden triangle" of air traffic between New York, Chicago, and Washington, D.C. The crisis peaked in July 1969, when, in one day, more than a thousand planes near New York were delayed for more than three hours, and stacks spread to all the other airports on the East Coast, into the Midwest, and on to Los Angeles.[8]

Three months before the "Great Stack-up," Volpe himself had been caught in a delay at LaGuardia. As his Coast Guard jet sat on the runway, Volpe grew more and more impatient. At last, he went to the cockpit to speak with his pilot. "Does the control tower know the secretary of transportation is on this plane?" he demanded. The pilot nodded his head. "Yes, sir, they do. But we're still eighteenth in line."

As a temporary solution, the FAA put in effect short-term rules limiting the number of instrument flight regulation (IFR) operations. The long-term solution had to be more and bigger airports, the goal of the Airport/Airways Improvement Act. The federal financing for airport improvements came from user taxes and thus did not affect the federal deficit.

On his first visit to an FAA control tower in 1969, Volpe was shocked by the primitive technology and poor working conditions under which the controllers performed increasingly demanding tasks. Radar screens could not differentiate between planes, and controllers moved markers called "shrimp boats" on tables in front of them to show planes' locations, while at the same time speaking to the pilots and communicating with other controllers by scribbling notes and passing them along.

At the NASA installations Volpe had visited, there was state-of-the-art technology in place to safeguard the lives of a few astronauts, yet thousands of Americans every day were entrusting their safety to an antiquated and often inefficient control tower system. Yet when air traffic controllers, first at Chicago and New York, then across the nation, went on a "sick-out" to protest poor working conditions and demand pay increases, Volpe took a hard line, as he had in Massachusetts during the MBTA strike. Flexibility in dealing with unions working on construction jobs or other nonessential business was necessary, Volpe believed. But to strike against the public, especially with the possibility of endangering lives, was morally wrong as well as illegal. He suspended striking controllers immediately and even ordered that those who had broken any regulations be penalized.

As the strike went on, Volpe came under fire from the press and even from a fellow cabinet member, Labor Secretary George Schultz, who objected to his "harshness and inflexibility." Nixon called Volpe and Schultz into the Oval Office to iron out their differences. Schultz defended his position, telling the president that Volpe should be more flexible. "Flexibility has nothing to do with it," Volpe argued. "The controllers have either broken the law or they haven't. You're either pregnant or you're not. If we give in, the post office workers may decide to go on strike, too. I've taken them to court, and I think we'll win."

While Volpe was dealing with the press, DOT's legal staff was fighting the air traffic controllers' lawyer, F. Lee Bailey. The presiding federal judge ordered Bailey to appear on national television and ask the controllers to return to work. He made the appearance, but many continued the sick-out, and it was widely believed that Bailey had used a code word in his speech that tipped off the controllers. The judge ordered a second television appearance, threatening Bailey with imprisonment, and he complied. Although a few controllers continued to stay off the job, the strike was broken. As the Airport/Airways Improvement Act was implemented, equipment and working conditions for controllers improved.

Volpe's safety campaign extended to his highway programs as well as to airports. Highway safety had been a prime concern of Volpe's ever since his days at the Massachusetts DPW. At DOT, he was in a position to implement changes on a much greater scale. Before he came to DOT, highway safety was the concern of a small office in the Bureau of Public Roads. Within a year, Volpe had created the National Highway Transportation Safety Administration (NHTSA), with authority to develop and finance federal programs on the national level and assign pilot programs to state and local governments.

Early in his term as secretary, Volpe began a program at NHTSA to develop a fail-safe car that would protect its passengers in high-speed crashes on interstate highways. Volpe observed several crash tests of seat belts, bumpers, and other shock-reduction devices. After the first seat belt demonstration, he began to use a seat belt himself, but he believed that the device with the greatest potential for saving lives was the air bag. In 1969, Congress passed legislation mandating the development of "passive restraint systems" for automobiles, but only two such systems seemed workable. One was a seat belt and harness system that secured the passengers in place once the door was shut. This appeared to Volpe to be too easy to disconnect. The other was the air bag. Air bags were simply large balloons, installed in the steering wheel hub or inside the dashboard and behind the front seats, that inflated automatically in the event of a crash, then deflated immediately.

In 1970, Volpe put American automakers on notice that they must begin installing air bags in all new cars by January 1, 1972. In January 1970, he ordered construction of an experimental safety car he hoped would be a model for the entire industry. But auto manufacturers resisted the air bags on the grounds that they were an added expense and that the public feared accidental inflation of the devices. The order was postponed until 1974. The three largest auto manufacturers fought the order during the entire time Volpe held office, and they were not opponents to be taken lightly. Imports then amounted to only a tiny fraction of the U.S. market, and the three corporations wielded enormous power over the entire economy through their impact on employment, commodity prices, and the stock market. Eventually, the issue reached the White House, where Henry Ford II reportedly intervened against Volpe's order. Only General Motors installed air bags in one 1972 luxury car, the Oldsmobile Toronado, as an option.

Volpe's other, less controversial, highway safety programs were more successful. He pushed the Traffic Operations Program to Increase Capacity and Safety (TOPICS) effort begun in 1967 by the Bureau of Public Roads to improve urban arterial streets with better designed signs, lights, and other construction work. Changes were made in the construction of guardrails and bridges to reduce crash impact.

Volpe also began the Alcohol Safety Action Project (ASAP) under NHTSA to deal with the problem of drunken driving at the local level, as well as funding research and publicity efforts on a national scale. In 1970, NHTSA contracted with nine cities and towns to implement detection and enforcement programs, treatment programs, and public awareness campaigns. The effects of the first ASAPs were dramatic. In Seattle, arrests for driving while intoxicated (DWI) increased 250 percent. In

Denver, DWI arrests tripled, and highway fatalities decreased by 25 percent. By the end of Volpe's administration at DOT, thirty-five ASAPs were in place throughout the country, and their programs were being copied by local authorities who were not receiving federal help.

Volpe's plans were projected through 1976, for he fully expected Nixon to be reelected in 1972, even though "peace with honor" had not yet been achieved. Volpe did not participate at all in the reelection campaign strategy sessions but made a few speeches during the campaign. Excluded from the White House staff's inner circle, Volpe knew nothing of the reelection committee's burglaries, wiretapping, and spying that would come to be lumped together as "Watergate."

At the first cabinet meeting held after the overwhelming Republican victory of 1972 — Nixon lost only the District of Columbia and Massachusetts — the secretaries rose to their feet and cheered when the president walked in. In a rambling speech, Nixon thanked them all for their loyalty. A few of Volpe's friends joked about the Massachusetts vote. Then Ehrlichman informed the secretaries that all their resignations would be required, merely for form. The president then indicated that he would like to talk to each secretary within the next two or three weeks. Volpe had already planned a speaking engagement at a highway safety symposium in Yucatan, Mexico, two weeks after the election. Nixon told Volpe not to cancel his plans and instead asked him also to visit Brazil, Venezuela, and Argentina, to exchange information on transportation problems, and to come to the White House for a talk when he returned.

In the days that followed, one secretary after another was invited to take the presidential helicopter to Camp David to confer on the shape of the new administration. Late one night, shortly after Volpe had returned from South America, Barry Locke received a call from him at his home. Being called at home was not unusual, even at late hours, and Volpe's staff had long ago accepted this as part of the job. But the content of the call was unnerving. "I'm supposed to see the president tomorrow," Volpe told him. "He'll probably be asking what I plan to do in the next four years. We'd better have something on paper." Volpe was optimistic, but Locke had heard rumors of impending cabinet shake-ups.

Early in the morning, the two men put together a rough agenda, and Locke typed it. Before Volpe left for the White House, Ehrlichman called, asking to see him fifteen minutes before his appointment. Volpe stopped in at Ehrlichman's office, and the White House aide delivered the news. He was to be offered the post of ambassador to Italy.

Volpe was surprised and angered at the breach of courtesy, but he hid his annoyance as he was ushered into the Oval Office. There the president congratulated him on his work at DOT and formally offered him the job in Italy. For years, Volpe had hoped to go to Rome as the last post of his career, but not so soon. He asked for four more months to see some of his crucial legislation through Congress, but Nixon told him that Graham Martin, then ambassador to Italy, was being sent to Vietnam immediately. The post could not be left vacant for long. Volpe returned to his office at DOT and shut the door. Locke found him sitting, silent, with the agenda on his desk before him next to the model of the SST. "The president wants me to go to Rome," he said, simply. Their years at DOT were over.

At home, Jennie saw things in a very different light. She had waited for four years in a strange and often unfriendly city, away from her children and her friends. Now she would be going to Rome, to preside over one of the city's most beautiful villas. It seemed like a fairy tale. "John," she told him, "go back to the White House and say yes before he changes his mind!"

The next morning, Ehrlichman called Volpe's office. "The president would like to know if you have made a decision yet." Volpe replied that he had not, but he would call as soon as he had. The following day, Ehrlichman was on the phone again. Had he decided? No, Volpe told him, not yet. By the third day, Volpe felt that he had kept Ehrlichman waiting long enough. "Yes," he said at last. "You can tell the president I will go to Rome."

NOTES

1. Theodore H. White, *The Making of the President, 1968* (New York: Atheneum, 1969), p. 466.

2. *The Boston Globe,* 13 December 1968.

3. John Ehrlichman, *Witness to Power* (New York: Simon and Schuster, 1982), p. 87.

4. *The Washington Post,* 4 December 1968.

5. *The Boston Globe,* 26 March 1969.

6. *The Christian Science Monitor,* 6 November 1970.

7. Joseph Bosco, "Transportation," unpublished manuscript, pp. 1–24.

8. Department of Transportation, *Annual Report 1969* (Washington, D.C.: Government Printing Office, 1969), p. 21.

CHAPTER XII

"Viva l'Ambasciatore!"

I N LATE NOVEMBER 1966, the stone village of Pescosansonesco still clung to its crooked hilltop in the Abruzzi, as it had since the wars of the Middle Ages. An earthquake in 1896 had destroyed some of the oldest houses, and in 1934 almost a third of the village had fallen into the valley below. The church dedicated to the Blessed Nunzio Sulprizio, the saintly village blacksmith who had died at nineteen, miraculously had been spared, but the back wall of the church now faced a sheer cliff.

The skies were bright, but the mountain wind was chill, and the distinguished women guests from America wrapped their mink stoles closely about themselves as the parade formed at the edge of town. A sign on the town hall proclaimed a welcome to "John Volpe, Governor of Massachusetts." The school and the town offices were closed, and the entire population of the village seemed to be following the mayor, the priest, the altar boys carrying religious banners, and the band as they climbed the main street past the row of shops up to the house where Volpe's mother had been born and where Vito Volpe had once lived. There was no electricity in the old whitewashed stone room, and the interior was as dark as a cave.

An uneven stone staircase flanked by a wobbly wooden railing led to the house's upper story. On an earlier visit, Volpe had taken a cousin aside and given him $500 to have the broken step mended and the place spruced up. But when he returned for the triumphal 1966 visit, the house was exactly the same as before. After attending Mass at the shrine of Nunzio Sulprizio, Volpe waved from the balcony the mayor had offered, but came down to ground level to give his address; the balcony reminded him too much of Mussolini. The mayor, Diodede Iezzi, gave an official welcome. "It is so rare and so very satisfying to see one of our compatriots reach such fame in America where unfortunately our names have often been linked to questionable conduct and even criminal activities," Iezzi concluded proudly. Volpe talked with his elderly cousin, Lucia Luciani, and her husband, and looked in on the little blacksmith shop they had preserved because the beatified Nunzio once worked there. Only five of Volpe's close relatives still lived in Italy: Lucia Luciani, Volpe's mother's two nieces (one in Pescosansonesco and one in nearby Pescara), and her two nephews (a retired Air Force officer in Padua and an accountant for the Defense Department in Rome). All the rest had emigrated.

After Volpe's address, the procession trooped out of the village to the patches of rocky ground where Vito once grew olive trees and tomato plants, and Volpe told Tauro how his father had spoken of the "grasping" soil that had barely sustained him. As they walked back to the town hall for the welcoming reception, he reached out to the elderly men and women of the village, asking them if they had known his parents. What did they remember? What, he wondered, would his parents have thought of the village now?

On the morning of March 3, 1973, Volpe's plane landed at Fiumicino Airport in Rome for the start of what would be his longest stay in Italy, as U.S. ambassador. Both Jennie and Jack were with him (Jack was to live with them on this tour for a little more than a year). The dignitaries were there to greet him: Minister Orlando Contucci, Italian chief of protocol; Boston's Cardinal Designate Medeiros; Cardinal Wright, an old friend from Boston; Cardinal Designate Luigi Raimondi; U.S. chargé d'affaires Wells Stabler. They spoke above the whirr and click of shutters and advancing film.

There was much work to be done and no time for sentimental journeys to the Pescosansonesco village. But there with the church and state dignitaries stood a village delegation — the mayor and the entire town council — to welcome the first Italian-American ambassador to Italy. Volpe spoke in Italian, with his parents' Abruzzese accent. "It is with vivid satisfaction and genuine pleasure that I return to Italy, birthplace of my parents and my wife," he began. His speech was short and concluded with a rousing "Viva l'Italia! Viva l'America!"

In his previous government posts, and in his business, Volpe had been able to choose his own immediate staff, but as ambassador he was allowed to take only one person to Rome. All other embassy employees were either career Foreign Service personnel or "locals." Volpe had asked Joe Bosco to come with him, but Bosco felt that he needed to start his own career as a lawyer. Thomas Trimarco agreed to come and found himself the object of suspicion from the embassy staff from the moment of his arrival. Volpe was an unknown and feared quantity: a political appointee rather than a career Foreign Service officer, a Massachusetts politician, and a former Nixon cabinet member arriving from Washington in the midst of the Watergate scandal. After a few months, however, the staff accepted Trimarco and used him as a sounding board for ideas they were not sure Volpe would approve of.

The contrast between the public style and personality of Volpe and his predecessor at the embassy was apparent from the first. Although he loved Italy, and even owned property there, Volpe's predecessor Graham Martin spoke little Italian and made no attempt to learn more. His public appearances were few, his manners were courtly, and he relied on a network of political contacts outside the embassy to keep him informed of the shifts and currents of Italian parliamentary politics.

From the first, Volpe was determined to speak Italian not only in ordinary conversation but also at press conferences and formal events. He began taking two lessons a week from the embassy's language teacher, Carolina Marchi. Marchi, who had worked for the embassy since 1947, was in her early seventies when Volpe arrived but was still called "la tigresa" by the staff. She rated the new ambassador's Italian as "fair," but decided that he would not give a speech without notes and preparation. At first, all his speeches were written in advance, and when he traveled, Marchi would brief him on the history of the city where he was going or on the culture of the region. One Italian newspaperman described his accent as "*italo-americano con cadenze abruzzesi.*" Another concluded in late 1973 that his speech was not perfect, "*ma resta sempre il fatto che sa farsi perfettamente comprendere*" (but the fact remains that he makes himself understood perfectly well).

When Volpe traveled to factory towns, southern villages, and large industrial centers and met ordinary Italians, his speech made him immediately one of them, a paesano, the embodiment of the emigrant's dream. But in a class-conscious European nation, his command of the dialect also created problems. Not long after Volpe's arrival, Italians on the embassy staff took Trimarco aside, asking him to request that, when Volpe addressed industrialists in Milan or intellectuals in Rome, he speak English. Trimarco agreed, though he did not find the task an easy one. Volpe clearly loved the language and was proud of his ever-increasing fluency. He took the suggestion with good grace, however, though it was painful. He consented to give some addresses in English, but in conversation with Italians, he still spoke Italian exclusively. They would have to accept him for what he was.

Although his speech retained the flavor of Pescosansonesco, Volpe now lived the life of an Italian nobleman and worked in a royal palace. The embassy at 119 Via Veneto, next to the Excelsior Hotel, was once the residence of the Queen Mother of Italy, Margaret of Savoy. The Palazzo Margherita boasted a main entrance with a high dome and busts of the twelve Caesars. A grand white marble staircase led to the ornate vaulted main gallery of the *piano nobile* (noble floor), where Volpe's office was located.

Volpe's embassy office was an enormous white and gold paneled rococo salon, three times the size of his old corner office, with a red Oriental carpet, a crystal chandelier, and a polished marble-topped desk. The embassy itself was in good condition, but the ambassador's residence, Villa Taverna, needed some work. Before Volpe left for Rome, Nixon had joked that he had heard the catacombs beneath the villa were falling in, and now he was sending his favorite contractor to repair them.

Villa Taverna, a rambling brick Renaissance structure with a red tile roof, had once been a Jesuit seminary, a papal property, and then in the nineteenth century the summer residence of the Roman Seminary. On the main facade, under the American flag, was a cardinal's coat of arms bearing an inscription Volpe found appropriate: "*In constancia et in fide felicitas*" (happiness lies in perseverance and faithfulness).

In the summer of 1963, President Kennedy had visited Rome and stayed at the villa. His first day there was hot, and he decided to have a swim. But there was no pool on the villa grounds. Kennedy ordered one installed, and so the villa swimming pool was built. Beside the pool, there was a house with a small kitchen and a playroom with a Ping-Pong table and a small conference room. During his first few months at the villa, Volpe and his son would play Ping-Pong there occasionally in the evenings. The conference room became the meeting place for any discussions that had to be very private.

The grounds also included a bocce court. When he arrived, Volpe found the court disused and hard as concrete, but he had it dug up and replaced. Several years later, New York Governor Mario Cuomo, staying at the villa, was surprised to find a bocce court — for the game that southern Italian immigrants had played in backyards in his childhood — in such grand surroundings. While Volpe was ambassador, the court was used often. On Saturday mornings, guests would come and play — Cardinal Raimondi was a regular — and then the party would have a leisurely lunch.

The villa's chef was Tuscan and prepared excellent Florentine dishes. Gradually, Volpe prevailed on him to cook Abruzzese dishes, but still the ravioli were not the kind he had enjoyed at home. Volpe did not want the staff to know that he could make ravioli himself but waited until his sister, Grace, came to visit. The cook let her show him the technique for making thin ravioli stuffed with ricotta cheese, and after a few tries, the villa's ravioli were to Volpe's mind practically indistinguishable from those he had eaten at home in Malden. Persuading the chef that all the ambassador wanted when he dined alone was a bowl of soup proved to be more difficult.

Although jogging and interest in health foods were becoming more popular in the United States in the early 1970s, Italians were astonished by Volpe's spartan lifestyle and amused at his enthusiasm for urging other people to try it. In Rome, heavy meals, ample wine, and a leisurely siesta in the afternoon were the norm for those who could afford it. Volpe did not "do as the Romans do." He was still up by six-thirty, worked out on his exercise bicycle in the bedroom in front of an open window, and generally went to 8 A.M. Mass then back to the villa to read his cables and have a light breakfast. Afterward he would go to the embassy. Lunch was for discussing business and lasted straight through the siesta. For guests who did not drink alcohol, Volpe began serving cranberry juice from Massachusetts. Most Italians had never tasted it before, and there was no word for it in their language, but soon they were asking for "whatever it was you served last time."

There was a disturbing difference between his routine as an American politician and daily life in Rome. In Italy, the threat of violence was always present. In Massachusetts, Volpe as governor used a state police escort, and at DOT, Coast Guardsmen were on duty for security. But in Rome, the political terror from extremist splinter groups on the left had become so commonplace that the Italian government insisted Volpe could not leave the villa grounds without an armed security aide next to the driver of his car and a police follow-on car carrying two men with submachine guns. The prime minister of Spain recently had been killed coming from Mass, and so, to Volpe's security men, church presented special problems. Going to morning Mass, the driver went to different churches by varying routes and parked the car in different places.

One spring morning during Volpe's first year in Rome, embassy employees found the skin of a fox (*volpe* in Italian) laid out on the sidewalk in front of the U.S. Information Service building next to the embassy. A short time later, a strange car tried to come between Volpe's limousine and the follow-on car but was edged out. The police never found out whether this was an assassination attempt or not. For the first two or three months, the heavy security made Volpe uneasy, but after a time he grew resigned to it. He resolved to take all reasonable precautions and then "leave the rest to the dear Lord."

Although Volpe had visited Italy nearly every year since the 1950s and had even run a business in Rome, he found the day-to-day workings of the Italian political process complex and often strange. He had arrived at a crucial time in postwar Italy, when the uneasy balance between the Church, liberal democratic institutions, and the Communist party was being challenged at the polls and in the streets by factions that ranged all the way from the extreme neo-fascist and monarchist right to the Maoists (the Chinese left) and anarchists. During the time Volpe was ambassador, both politically and ideologically, the left as a whole was increasing its influence at the expense of those elements that traditionally were close to the foreign policy goals of a Republican administration in Washington.

When Volpe arrived in Rome in 1973, Italy was functioning under the thirty-fifth government since the end of World War II. The center-left coalition led by the Christian Democrats had become seriously weakened by its apparent inability to control strikes and civil disorders. The Communist party (PCI) vote was edging upward with each election, and party secretary Enrico Berlinguer was moving to the right politically. In January 1973, Berlinguer had launched the new slogan *compromesso storico* (historic compromise), advocating participation by his party in the national government and reassuring the public that the "compromise" would still give Italy complete independence from the Soviet Union. As the PCI tried to move toward the center, disenchanted leftists split off into *grupposcoli*. These included Maoists, anarchists, the Red Brigades, and followers of Herbert Marcuse.

In the spring of 1972, the seriousness of the grupposcoli threat was made plain to the public when millionaire left-wing publisher Giangiacomo Feltrinelli's body was found under an electrical pylon he had tried to blow up. His vision had been "in every corner of Italy a Vietnam," and he had died trying to put his ideas into practice.[1] In the resulting crackdown, police turned up thousands of machine guns, maps, coded documents, and other paraphernalia of revolutionary activity. The Red Brigades were not just posturing radical students but trained cadres who appeared to command at least passive support among ordinary workers.

The 1972 elections, held just three months after Feltrinelli's death, went off without major problems, and the Communists, because of the scare, made no gains for the first time since 1948. But the uncertainty was great. Italian politicians quoted the French proverb *il n'y a que le provisoire qui dure* (only the provisional really lasts) but questioned how much longer Rome could hold on to the provisional coalitions without disintegrating. Five months after Volpe's arrival, the coalition headed by Giulio Andreotti, a journalist and former protégé of Alcide DeGasperi (Italian premier in the 1950s), broke down. Mariano Rumor formed a new government with the Socialists in a stronger position. There was little change in policy, only a shifting of cabinet posts.

Within a few months of his arrival in Italy, Volpe found that the embassy under the previous ambassador had been making clandestine payments to rightist Italian politicians through the former head of the Italian SID (Secret Service), Vito Miceli. Miceli had run for, and been elected to, Parliament on the neo-fascist Movimento Sociale Italiano (MSI) ticket and had been linked to an abortive 1970 coup attempt. (The so-called spaghetti coup was called off at the last minute when its leader, a prince who had commanded submarines under Mussolini, became uncertain of receiving Italian Army support. Instead of a coup, the prince and his followers held a spaghetti dinner.) The cover set up to funnel the approximately $5 million to the rightist politicians was a political magazine published in Rome.

At the State Department briefings Volpe attended before leaving Washington, he had been told that his predecessor was a sophisticated career diplomat who employed undercover operatives and that an important contact would be an Italian-American Colonel. Volpe, uncomfortable with possible direct involvement with clandestine activities, told Trimarco to see the Colonel first. At their meetings, starting in the spring of 1973, Trimarco found the Colonel to be a caricature of the secret agent. The two men would meet at the Piccolo Mundo restaurant on the Via Veneto, a well-known tourist spot, and the Colonel would sit at a table from which he could see the door at all times. He covered his mouth when he talked to prevent enemy agents from reading his lips and explained his program without ever giving names. Trimarco felt that the whole operation would have been laughable if it were not so potentially dangerous to American credibility.

Instead of taking the Colonel to meet Volpe, Trimarco consulted the CIA station chief in Rome. He found that the Colonel was neither reporting to nor being paid by the CIA, who knew virtually nothing of his operations and found him baffling. The funds for the Colonel's operations were apparently being channeled to the embassy from the Pentagon.

Volpe was appalled by the situation. If word of the Colonel's activities became public, the press would have confirmation of the communists' old accusations that the embassy was trying to bring about a fascist coup. This kind of revelation, Volpe felt, would be a godsend to the PCI in the next elections. Volpe cabled the State Department with the request that the Colonel's operations end by May 1973. Secretary of State Henry Kissinger replied by "back channel" (classified cable) that the operations were necessary as a check on the rising left. Volpe's predecessor in the embassy also cabled, appealing to Volpe's patriotism. Volpe replied that he still disapproved. By June 1973, Kissinger and Volpe were deadlocked. On his own authority, Volpe could not cancel an operation funded by Washington and approved by the secretary of state.

In the early summer of 1973, while the Volpes were vacationing in Priano, Kissinger sent General Vernon Walters to convince Volpe to continue the Colonel's operations. In their meetings, Walters leaned heavily on Volpe, appealing to his sense of patriotism, implying that Nixon himself wanted the operations to continue. Volpe also argued with Trimarco over the issue. Volpe was not against covert operations in principle; they were certainly justified in wartime, he believed. But this one was clearly ineffective, if not wildly dangerous. And if Nixon wanted it, Volpe's loyalty to the president was at stake. But, argued Trimarco, did Nixon really want it enough to risk the possibility of being linked in the press to neo-fascists? "They can't take the political embarrassment of your possibly resigning," Trimarco argued. "Kissinger will never call your bluff."

Volpe held firm. He would continue the operations through the embassy only if Nixon personally met with him and gave his approval. But Nixon was unwilling to have such a meeting. The operations were canceled.

After extricating the embassy from its entanglements with the Colonel, Volpe saw no benefit in becoming too closely involved in Italian parliamentary affairs. Italy was distancing itself more and more from the United States politically, and to Volpe this seemed a natural development of its greater participation in the European economic community. Yet he was disturbed to see anti-American demonstrations by Italian youths. The older generation, who remembered the liberation from fascism and American help through the Marshall Plan, still seemed sympathetic to the United States' ideal, if not always to its immediate foreign policy goals. But the generation then in schools and universities was too young to remember the early postwar years and was thinking of the United States only in terms of Vietnam and Watergate. In Massachusetts, Volpe had been forced to bypass the traditional political machinery to gain broad support. In Italy, he decided to do the same thing. He would take his case directly to the media and the people. Now Volpe was not running for himself, however; he was campaigning for America.

Volpe's trips around Italy, at first simply responses to invitations, came to follow a pattern. The journey would be carefully scheduled in advance, just like a campaign stop. He would call on the ranking church official, then on the local prefect, and always make a stop at the city's newspaper offices to meet with the editorial board. At first, Italian newspaper reporters were somewhat baffled by Volpe's public diplomacy. Although routine in Massachusetts, a politician or diplomat meeting with newspaper editors in their offices was unheard of in Italy. And at the meetings, he opened himself up for questions — a risky business for a diplomat.

At the first few press meetings, Volpe and Trimarco were surprised that few reporters asked about the developing Watergate scandal, but they learned that sophisticated Italians took the Americans' reactions as a sign of their political naiveté. Volpe was relieved to find that, instead of hostility, many Italians displayed sympathy for Nixon's predicament. They expressed admiration for the president as a tough man who knew how to deal with the Soviet Union. Spying on his opponents? Italian reporters would laugh. Here they do that every day of the week! Instead of grilling him on Vietnam and Watergate at press conferences, reporters began to ask jokingly what office in Italy he was running for.

Volpe spent considerable time establishing contacts within the Italian press. Although he was careful not to become too closely involved in Italian politics, his anticommunist, moderate views became well known in the media. In 1975, when Indro Montanelli, editor in chief of Milan's *Corriere della Serra,* resigned with forty other staffers because they believed the paper was too leftist, Volpe encouraged them when they decided to establish a new paper, *Il Giornale.*

One of his first attempts at public diplomacy came about six months after his arrival, in September 1973, on a visit to the port of Naples. The local officials had arranged for a reception at the Port Authority. Looking over the schedule, Volpe asked if any union leaders had been invited. The dockworkers union was communist, and their local representatives had not been put on the list. Volpe insisted that they come, and the invitations were sent out.

Volpe's staff worried about possible anti-American demonstrations, but Volpe insisted on the trip, despite a cholera outbreak in Naples. Volpe and Trimarco drove to Naples. It was lunchtime as they neared the port, and a group of thirty or forty longshoremen were eating their lunches with their bottles of wine. When they spotted the car with the American flag, they ran toward it. Trimarco cringed, horrified to see them racing toward the car. Volpe began to laugh; as the men came closer he could hear them shouting *"Viva l'Ambasciatore!" "Viva America!"* Volpe ordered the driver to stop, got out of the car, and began shaking hands. There were no anti-American demonstrations at the port that day.

Shortly after the visit to Naples, Italy was struck by the energy crisis, and Volpe had to curtail his travels temporarily. The OPEC oil embargo had an enormous effect on the Italian economy, which was already suffering from double-digit inflation. Only 15 percent of Italy's energy needs were met by its own gas and electric power; for the rest, Italy relied on imported oil from the boycotting Arab nations. Premier Mariano Rumor, who had come to power in July after the dissolution of the center-left Christian Democratic coalition, went on television and announced the beginning of *l'austerità.* The press immediately used the English word "austerity" because the concept was, they believed, a foreign one. The measures imposed were hardly draconian: a ban on private driving on Sundays and holidays, lower room temperatures, less siesta time (which bothered Volpe not at all, since he never took a siesta), and an hour less television each night. To do his part for austerity, Volpe gave up the embassy limousine, using a smaller car for the rest of his term.

On the day Rumor announced l'austerità, Volpe happened to have an appointment with him. Volpe mentioned that even though the diplomatic corps was exempt from the ban on private Sunday driving, he intended to comply with the rules. Rumor told Volpe this would not be necessary, but Volpe insisted.

Each Sunday for the duration of the austerity program, Volpe walked to Mass with his guards. The guards were annoyed, for they could not carry submachine guns on the street. But Volpe thoroughly enjoyed both the exercise and the freedom. He was not alone in this. For the first time since the war, Romans awoke to the sound of church bells — instead of car horns — on Sundays. People roller-skated, strolled, bicycled, and even rode horses in the empty streets.

Seeing firsthand the effects of the energy crisis in Italy and reading about similar problems in the United States, Volpe was glad that he had pushed mass transit and Amtrak so vigorously. Although he had not foreseen the OPEC boycott, his sense of urgency now seemed justified. He no longer feared that his mass transit programs in the United States would be dropped now that he was not there to push them. The lines at gasoline stations and natural gas shortages made the energy crisis an issue that could not be soon forgotten.

By the spring of 1974, the restrictions on auto travel in Italy were removed, and the energy crisis faded. But the political instability caused by the increasing influence of the left continued. In other European countries, the right seemed to be losing ground. In April 1974, a revolutionary officers' group overturned the fascist government of Portugal. In early summer, the military dictatorship in Greece collapsed, and the new government began threatening to deny the Sixth Fleet access to its bases in Greece, making the American naval bases in Italy more important. In Spain, Franco's fascist government had lost power after its leader's death.

Rumors of the United States' covert activities involving the extreme right began to surface in the summer of 1974, and a few writers speculated on the possibility that Volpe, too, might be involved. The Rome weekly *L'Espresso* ran an unflattering article under the headline "*Per favore non chiamatemi John Golpe.*" ("Please don't call me John 'Golpe'." *Golpe* is Spanish for "coup.")[2] Volpe denied any involvement but could not defend himself by mentioning the former ambassador's activities and his stand against them. Criticism gradually died away as Volpe kept to a very public and very moderate course. The extreme right, he believed, lacked a base of support — too many had suffered under fascism to make it attractive. Although Italians might vote for the far left to get clean municipal government, Volpe believed that the Catholic Church and democratic ideals were too strong for Italians to trust their national government to communists, especially in matters of foreign policy.

The Volpes returned briefly to Boston in the summer of 1974 for the dedication of the $39 million international terminal building at Logan Airport named for Volpe. Ground-breaking had begun in 1969, just after he had been named DOT secretary. Also during the summer of 1974, Jean brought her four teenage children to stay at the villa. Volpe taught them to play bocce and spent as much time as he could with them. A reporter interviewing Volpe at the villa while the grandchildren played in the pool dubbed him "*Il Nonno d'America*" (the Grandfather of America).

Throughout the rest of his term, Volpe kept up his travels and campaigning. By June 1974, he had visited forty-six of Italy's ninety-three provincial capitals. When Secretary of State Henry Kissinger visited Italy in early 1975, he began a speech at a state dinner with what was by then a hackneyed joke. "I hear that John Volpe is running for president of Italy. Well, you can't have him!" His audience laughed politely, but Volpe winced. He had always been careful to refer to himself as an American and to respect Italian sensibilities. Italy, he knew, did not have to look to the United States for leaders, as Kissinger's joke implied.

June 1974 also was the time of another national election, and the Communists scored another success. Their vote jumped from 25 percent to 33 percent, only a little more than two percentage points behind the Christian Democrats. Still, political analysts believed that even if the PCI equaled the Christian Democratic vote, they would not seek parliamentary supremacy, fearing that such a move might trigger reaction from the center and the right.

Volpe himself chose not to initiate contacts with the PCI but allowed some State Department (not CIA) officials to begin talks on a lower level. Instead, he invited some of the younger Socialist party officials to the villa, over the objections of the more conservative political officers at the embassy. Although leftist, the Socialist party, Volpe believed, was solidly within the democratic tradition. In the context of European politics, he saw nothing wrong with opening up a dialogue with the noncommunist left. Volpe was especially impressed with Bettino Craxi, a Milanese leader. His hunch was to prove correct, for only a year later, when the Socialist party central committee voted out the whole senior leadership and elected men in their forties, Craxi became secretary general.

The summer of 1974 saw even more momentous events played out in Washington, as the Watergate scandal drew toward a climax. Personally, Volpe believed that Nixon was innocent of any wrongdoing, that the fault lay with Haldeman and especially Ehrlichman, whom Volpe despised. Publicly, he avoided commenting directly on events of which he had no firsthand knowledge but continued to express his support of Nixon. His position remained the same as it was in October 1973, when he told a reporter from the Turin *Gazetta del Popolo* that "the guilty ones are few, and they will probably be punished for their transgressions."

Speculations that Volpe himself might resign were floated in the Boston press and picked up by Italian communist newspapers, but Volpe denied them. Trimarco and many of his staff were thankful that Volpe was in Rome, far enough away not to be drawn into the defense of an administration whose top leadership had never consulted him on important policy decisions. He had not been on board for the takeoff. Now he would not be on board for the crash.

When Henry Kissinger visited Rome that summer, he and the Volpes attended a formal dinner given by an Italian baroness. The guests were artists and literary and film people, among them director Federico Fellini and American actress Audrey Hepburn. Halfway through dinner, the hostess turned to Kissinger and asked: "Why is it, Mr. Secretary, that a man as intelligent as Richard Nixon could have chosen two men such as Haldeman and Ehrlichman as his two top aides at the White House? With Watergate at hand, it certainly does not appear to have turned out very well." To Volpe's surprise, Kissinger turned to him and said, "John, I think you can answer that question better than I." Volpe smiled, suppressing the urge to say: "Henry, I think *you* can answer it better than I because you were right there at the White House and I wasn't." Instead, Volpe answered: "You know, Baroness, every man, no matter how intelligent he is, on occasion has a blind spot. I would say that on that particular occasion, when President Nixon selected those two men, he had a blind spot. Had he thought more seriously about the caliber of men required in those particular assignments he might have chosen differently." After a minute, Kissinger whispered, "John, that was a hell of a good answer. I'm glad you pulled me out of it."

Nixon could not, in the end, be pulled out of Watergate. Up to the very end, Volpe still believed that Nixon himself was innocent and sent cables expressing support, urging him to remain steadfast and to do the right thing. On August 9, 1974, the embassy received word that Nixon had resigned. Volpe was saddened but not surprised. At least the country, and his friend, had been spared the trauma of impeachment. But he was pained to see that Nixon's vilification in the press continued unabated. A few weeks after Nixon's resignation, Volpe met with Pope Paul VI. After they had talked for a while, the pope said suddenly, "I'll never understand you Americans, never understand your treatment of President Nixon. After all he's been through, after hounding him from office, they aren't content to leave him alone. They have to stomp him into the ground until the blood comes out!"

"Your Holiness," Volpe answered, "that's true of the media and of some Americans, but not *all* Americans. When the media play something up, people follow."

"I've lived through this entire century," the pope replied, "and I will say that it may take ten years, or twenty years, or more, but someday people will recognize that Nixon did more to bring about a climate in which peace could be achieved than any other person in this century. I can't judge his personal guilt or innocence. Only the Lord can do that."

Volpe's position as ambassador was not affected by Nixon's resignation. In the first weeks of the Ford administration, there were rumors that the new president might recall men of Nixon's first cabinet who had left in his second administration: Romney, Hickel, Richardson, and Volpe. But Volpe remained in the embassy in Rome.

Throughout the rest of 1974 and into the summer of 1975, the pressure from the left continued in the Italian parliament, and Volpe went on with his campaigning. On July 12, 1975, the Italian and Spanish Communist parties issued a joint proclamation of "Eurocommunist" commitment to parliamentary democracy. Yet the senior Christian Democratic leader, Aldo Moro, continued to reject the historic compromise even while he kept in communication with PCI leadership.

By early 1976, the election scheduled for June was assuming a very serious importance. For the first time since World War II, the communist vote might equal or surpass that of the Christian Democrats. But just as the election campaign was beginning, natural forces intervened.

At 3 A.M. on Sunday, May 17, Volpe's private telephone rang. Minister of the Interior Francesco Cossiga was on the line; there was an emergency. At nine o'clock the previous evening, the first of a series of earthquakes had struck the Friuli area of the Tagliamento River Valley in the Dolomite Mountains northeast of Venice. At least twenty villages were badly damaged, several hundred people dead, and many more injured. The rescue workers on the scene had informed Cossiga that they needed five thousand to ten thousand tents, along with medicine, blankets, and supplies as soon as possible. Could the American government help? Volpe assured Cossiga that he would do all he could.

To send cables and go through regular State Department channels would take time. Instead, Volpe waited until 6 A.M. and telephoned General Alexander Haig, chief of NATO allied forces in Brussels. There was a U.S. Air Force base at Aviano, near the center of the stricken area, only twelve miles from one of the worst hit villages. Within hours, the U.S. Air Force had brought blankets, cots, tents, food, and medicine to the disaster area — before the arrival of the Italian Army.

Soon after, U.S. and Italian helicopters began to fly out the seriously wounded. Within forty-eight hours, virtually all the extra U.S. military tents available in West Germany, France, and Belgium were being shipped to Friuli, and more supplies were on their way from the United States. The disaster proved to be the worst earthquake in Italy since 1915. Almost a thousand people died, and thousands more lost their homes.

Only five days after the earthquake, Vice President Nelson Rockefeller and his wife, Happy, flew to Aviano. Volpe met them at the air base and went with them by helicopter over the earthquake area. They landed in villages where 30- by 25-foot military tents were the only shelter. The children huddled on cots set up on the muddy tent floor, while the adults and rescue workers dug for bodies in the rain. The town of Osoppo, the hardest hit, was a mass of gutted homes, rubble that had been roads, graves covered with crushed lime, and fields of mud. The villagers had been poor before the earthquake; now they were destitute. Near Osoppo, they visited a hospital where the injured had been taken. Rockefeller had intended to speak with the hospital director, but instead, with Volpe as his translator, he proceeded to shake hands with anyone who had a hand to shake and to say something encouraging to each patient in the wards. As the Rockefellers left, Volpe saw that both were in tears.

In Washington, Congress appropriated $25 million for reconstruction aid to the Friuli area. Volpe felt that amount would be insignificant when compared to the enormous need for housing and recommended that the Agency for International Development (AID) program replace some schools and build a new community center for Osoppo. When the plans for the schools and community center were finished, the town made Volpe an honorary citizen, and he spoke at the ground-breaking ceremony beside a sign welcoming him and announcing that the project was a gift of the United States.

After the earthquake emergency had passed, the election campaign of 1976 began again in Italy. This election was widely believed to be the Communists' first real chance at national power. The Church reacted predictably, urging its supporters not to let the PCI supplant the ruling Christian Democrats. Again, Kissinger brought power to bear on Volpe to allow covert support for anticommunist politicians. And again, Volpe found the notion that the United States should try to "save" the democratic process in Italy with cash contributions deeply insulting.

Although he would not allow covert operations, Volpe stepped up his own open efforts to win support for U.S. interests. During the campaign, Volpe held more than the usual number of receptions at the villa, with more Italians on the guest lists. Often Italians would sound him out on the political situation. The communists may be taking over. Should I send my children abroad to school, sell my business? Volpe had the same answer for all these questions. "Are you Italian?" he would ask. "If you're really Italian, you'll stay here and fight. If you want to hand it over to the communists, you'll leave."

Volpe's speeches, too, took on a more militant tone, but he always stopped short of actually advising Italians how to vote in their own elections. At a joint meeting of Italian Rotary, Lions, and Soroptomists clubs in Bari in June, he began his speech bluntly: "I suppose you think I'm going to tell you how to vote. Well, I'm not, that's *your* privilege. In some countries, people don't have that privilege. I can only say that now the United States and Italy have good relations. If the Communist party becomes dominant, I can only say that my country would have to reevaluate its relationship with Italy, in terms of economic relations, the NATO alliance, even cultural relations. In the final analysis, the decision is yours."

Volpe was confident that even if the Communists polled a larger vote than the Christian Democrats, they would have difficulty forming a coalition to govern. Under the Italian constitution, the president of the republic asks the largest party to form a government; if the party can't, the leadership passes to the next-largest party. A Communist victory would not have meant the creation of a Marxist state but would have given the PCI the presidency of the Assembly and the Senate and some cabinet posts. It also would have jeopardized the NATO alliance and seriously disrupted relations with the United States.

In the end, it was the smaller parties of both left and right that lost ground in the June 20, 1976, election. Without American covert aid, the Christian Democrats gained ground, achieving 38.7 percent of the total vote. The PCI was close, with 34.0 percent. Christian Democratic moderate Giulio Andreotti emerged as the coalition-builder and was able to put together a center-left cabinet with the communists still in opposition. Although the worst of the energy crisis was now over, the political situation was still unstable. Student demonstrations continued, and on the far left the Red Brigades were always ready to disrupt the precarious balance.

Volpe did not take part in the 1976 campaign for the American presidency; he was busy in Rome except for short vacations. The Democratic victory in November was a deep disappointment for Volpe, who had planned to spend possibly another two years in Rome. He had renovated parts of the villa (changing the name from Villa Taverna to the older name Villa La Pariola) and repaired the catacombs under the property. Jennie had made the gardens a top priority and closely supervised the running of the kitchen and the rest of the household staff. The villa now ran more smoothly than it had in years. When Volpe had accepted the appointment to Rome, he had joked to Nixon that he had once carried a hod and hoped that the expenses of entertaining in Rome would not force him into carrying one again. Nixon had assured him that the entertainment allowance would be adequate. This was not the case, and every few months, Volpe withdrew funds from his blind trust to pay for the villa's expenses. By 1976, he had spent more than $250,000 of his own money.

Shortly after the November election, Volpe, as a matter of form, asked the State Department to inform him of the approximate date when he should leave his post. Yet he hoped that he might stay on for six months or even a year. He had dealt with Jimmy Carter and his close advisor Burt Lance over highway issues and at governors' conferences, and he hoped Carter might make an exception in his case. Volpe returned to Boston for Christmas with the family, still hoping that he could stay on, but young Joe Tauro and Trimarco tried to dissuade him. Tauro advised him to begin preparing for his next job — Carter would want the embassy for a Democrat, no matter how good a job Volpe had done. The official word from the State Department was an estimate that confirmation proceedings for his successor would not be finished until March, and so Volpe returned to Rome after the New Year. Volpe had no wish to retire. His health was good, and he remembered that his father had kept busy until five months before his death.

Less than a week after he had returned to Rome, Volpe was called by a member of President-elect Carter's transition team and told that his replacement would be announced within twenty-four hours. Protocol dictated that an ambassador resign before his successor was named, so to prevent diplomatic embarrassment, Volpe sent his resignation to President Ford on January 7.

A week later, U.S. Deputy Assistant Secretary for European Affairs Richard Barbour telephoned Volpe with the news that Vice President-elect Mondale would be visiting Italy soon after the inauguration. At such times, the visiting dignitary stays in the villa and the ambassador's family in a hotel. But Barbour told Volpe bluntly to leave Rome entirely and stay in northern Italy during Mondale's visit. Volpe was hurt and angry but restrained himself. "Rather than say something I might later regret, let me think about your request and call you back in an hour," he told Barbour. After telling Jennie and Trimarco the bad news, he called Barbour. He would leave Italy well in advance of the visit, so there would be no embarrassment.

215

In late January, Volpe was honored at a series of farewells to the "activist ambassador." President Leone in his farewell speech referred to their private talks in Neapolitan and Abruzzese: "By speaking in dialect, I meant to show you that our country was opening its soul to you." The Volpes shipped their belongings back to Boston and left for two months in the Virgin Islands, their first long vacation in several years.

After the return to Boston, Peter Volpe asked John to return to the Volpe Company as a part-time consultant at any salary he wished to name, but John had spent too much time in public service to feel comfortable in the construction business again. He began looking at houses on the North Shore and eventually settled in Nahant.

For a few months, Volpe went on the lecture circuit, but he found the schedule tiring. Giving speeches without a purpose seemed meaningless. Nearly a year after he returned to the United States, he was approached by the Italian-American Foundation. While he was still ambassador, businessman Jeno R. Paulucci had approached him with the idea of establishing an Italian-American cultural foundation with a Washington office. Volpe had advised him to keep the foundation nonpolitical and to concentrate on coordinating existing groups rather than on building membership, so as not to compete with organizations such as the Sons of Italy. The foundation was started by Paulucci and Congressman Frank Annunzio of Illinois in 1975, with Monsignor Jino Baroni as president.

When Baroni was appointed secretary of HUD by Carter, Paulucci approached Volpe to take his place. The organization was still small, supported financially by a Council of One Thousand, with a budget of $50,000 a year. Yet it was already running literacy programs for immigrants, awarding scholarships, and organizing exchange programs between the United States and Italy. When *The Boston Globe* had questioned Peter Volpe about his brother's plans when he left Rome, Peter had joked that he "hoped he would take it easy." Instead, a year after his "retirement," he was back at work, in Washington and Boston, still traveling to Italy, going to Mass every morning, following his health regimen, and giving speeches, now with a cause. The journey was not yet over. Retirement could wait.

NOTES

1. "The Feltrinelli Case," *The Atlantic Monthly,* July 1972.

2. Norman Birnbaum, "The 'Z' Script: Italy Fears a Coup," *The Nation,* 7 December 1974.

Epilogue

F OR THREE YEARS, Volpe served as president of the National Italian-American Foundation, traveling and inviting people to become members of the Council of One Thousand. Then on a Sunday night in the first week of December 1980, events forced Volpe out of his "retirement." The worst earthquake in sixty-five years struck southern Italy near Salerno. Tremors radiated through Naples and across Campania and Basilicata. The death toll exceeded three thousand, with two hundred villages damaged and more than three hundred thousand people left homeless. The effects of the earthquake were most devastating in the remote medieval hilltop villages, where the close-packed stone houses collapsed on the villagers and there was no escape in the narrow, twisting streets.

The tragedy was compounded by the Italian government's inability to quickly mobilize help for the isolated villages. Despite Italy's long history of earthquake activity, no disaster relief plan had been formulated, and at first the government even refused international relief, unaware of the magnitude of the disaster. As word of the tragedy spread, the usable roads were blocked by cars full of people from the north looking for family members. Lacking equipment, villagers dug for their relatives with their bare hands in the sleet and snow.

As it had in the 1976 Friuli tragedy, the United States supplied military helicopters and tents. But rescue efforts often were stalled by the Italian bureaucracy. Giuseppe Zamberletti, who had supervised the Friuli relief operations in 1976, appealed directly to American citizens for help.

In several American cities, earthquake relief committees sprang up. Volpe was asked to become chairman of the Italian-American Foundation's Earthquake Committee. With five other people, he flew to the disaster area and visited with Pope John Paul II, who had been touring the area by helicopter.

Bypassing the government and relief agencies, Volpe dispensed the money raised in the United States to the mayor and a committee of leading citizens (the doctor, the priest, and shopkeepers) in each village, who could give out money to needy families with little paperwork. Volpe also met a priest of the Order of the Sons of Divine Providence, the same order that ran the Don Orione Home in East Boston, and gave him money to distribute. Upon his return from Italy, Massachusetts Governor Edward King asked Volpe to serve as chairman of the Massachusetts Earthquake Relief Committee, and he agreed.

After coping with chaotic and uncoordinated relief efforts for several weeks, the Italian government required that all foreign relief funds be channeled through a charity with a permanent office in Italy. Only four agencies met this criterion: the American Red Cross, Catholic Relief Services, Save the Children Federation, and the Salvation Army. The Massachusetts committee chose the Red Cross for some projects and Catholic Relief Services for others. Under the aegis of the Red Cross, the committee financed the building of three clinics for the mentally retarded. While Volpe was visiting the construction sites, he found that the skilled workers came from other parts of Italy; few workers in the *Mezzagiono* — the largely poor region of southern Italy — had appropriate training. With Catholic Relief Services, the committee built a technical institute to train young people in the construction trades. The project finally was completed in October 1985, and Volpe flew to Italy to dedicate it.

A month after the disaster, Vice President Walter Mondale called a meeting of all the American groups raising money for earthquake relief to form an umbrella organization to coordinate private and governmental efforts. Mario Cuomo, then lieutenant governor of New York, called a meeting in New York City of the Italian Disaster Earthquake Association (IDEA), which was already operating in New York but would soon become a national organization. Volpe assumed that Cuomo would become chairman of the new group. On the day of the first meeting, Volpe flew to New York, but his plane encountered poor weather, circled the city for an hour, and finally was forced to return to Boston. He reached Cuomo by phone from the airport just as the meeting was breaking up. "We've just elected you chairman," Cuomo told him.

As chairman, Volpe went to New York every two weeks to review project proposals. The Agency for International Development (AID) built several schools and made matching funds available for other projects, but much of the money was raised through private donations in Italian-American communities. The IDEA committee wound up with a $35,000 surplus. To use the extra money, Volpe asked Catholic Relief Services to come up with a small project. CRS found a home for delinquent boys, operated by Jesuit fathers, that badly needed repairs. Volpe agreed to allocate the money with one condition: that the name be changed from "Home for Delinquent Boys" to "Home for Boys."

Volpe's workload on the earthquake rebuilding projects was diminishing by 1982. On April 14, Secretary of Transportation Drew Lewis asked him to come to Washington to chair a presidential commission on drunk driving. This issue had long interested Volpe, and he accepted the position. While secretary of transportation, he had greatly increased funding for the National Highway Traffic Safety Administration. He also had funded the Alcohol Safety Action Projects (ASAPs) and had pushed the drunk driving issue during his administration. But the ASAPs had been discontinued in 1976, and since then, efforts on the issue at DOT had been sporadic. Now political pressure was coming from other sources. Mothers Against Drunk Driving (MADD), a grass-roots movement, had been formed a few months earlier, and impetus for action on the federal level also came from Congress.

The thirty-two commission members President Ronald Reagan appointed included lawyers, teachers, doctors, volunteer organizers, judges, and even advice columnist Ann Landers. The commission was to produce a report in a year, but after nine months' work, Volpe realized that the deadline could not be met. The commission was authorized to work until the end of 1983. The commission held public hearings in major cities across the country and received considerable media attention. The creation of organizations such as SADD (Students Against Drunk Driving), which Volpe helped start in Massachusetts, and RID (Remove Intoxicated Drivers) in New York also helped the commission's work. Volpe's leisure time virtually disappeared as he traveled for hearings, meetings, and speaking engagements.

On December 13, 1983, the entire commission was present to give its report to President Reagan in the Roosevelt Room of the White House.

Among the report's recommendations was that Congress deny some federal highway funding to states that did not adopt a minimum drinking age of twenty-one. Congress passed the legislation in 1984.

Reagan gave Volpe a Presidential Citizen's Award for his work. But the job was not over. Volpe and some of the other presidential commission members formed a private sector commission, with Volpe again as chairman. After a year, Volpe turned the chairmanship over to former president of the American Automobile Manufacturers Association James Adduci, but remained on the commission as Chairman Emeritus. In December 1985, the commission issued another report, and its work continued.

In July 1986, Volpe was drawn once again into Massachusetts gubernatorial politics. The two leading contenders for the Republican nomination for governor suddenly withdrew from the race. One candidate left the race because of allegations of bizarre behavior on the job and irregularities in signatures on his petitions, the other because news reports revealed that he had lied about his military record. Volpe was urged to run but felt that, at seventy-seven, he was too old to campaign. Instead, he agreed to chair a blue ribbon committee to find a replacement.

In September 1986, Volpe traveled to Italy to dedicate the Jesuit Home for Boys renovated with funds from the 1980 earthquake relief committee.

Index

221

223

About the Author

Kathleen Kilgore is a writer living in Mattapan, Massachusetts. Born and raised in Washington, D.C., she graduated from Oberlin College and the Fletcher School of Law and Diplomacy and soon after began her active involvement in politics, working in the unsuccessful 1970 congressional campaign of her husband, Daniel Houton.

Her writing has appeared in numerous newspapers and periodicals, including *The Boston Globe, The Boston Herald American,* and *Yankee* Magazine. In addition, she served previously as a contributing editor to *Boston* Magazine and has published two novels, *The Wolfman of Beacon Hill* (1981) and *The Ghost-maker* (1983).

She and her husband have three children: a daughter, Mariah, and two Vietnamese sons, Hong Duong and Hoa Duong. Ms. Kilgore has said that she thought often of her sons' plight as refugees while writing the early chapters of this book about the struggles of John Volpe's immigrant parents.